EXPLANATION AND HUMAN ACTION

EXPLANATION AND HUMAN ACTION

A. R. LOUCH

UNIVERSITY OF CALIFORNIA PRESS

BERKELEY, LOS ANGELES, LONDON

UNIVERSITY OF CALIFORNIA PRESS

BERKELEY AND LOS ANGELES, CALIFORNIA

UNIVERSITY OF CALIFORNIA PRESS, LTD.

LONDON, ENGLAND

ISBN: 0–520–01454–5

LIBRARY OF CONGRESS CATALOG CARD NUMBER: 66–19352

SECOND PRINTING, 1969

THIRD PRINTING, 1972

MANUFACTURED IN THE UNITED STATES OF AMERICA

'In psychology there are experimental methods
and *conceptual confusion*.'

Ludwig Wittgenstein,
Philosophical Investigations, II, xiv.

PREFACE

IF THE social sciences are added to the motto that stands at the head of this work, its aim as well as its indebtedness will be sufficiently indicated. Much of what goes on under the label of behavioural science is cause for suspicion; I have tried to give substance to these doubts by tracing current practices of psychologists and social scientists to confusions about the nature of explanation.

A fair share of what I have done is due to the work of Wittgenstein, Ryle, Austin and those who have followed their lead in exploring in a fresh way many matters which a previous generation of philosophers had taken for granted. I should claim as my own the attempt to outline a view of the nature of explanation and description of human action which brings together questions of fact and of value. I believe that a coherent account of human action cannot be given by separating these interests, though much of epistemology and ethical theory has had the effect of dividing them irrevocably. Observation, according to a prevailing orthodoxy, is one thing, appraisal quite another. Consequently, the activity of appraisal or evaluation gives us no new information about the world. I shall maintain against this view that observation, description and explanation of human action is only possible by means of moral categories. The concept of action itself, I hope to show, is in a broad sense a moral concept. I shall thus be involved in argument against two prevailing philosophical views, that observation is to be defined in terms of the perception of physical events or sense-data, and that explanation is a matter of bringing a particular event under a general law or theory. And I shall be arguing, further, that a study of human behaviour construed along these philosophical lines or supported by analogies to the science of mechanics is radically misconceived.

There are two ways in which such a book might be written. It would have been possible to do an inventory of the behavioural sciences in the light of the philosophical thesis of moral explanation. Or it would be equally possible to utilize typical themes in behavioural science to illustrate the various stages of the philosophical argument. If I were able to assume that the philosophical thesis were orthodox, and not standing in need of major defence, it would have been possible to pursue the first plan. The second plan is necessary in the present case, for it is the philosophical thesis that requires major defence. Without that defence, objections to the practices of psychologists and social scientists might appear anti-scientific and nothing more. The result is that psychology, psychiatry, sociology, anthropology, economics and political science enter, exit, and re-enter the argument in a manner that would be bewildering if it was supposed that my sole object was to launch a systematic critique of the behavioural sciences discipline by discipline.

But the manner of presentation should not lead to an improper estimate of the relative importance of the two aspects of this essay. The philosophical thesis is the result of reflections on what was felt, rather than seen clearly, to be the unsatisfactory state of most studies of human action. My main intent has been to show that the idea of a science of man or society is untenable. I defend this view by developing a philosophical thesis as to the nature of explanation, contrary to that which would be required to support the scientific claims of psychologists and sociologists. But this argument has philosophical ramifications for epistemology, ethics and the philosophy of mind, which cannot be passed by without notice. Consequently, from time to time, the sustained attack on the notion of a science of behaviour is interrupted by more purely philosophical reflections, on the meaning of explanation, purpose, mind and consciousness.

I am exceedingly grateful to Mr. Bernard Mayo, who gave the book a close and thoughtful reading. Substantial portions of the first three sections of Chapter VIII have appeared in two articles, in *Inquiry* (Vol. 6, 1963) and in *The Monist* (Vol. 47, 1963). I wish to thank the editors of *Inquiry* and the Open Court Publishing Company for permission to use somewhat revised versions of that material here.

CONTENTS

Chapter One

INTRODUCTION

In daily life we succeed in accounting for our actions without recourse to general theories or statistical regularities. When we appeal to wants, plans, schemes, desires, intentions and purposes we render our actions intelligible to ourselves and our everyday auditors. More often than not, it would seem absurd to render our accounts explicit; they are implied in the ways we observe and describe behaviour. A student in my office reaches for a cigarette and matches, he strikes a match and lights the cigarette, inhales and exhales the smoke. It would not occur to me to accompany this set of observations of his actions with further comments designed to explain what he did. If I had to do so, I should appeal to his reaching for a cigarette as indicating a desire to smoke, and the rest of his actions as contributing to the same end. It would not occur to me or to my interlocutors to offer or demand general laws from which this action can be shown to follow, or regularities of which the connexion of this action and its motive would be an instance.

'Behavioural scientists' (i.e. psychologists and social scientists) and philosophers have put obstacles in the way of *ad hoc* explanations by demanding that any explanation lean on generalities for its support. When these demands of philosophers of science or 'methodologists' are taken seriously, as they are very frequently by psychologists and sociologists, theories are developed which meet the formal requisite of generality, but which pay the price for it rather heavily. For these theories are often redundant and platitudinous or totally irrelevant to the behaviour they are designed to explain. When we say that a man seeks food because he is hungry, or kills his father because he has been cut out of the will, or equally, when we say that men band together in economic or political enterprises and religious and social ceremonies because of their beliefs, needs, or roles, we are offering explanations of cases which do not require the support of general or theoretical statements. Often enough, of course, patient and detailed observation is necessary to describe adequately what we wish to explain; but no further research or generalizing technique is required to add an explanation to this description. It is true that men generally seek food when hungry, but it would hardly be necessary or relevant to establish or invoke this generalization in order to proffer the claim that hunger led me to cook my dinner or Jean Valjean to steal a loaf.

1

But philosophers are inveterate generalizers and criterion-mongers, and *ad hoc* answers thus leave qualms. The qualms grow as we extend the discussion to more complicated questions. If someone asks me why I took up philosophy it might seem reasonably decisive to say that I became concerned with conceptual difficulties that stand in the way of empirical discoveries. But if an unflattering psychiatrist should suggest that I was temperamentally unfitted for the more arduous work of the laboratory or market place I should find it difficult to challenge him with my *ad hoc* reasons. In some sense my reason is the reason, yet in a sense that leaves open a host of alternative explanations.

Moreover, it is not only professional or professed scientists who find themselves ready and able to challenge *ad hoc* reasons. The accounts we give of our own behaviour are frequently challenged in an unanswerable way by wives and mothers and friends. A wife scorns her husband's account of his night of drinking (a business deal, of course) or his animated conversation with a pretty girl at a party (her intelligent conversation) as transparent rationalizations. But we don't know when to speak of his excuses as reasons and when as rationalizations. It may be that a new contract as well as a headache was the consequence of the evening's entertainment, and that the girl had brains as well as looks, though nothing is remembered of what she said. Quite outside the needs expressed by philosophers and scientists, to tidy up or generalize or verify our hypotheses, we do want to accept some reasons as appropriate or plausible or correct, and reject others as rationalizations. But we are in a quandary if we attempt to draw the line, or frame criteria which would enable us to draw the line, between reasons and rationalizations.

We are tempted in such circumstances to deny the propriety of reason-giving accounts altogether, and suppose that human nature must await, as the sociologists say, its Galileo. Much of the rationale of work in the behavioural sciences has to do with this sort of expectation, and so it is that psychologists and sociologists feel their actions justified if they spend lifetimes collecting statistics and framing indices, computing the mathematical values of correlations and devising hypothetical constructs: it will all bear on the Galilean revolution in the human sciences just as Brahe's tables of planetary motion contributed to Kepler's hypotheses.

Still, much of the time our reasons are not challenged. At least some of the time such accounts must stand; otherwise we should hardly have grounds for singling out some instances as rationalizations. If I said I enjoyed complicated fiction like that of Proust or Faulkner as an explanation for having their volumes on my shelves, yet when alone ferret out whodunits and scatological tracts, I should be rationalizing my possession of solemn novels. By the same token I should be giving an adequate account of my possession of whodunits and salacious paperbacks if I said I enjoyed them. So we distinguish between good and bad, or better and worse reasons; the problem is to see them formulated in such a way as to make clear why some of them are good and others are bad. And this is the difficulty.

How, then, can an explanation be adequate and yet have no implications beyond the case? One solution, quite popular among philosophers of history around the turn of the century, preserves *ad hoc* accounting, but does so by shrouding the business of explanation in mystery. According to the advocates of this kind of view, explaining human action is a matter of plumbing motives by means of a hypothetical experiment enabling the historian or sociologist to relive the actions of those whose lives he investigates. It is not at all clear, however accurate an account this may be of the historian's procedure, how successful divinations can be distinguished from the failures, and this seems to disqualify Collingwood and Croce, Rickert and Dilthey and Bergson, as responsible critics of the historian's, the social scientist's and the psychologist's trades.

The mystical and divinatory excesses of these philosophers have contributed much to the power of the opposite thesis that all explanation is general and theoretical in nature. Sometimes the advocates of this view follow a Humean line, according to which the strategy of any explanation consists in an appeal to regularities. At others it is supposed that explanation consists in bringing an event under a law, without claiming that the law is descriptive. An adequate explanation, on either form of this account, is one that can be shown to extend the account beyond the case in question, which, in its most usual form, is to predict. If either the inductive or the hypothetico-deductive strategies are taken as paradigm, something must be done about putative *ad hoc* accounts. Sometimes they are dismissed as irrelevant, being treated as rather trivial and uninteresting approximations of knowledge. At other times it is supposed that they disguise generalizations which could be brought forward in their defence, but which, because of their transparency or unimportance, do not need to be.

Neither of these alternatives, it seems to me, does justice to the business of *ad hoc* explanation. History, anthropology, journalism and our day-to-day observations attest the prevalence and importance of *ad hoc* accounts. We have, in fact, a rather rich knowledge of human nature which can only be assimilated to the generality pattern of explanation by invoking artificial and ungainly hypotheses about which we are much less secure than we are about the particular cases the generalizations are invoked to guarantee. Moreover, when we move, as we shall in the next chapter, to a review of attempts by psychologists and sociologists to seek law-like explanations, we shall discover that these attempts normally result in redundancy and platitude, or else are irrelevant to the behaviour to be explained. Still further, it is not at all clear that theoretical or inductive support is implicit in perfectly normal cases of physical explanation. The paradigms of causal explanation, I shall suggest in Chapter III, are observed collision, effort, and continuity, cases in which a correct account can also be given *ad hoc*. The view that causal explanations depend upon repeated observations of temporal succession derives its support chiefly from an atomistic view as to what we may be said to observe, a view which I hope to show cannot be intelligibly stated.

Physical interaction, of course, is not directly germane to explanations of human action. But if we can attack successfully the major claim of the generality thesis of explanation it may be possible to break the hold that this thesis has had on philosophical thinking about explanation, and so consider explanations of human behaviour on their own merits without being distracted by the generality thesis and its supposed paradigm in physics. The thesis I shall advance, in Chapter IV, and work out in detail in the remainder of the book, is simply this: when we offer explanations of human behaviour, we are seeing that behaviour as justified by the circumstances in which it occurs. Explanation of human action is moral explanation. In appealing to reasons for acting, motives, purposes, intentions, desires and their cognates, which occur in both ordinary and technical discussions of human doings, we exhibit an action in the light of circumstances that are taken to entitle or warrant a person to act as he does.

This view may help to clarify and even resolve a number of issues in philosophy and the behavioural sciences. First, it may serve to straighten out the role that generalizations do play in explaining particular human actions, by considering the role of rules and aims in their logical bearings on action. Second, it may contribute something to a view, much in evidence nowadays, that what we observe depends as much on language as upon eyes, on techniques as much as on events. To identify a piece of behaviour as an action is already to describe experience by means of moral concepts. This view has been obscured by the is/ought dichotomy that plagues contemporary ethics, and so this discussion may lead to some revamping of traditional conceptions of a subject which has been the target for a good deal of abuse in the last hundred years. Third, it may help to dissolve the paradoxical flavour of many of the comments of contemporary philosophers on the subjects of consciousness, private experience, purpose and intention, by showing that such terms exact different requirements depending on whether they are employed to describe, explain, or perform other linguistic tasks. Finally, I should at least expect that the thesis offered in these pages might serve to counter some of the more extravagant views denying a role to scientific method in explaining human affairs. For this rejection of science often leaves us with nothing but expletives and appreciations where we had hoped for knowledge.

The behavioural sciences have become established features of academic life. They play a crucial role in the political and social strategy of governments. Experts in these disciplines are looked to for professional advice. To oppose their influence is thus to find oneself opposed to intelligent action in government and social policy. And if one denies to them the right to frame hypotheses and form laws of human behaviour, one undercuts their status as scientists and experts.

But the truth, I think, is somewhat different. The intelligent and well-informed rearing of children, treatment of the mentally ill, and fashioning of policy is, no doubt, highly to be desired. But the observations pertinent to these areas are piecemeal, the conclusions tentative, and dependent upon a moral point of view. The machinery that behavioural scientists bring to bear on human action is, in contrast, general and theoretical, and in principle free of the context of moral discussion. Consequently, I will suggest, their efforts pass by the problems to which they are ostensibly addressed. Behavioural scientists are forced into a mistaken view of their subject-matter as a result of their preoccupation with a method they take to be necessary to any respectable inquiry.

CHAPTER TWO

THE SCIENCE OF BEHAVIOUR

MY OBJECT in this chapter is to describe how a conception of methodology has prevented sociologists and psychologists from offering significant accounts of human behaviour. This is necessary, to prepare the way for a rather different analysis of our manner of acquaintance with human doings by showing how methodology leads only to formulae for possible theories, but not to any genuine accounts of human behaviour. A sterile scholasticism has possessed the behavioural sciences, for which philosophers with their theories about the nature of science are very much responsible.

It might be supposed that the object of philosophers of science is to describe the moves scientists make in order to discover, invent, or verify hypotheses. But there is always the further note in the philosopher's account, which suggests that he is in a position to impose certain criteria and restrictions on what the scientist can do or say with propriety. Certainly psychologists and sociologists of a methodological bent have taken some philosophical writings in that spirit. *Language, Truth and Logic*, the *Encyclopedia of Unified Science*, the writings of Reichenbach, Hempel and Bergmann have, among others, served as scriptures to the methodological exegeses of many psychologists and social scientists. They find in these writers sustenance for the view that all explanation consists in bringing phenomena under laws. Accordingly, all explanation will depend upon generality or scope, which ordinarily will take the form of successful forecast of new phenomena.

This story falls into two parts. The first states, as it were, the moral qualifications for any investigation, taking the form, for example, of the verification principle of meaning, or, earlier, Hume's dictum, 'no idea without a corresponding impression', or, still earlier, Bacon's insistence on the method of experiment. The second outlines the procedure for passing this test. Now there are points, and important ones, made by these demands. But they need to be understood in context. Bacon's demand for experiment, for example, needs to be seen as an argument against the appeal to scriptural or Aristotelian authority which is supposed to have characterized the science of the Middle Ages. The special cases of 'torturing nature' to find out her truths must be taken as illustrating his point, not constituting it. In the same way, Hume's appeal to induction needs to be seen as a polemic against the view that deductive reasoning is sufficient to establish the truth of any proposition. The verification principle needs to be viewed against the kind of philosophy that purported to describe how the world really is by invoking concepts that were suspiciously elastic or impossibly vague. All of these arguments are illustrated in ways that make the intended contrast more explicit. Difficulties arise when the vehicles for drawing the contrast are taken as embodying the rules for any investigation. The extreme case, employed to make the contrasting point, is taken as the standard or universal case, and thus the condition for any inquiry whatever.

The same might be said of more recent attempts to describe the nature of science. First, within the context of the claim that the meaning of a statement is its manner of verification, it becomes necessary to do something about laws which, because of their central role in science, ought to get full marks for empirical meaningfulness. If laws are treated as generalizations, however, they are not conclusively verifiable, for they cover any possible case of a certain sort, and thus include cases beyond those for which verification has been offered. So laws come to be treated as tools, ways of getting round reality in Schlick's phrase, or models that order the data, or mathematical devices that facilitate prediction. In much the same spirit these same descriptions of law-like statements are framed in contrast to Hume's inductive view of laws. It is claimed that laws are really hypotheses, from which consequences in the observable world can be deduced, and not inductive consequences of a host of observations. These remarks bring out an important feature of numbers of moves of physicists and biologists which tend to be overlooked by writers like Hume and Mill, who are anxious to avoid the *a priori* excesses of rationalist accounts of science. But these instructive contrasts do not entitle us to draw the moral that the methodologists in psychology and sociology tend to draw from them. Many scientific laws serve as bridges to predictions, or models which join otherwise disparate observations, or parts of deductive systems from which observations can be shown to follow. But it does not follow that anything counting as adequate description or explanation of phenomena must take this shape. To suppose so betokens an insensitivity to the content of an investigation as a result of a preoccupation with its form.

It might be said that before playing a game the rules must be laid down and understood. But imagine that the rules are laid down for a game before it has been decided whether we are to play with counters, nets and rackets, or cards, whether it is to exercise mind or body. To advance a theory of games under such circumstances would require saying something that would apply to any procedure and aim that one might conceivably want to employ or follow. To stretch so far, such a theory must accommodate itself to anything, and thus be tautologous, and so uninformative. To apply more specific prescriptions is to decide how to play a game when it is not clear what the aim or the equipment or the competitors in the game may be.

The sociologist, and the historian with scientific pretensions, are apt to take the philosopher's polemics as prescriptions for carrying on their investigations. If, for example, they can produce any generalization at all, or any hypothesis that allows them to predict, they are prone to claim that they have accomplished something new and of significance in the study of society or of history. A classic case of the confusion of methodological propriety with new knowledge is F. J. Teggart's study, *Rome and China*, in which he shows how Roman invasions of Armenia were invariably followed by barbarian uprisings on the lower Danube and Rhine, and Chinese imperial wars in the eastern T'ien Shan by disturbances on the Danube between Vienna and Budapest.[1] These coincidences occurred forty times during a period of 165 years. This is the generalization, which in turn is explained by appealing to the interruption of trade routes occasioned by the wars. Teggart's analysis is designed to show that such an explanation could not have been given without the generaliz' tion. But the generalization does not in this case establish the explanatio .. Had we bothered to trace the chain of events in one case, we would have seen that the military movements created obstacles to a free flow of trade, and that these obstacles required the barbarians to move in order to restore their perishing economies. That such a chain of events was repeated indicates only that the dependence of the barbarian tribes on east–west trade continued through the whole 165 years. The explanation has its ties with a particular sequence, and any such sequence, of events. It had been given, in fact, before Teggart constructed his table of coincidence, as he fully acknowledges in his bibliographical data. It is only the view that all explanation is generalization that could make it appear that the barbarian movements had only been explained once the repeated sequence had been discovered.

Often the sociologist and the psychologist go further along the road to specifying the rules of the scientific game, by identifying the essential procedure of science with quite specific theories in it. Kepler's laws have been especially popular in this respect. There is good reason for this, for the theory of planetary motions has the virtue of predicting from the laws and initial conditions the specific positions and motions of individual

---

[1] F. J. Teggart, *Rome and China* (University of California Press, 1939), p. 244; and 'Causation in Historical Events', *Journal of the History of Ideas*, Vol. 3 (1942), pp. 8–9.

bodies. Since the psychologist feels that his study has a bearing on what individuals do in special circumstances, his hankering after general theory has often taken Keplerian shape. But Kepler's laws scarcely illustrate any general truths about scientific procedure. They are, particularly with respect to their reference to individual bodies, rather unique in the catalogue of scientific theories. But this has not prevented many psychologists from supposing that their aim is to bring human behaviour within the laws of a Kepler-like universe.

The results of this preoccupation with methodology, i.e. with what is taken to be the proper and scientific form of any investigation, have been, in my view, disastrous in the disciplines investigating human behaviour. It has led to a formulation of methodological codes for investigation, in which everyone adds to or subtracts something from the code, but no one applies it. It has led sociologists and psychologists to design their studies in accordance with some conception of proper form and almost wholly without reference to the subject-matter in consequence the putative laws are often thinly disguised tautologies. It has sometimes led eager theorists to embrace symbols, without the ghost of an idea as to the range of the variables or the function of the constants. To put it in a form acceptable to sociologists: methodological soundness is inversely proportional to factual significance. Triviality, redundancy and tautology are the epithets which I think can be properly applied to the behavioural scientist.

Sociology

Let us make the charges stick by appeal to cases in which methodological exactness replaces empirical significance. In a recent collection, Paul Lazarsfeld indicates the supposed advantages for our understanding of human doings that comes with a proper scientific technique.

It has been found that the more fire engines that come to a fire (x) the larger is the damage (y). Because fire engines are used to reduce damage the relationship is startling and requires elaboration. As a test factor (t) the size of the fire is introduced. The partials then become zero and the original result appears as the product of two marginal relationships; the larger the fire, the more engines and also the more damage.[2]

I don't suppose anyone would quarrel with the conclusion. But it is a rather unnecessary employment of the sophisticated techniques of mathematical or at least symbolic formulation of hypotheses. Lazarsfeld's example may perhaps be intended only to illustrate the technique, and so such common or garden acquaintance with the world may only have been chosen in order to exhibit the technique without the distraction of

[2] Daniel Lerner (ed.), *Evidence and Inference* (Free Press, 1959), p. 129.

the case. But it will appear, I think, that the technique is, for Lazarsfeld and for other sociologists, sufficient unto itself. Indeed, Lazarsfeld expresses himself as being rather satisfied with this outcome of his techniques, as if it had produced here something we didn't already know. Lazarsfeld's whole approach suggests that there is novelty enough in discovering that his techniques can produce the same results as those already obtained, quite convincingly, by more pedestrian methods. So much, for the moment, for the redundancy of the sociologist's account of human doings. But we can see now how the symbolizers in sociology come to be satisfied with their work. It is because their criteria for adequate theory derive wholly from a conception of the proper form of a theory and totally ignore its content or object.

Some of these equations are ambitious indeed. Dodd, for example, has been adequately excoriated for his symbolic writing of social processes, by Kaplan,[3] but the gist of Kaplan's criticisms might be inserted here with profit. In the *Dimensions of Society*, Dodd offers the formula $S = {}_s^s(T;I;L;P)_s^s$ where S means situation; T, time of duration; I, indication of characteristics; L, spatial region; P, population; $;$, mathematical combination; and ${}_s^s$, qualification factors. This appears to say, then, that a situation varies with respect to its duration, its characteristics, its geographical place, and its population, qualified by its social factors. One might say, surely, all of this goes into what we mean by a social situation. But it is not a law of social process, nor even, for purposes of further symbolization, helpful as a definition. The mathematical function '$;$' remains uninterpreted. Perhaps we should read it as 'varies with', but we are totally in the dark as to whether it varies directly, inversely, arithmetically, geometrically, or in any number of other ways. At best we could only say, something like this might be the form that a law of social change would take, if it were possible to generate such a law. But this is a hypothetical perfectly consistent with the impossibility of such a law, or the possibility that it might take a quite different form. It bears much the same relation to the laws of science that La Mettrie's speculations about mechanical man bear to Newtonian mechanics. It is a kind of speculation which allows us to dwell on what a Newtonian science of man might look like, if there could be such a science, but it does nothing to decide whether there could be or not. At worst, it looks as if Dodd's formula is the result of an effort to leave nothing out, and not to be caught out in any way, an aim achieved by giving his law tautological elasticity.

[3] A. Kaplan, 'Sociology Learns the Language of Mathematics' in P. F. Lazarsfeld and M. Rosen (eds.), *The Language of Social Research* (Free Press, 1955).

There are many instances of the same sort of thing. In *Sociology Today*, Alex Inkeles offers another Dodd-like formula of even grander sweep and simplicity.[4] It is: (S) (P) = R, where S is the state of society, P the personality factor, and R the rate of social process. The emptiness of Inkeles' formula parallels Dodd's. In both cases a mathematical look is given the formula, without mathematical sense. It is not clear how these factors are to be quantified, nor what exactly their range of application is. But it does look, surely, as if one could say, whatever happens in society is a consequence of its state and the personality of its members. The verbal formula is all-inclusive and for that reason both true and unimportant. The symbols only serve to disguise the triviality.

These are perhaps sociological sports, but they illustrate something going on at the heart of the discipline. Methodology exercises its perverse influence by disguising itself as theory. The point of theory, sociologists are fond of repeating, is to order the data and open possibilities for liaisons with new data. The point of methodology might be presumed to be statements like the preceding sentence, i.e. statements about the point of theories. But there is also a kind of scholastic intermediary, in which the sociologist lays down ground plans for analysis or chapter headings for books of as yet unknown contents. It is here that methodology keeps a foot in both the philosophical and the scientific doors, and does much to muddy both floors. Again from *Sociology Today*, hear what Parsons has to say about the ground plan for 'the systematic analysis of the structural components of large-scale and complex societies in terms of their relations to one another'. Parsons derives a scheme on the basis of two 'axes', the internal-external and the instrumental-consummatory. In a purely logical way 'problems or dimensions of a system structure' can be generated by the four possible intersections of the axes. Thus, where the external end of one axis intersects the instrumental end of the other, one has 'adaption'; external-consummatory or goal attainment; internal-instrumental or 'pattern-maintenance and tension management' and finally, internal-consummatory or 'integration'. With some temerity, I translate these impressive rubrics as follows: sometimes an individual adjusts to social pressures, at other times he manipulates other individuals and the institutions of his society to accomplish his ends, at still further times he attempts to reconcile external pressures and demands with his own desires and conceptions (e.g., sublimation?) and sometimes he achieves internal satisfaction (e.g., by a creative act?). Put in this way one wonders, what's the news? for surely the business of living has made us cognizant of the

[4] Robert K. Merton, Leonard Broom, and Leonard S. Cottrell, Jr. (eds.), *Sociology Today* (Basic Books, 1959), p. 255.

various strategies we employ, the satisfactions we achieve, and the pressures and demands made from without. That one can phrase these categories in technical jargon—presumably for the purpose of greater precision—and derive them from co-ordinating axes is only interesting if something follows from such terminology and organization that we did not know before.

What can be deduced from this scheme? In conjunction with some unspecified observations, it is discovered that the modes of social interaction are hierarchical, with the individual at the bottom and the nation at the top. (Parsons puts inverted commas around 'top' as if somewhat ashamed of his use of such a short and ordinary word.) It follows, for example, that 'The "decisions" [note again the embarrassed use of inverted commas] which bind larger and larger sectors of the social structure are made at progressively higher levels in the organizational system'. Now we all know that federal law has wider scope than state law, that state law, applies also to towns, and that the rules a father lays down for his offspring do not apply to others' progeny. So Parsons' labours appear to be redundant. But worse, it is not quite clear what would count as higher levels in the organizational system except those bodies and corporations which make decisions of wider and wider scope, and so the law appears to be tautological. The theory is, so far, only a set of definitions whose usefulness in accounting for social phenomena is yet to be demonstrated.

Let us turn now to a special application of the theory. Parsons refers to it as an insight (p. 9), consequently I suppose it should be here if anywhere that we should see how the theory discloses new information. 'The two main axes of differentiation . . . could also be identified in the generation and sex axes of the nuclear family.' The roles of various members in the family can be talked about by reference to the internal-external axis, if we are organizing the family by generations; to the instrumental-consummatory axis if we are thinking of differentiation by sex. I think this means that parents have authority over children, and that men tend to be the wage-earners. Once again, what's the news? Parsons' elaborate structure turns out to be a way of classifying the various interactions among individuals and groups, and any surprise arises only in that what we know already about human activities can be re-phrased in this terminology and classificatory system.

Now classificatory schemes may be useful adjuncts to scientific or scholarly inquiry; by a principle of ordering materials, they facilitate the location of any wanted item. But indices, tables of contents, or card catalogues, however ingeniously ordered and cross-filed, are not parts of scientific theories. (Except what is nowadays called Library Science: everything has to be a science.) In another sense, however, classification is an integral part of scientific theory. Linnaean family resemblances contribute to and are modified by evolutionary and genetic theories, the distribution of fossil and living types, and embryological development. But Parsons' scheme is not a consequence of theory; it *is* the theory. Consequently Parsons' pronouncements must be demoted from the status of theory to that of inventory. It is a system of arranging evidence so that it will be possible to locate the facts for which one is looking. But it is not clear that it is even successful in this role, for it is never quite clear what facts or items on his list Parsons is looking for.

There is, perhaps, yet a further point to taxonomy. For a classification is a way of reducing complex and confusing observation to something manageably simple. Parsons' system might be defended as the first gropings in the sociological field; it would be a mistake, then, to judge his taxonomy until it has either borne fruit or been replaced by something better. For the success of a taxonomic system cannot be judged beforehand. But even at its inception a taxonomic scheme, if it is to be more than an alphabetical or a subject inventory, should reveal unsuspected patterns; it should have, as it were, some theoretical standing. And this should show up in the consequences that Parsons draws from his system of concepts. Parsons attempts to show just such results of his taxonomy. He uses the concept of input–output to show (pp. 16 ff.) the way in which a variety of social interactions can be accommodated to this model—in politics, the economy and education. Learning in the classroom can be regarded as output, educational 'deflation' can occur if students 'hoard' the output, and so on. The game could be carried on indefinitely. The question is, do we learn anything new about the educational process by applying this system, or is it rather that we understand the theory a little better when it is applied to a case that is *wholly familiar*? Parsons applies his theoretical or taxonomic superstructure to cases which are not illuminated in any way by the application. Quite the reverse; we understand the verbiage of the superstructure a little better when we see what count as instances of his terms and rubrics. In this sense the theory has no explanatory power; and as a description is unnecessarily complex.

The outrageous vocabulary clothes the essential barrenness of the theory. So:

. . . when the structure of the larger system is undergoing a relatively continuous process of change in the direction of increasing differentiation, the mechanisms involved in this change will, under certain circumstances, operate to dichotomize the population of units receiving the primary 'real' output of the focal system of reference and to produce an orderly alternation of relative predominance of the two nearly equal parts (p. 22).

That is: given social change in a democratic society parties in power will tend to swing from liberal to conservative and back again. I do not know why such simpler formulations will not do in place of the bewildering complexity, unless it is that the terminological display clouds the paucity of information. But one can see also how a sociologist might be led to such relatively arid pronouncements about social structure by virtue of just those considerations which trouble philosophers of science. Even when the particular sequence of events is better understood than the pattern or theoretical structure under which it is subsumed, an appeal to the theoretical structure is necessary in order to make our understanding of social processes fit a preferred account of explanation and description.

Many sociologists deplore Parsons' over-theorizing. Merton feels that what is needed first are laws of 'middle range', applicable to special segments or aspects of the social situation.[5] With a firm foundation of such middle range laws, a more general accounting might be possible. Statements about society are needed, not Parsonian concerns with statements about the nature of sociological inquiry.

One such theory of middle range is to be found in George Homans' *The Human Group*.[6] Homans wishes to generate a number of laws for the small group (in this case Hilltown, a small New England community) which may then be extended to apply to a suitable class of such groups. The 'variables' he wishes to join into laws are 'activity', 'interaction' and 'sentiment'. It will be my contention that his so-called laws are tautologies, sustained not by the evidence, but by the interdependence in meaning of the terms out of which his laws are formed.

An activity is any element of behaviour (pp. 34 ff.). This itself is somewhat obscure if it is taken in anything more than a commonsense way. For example, verbal interchange is an activity. But is the word or the sentence or the whole conversation the activity? In ordinary talk about the doings of men, this is not troublesome. What will count as an activity, what will count in other words as the unit of discourse, is made clear by the context. Whether I am talking to you about the motion of your arm in making a turn, or about the whole operation of turning the car, or the activity of driving, will ordinarily be made clear by the kind of questions I am asking you, or the kind of conversation we are having. But Homans wishes to establish laws expressing functional relationships

[5] Robert K. Merton, *Social Theory and Social Structure* (Free Press, 1957), pp. 5–11, *passim*.
[6] George C. Homans, *The Human Group* (Harcourt, Brace and World, 1950).

between activities and the other factors; consequently he needs more than contextual clarity.

Interaction is defined as the amount of shared activities, and sentiment as the liking of people for one another. The imprecision in the use of activity thus allows for a good deal of overlap between this concept and interaction. For many of our activities are shared by definition; they are social activities. Activity and interaction are inseparable without a criterion which would restrict activities to some sort of movements of the individual organism. Many of Homans' generalizations rely exclusively on this overlap. It is also very difficult to separate Homans' use of sentiment from his use of interaction. For the purpose of general laws, he needs a behavioural criterion for sentiment, for he can hardly rely on that kind of particular judgment we make as to the likes and dislikes of a person, which is a function of context and long acquaintance. But this behavioural criterion turns out to be suspiciously like that for identifying interaction. The mark of sentiment is the quantity of shared activities. Thus the way in which he defines the building-blocks of his theory provides the basis for the generation of a series of tautologies masquerading as empirical generalizations. Let us examine some of these.

(a) 'A man will do more [output, in sociologese] if he is interested in his work' (p. 102). It may be possible in ordinary talk and contexts to attribute a person's work to his enthusiasm for his task without running the danger of pleonasm. We read it in his style of work, his facial expressions and his avowals. But as these readings depend upon a kind of impressionistic and circumstantial evidence that a practising scientist would deplore, Homans is forced to interpret sentiments behaviourally and measurably, that is, by the amount of participation in the activity. Interest in work is identified by the amount of time spent in, or the intensity of, its pursuit. It is, then, not surprising that the amount of time spent at work increases directly with the amount of time spent working.

(b) 'If the scheme of activities changes, the scheme of interactions changes also' (p. 102). A man, let us say, plays golf with his business associates, but after his nefarious conduct of business affairs has been revealed and he is ruined we find him playing pool with a group of derelicts. His game is adjusted to his associates. This fragment of the larger generalization is a sociological truth. Games go with incomes. They are, if you will, status symbols. But it is not this or any assemblage of such observations that concerns Homans. These are the piecemeal observations which constitute amateur sociology, and have point when embedded in novels, newspaper columns, and travelogues. These are undoubtedly interesting observations, so long as one does not have to read a catalogue of them, that is, so long as they occur in a story. But to convert them into the kind of formula Homans desires, it is necessary to consider activities and inter-actions as variables bearing a constant relation to one another, and for which one may substitute any activity or instance of interaction. Such a formula either tortures the piecemeal observations of which it is made up, by exacting of them more than they can give, or degenerates into the pleonasm that one's activities with *ABC* are distinct from one's activities with *DEF*, in virtue of the fact that they are performed with different people. The first alternative is the familiar move to general formulae as a way of accounting for or describing human actions already well enough described and accounted for by piecemeal observations. The second reflects a concern over the appropriate way of defining action; it turns out that it is to be defined in terms of interaction.

(*c*) 'Persons who interact frequently tend to like one another' (p. 111). This statement tries to vault the horns of a dilemma. We all know very well that sometimes familiarity does breed contempt, and even hate. Consequently, if his thesis is factual, it is surely false.

But Homans uses interaction as the sign of sentiment, hence the conne-xion between the interaction and likings of people for one another is tautologous. Homans is not offering this hypothesis in a 'sometimes, but then again often not' spirit, which would be the modest requirement for factual status, for on the following page he reformulates his thesis in a law-like manner: 'If the frequency of interaction between two or more persons increases, the degree of their liking for one another will increase, and *vice versa*.' The percentage of cases in which this hypothesis is likely to be false makes it a poor candidate for a law of social groups, and its universality is guaranteed only by depriving it of empirical significance.

(*d*) The next of Homans' laws requires a new distinction, drawn be-tween the 'internal' and the 'external' system. The external system (pp. 90–94) consists of those activities, interactions and sentiments that allow the group to survive in the environment. The internal system, by con-trast, is characterized by behaviour that is an expression of sentiments 'developed by the members of the group in the course of their life together' (p. 110). With this increased arsenal of terms and distinctions Homans states the following 'law': Frequency of interaction in the external system varies directly with sentiment which in turn varies directly with interaction in the internal system. I think it is also Homans' intention to give this formula a causal sense, that is, these circumstances follow each other in this invariable sequence, so that frequency of interaction (external) has frequency of interaction (internal) as a consequence. An instance might be the sharing of parties, lawn-mowers and whisky by men who also share workbench, office-space and tools. But so rendered the hypothesis is surely suspect. Of course we know people who do associate at home with the office personnel, but we know just as well of people who don't. To save the generalization from such a disaster—one might call it the Pooh disaster, for, you will recall, Pooh is addicted to the solemn generalization: 'Some do and some don't'—Homans can only shore it up by defining his words in such a way that they no longer refer to independent factors in the situations allegedly described by the law. What will count as interaction in the internal system is determined by its bearings on interaction in the external system, and conversely. In this way the only case that will satisfy Homans' concepts will automatically support his law.

(e) One final instance: People who interact frequently are more like one another in their activities than they are like other persons with whom they interact less frequently. Since activities are cases of interaction, this law too is tautologous. It might be claimed with some point that sharing sharing specified activities (job, club) or neighbourhoods augurs other similarities, like religious or political beliefs. Political experience fortifies our belief in the relatively conservative politics of the wealthy. Such facts, as others that come to mind with each of Homans' laws, are perfectly in order and defensible. But they neither require nor add up to the sorts of laws of universal scope that Homans finds necessary in order to carry out the scientific study of society.

At times Homans reaches through this structure of theory to actual descriptions of social behaviour. For example, he notes (p. 141) that the higher the rank of a person in a group the more nearly is his behaviour likely to conform to the standards of the group, although here too, seeing the generalization expressed in naked English gives us qualms. We think too readily of the many cases in which the boss dictates the moral code stringently to others but applies it rather loosely, if at all, to himself. The observations do not lack point by reason of the exceptions. It is in being forced to do duty as general laws that they are emptied of significance.

At the end, Homans voices Durkheim's thesis that civilization decays through lack of social cohesion. This is the justification as he sees it of his enterprise in the meticulous analysis of small groups. For now the analysis bears an important relation to the preservation of society, a way of life, a civilization or culture. But the same difficulties beset him here in making a conceptual truth play the role of scientific law. Surely social cohesion and the prospering of a civilization go hand in hand. But not in the sense that the one is the harbinger of the other, but in the sense that the one is the other. We ought to be able to demand more from a science of society than this.

In writing the history of their subject sociologists are apt to see the following approaches succeeding one another. (1) Dynamic sociology, or the attempt to account for social change; (2) static sociology, or the analysis of social structure, samples of which we have just considered; and (3) neo-positivism, a movement characterized by alleged improvements in the manner of observation of social phenomena, through the employment of questionnaires, statistics and other quantitative refinements. Practitioners of the last of these styles congratulate themselves on being sophisticated enough to shun sweeping generalizations and causal hypotheses, and substitute for them what is needed first, scrupulous observation. Theory without observation has an exceedingly bad reputation, of course, and this justifies many sociologists in pursuing what to the outsider might appear to be inconsequential details and arbitrary correlations. We shall see in due course that the apparent triviality of this research is real indeed, in the sense that our identification of social facts takes place in a way to which these precise methods have no relevance. In any case, since such writers eschew explanatory impulses, we can pass over them here.

We can also overlook so-called dynamic theories. The theories we have looked at so far are static theories. They show a morbid preoccupation with form at the expense of significant relation to social facts. This preoccupation has another side. Most social theorists of the past thirty years or so have wished to avoid the excesses of the dynamic school, in which the object was to explain or devise the laws of large-scale social changes. Now many of these dynamic theories were significant, but false. The supposed evolution of society from hunting through herding to tilling the soil is an instance. The wrecking of the fortunes of dynamic theories on the shoals of evidence led, on the one hand, to static theories with their redundant, trivial and tautologous formulae, and on the other to new dynamic theories, which protected themselves against damaging evidence by much the same elastic and interchangeable use of concepts, which led to tautologies masquerading as laws in social static theory. Toynbee's curious intermixture of the concepts of religion and social order is an obvious case. But so also is the Marxist thesis. There is the tendency here to confuse a methodological directive, 'seek out the economic changes', and the substantive theory that all social change is due to changes in the mode of production. Every society exhibits some distinctive economic arrangements alongside equally distinctive cultural forms and processes; consequently by invoking the methodological principle as a law, the possibility of discovering disagreeable evidence is avoided.

Laws of social process characteristic of dynamic theories, then, show the same defects as the laws of social statics. They have been amply and ably criticized, by sociologists themselves, but with special force by Karl Popper in *The Open Society and Its Enemies* and *The Poverty of Historicism*. I shall not impede the progress of my argument by repeating his, though I should like parenthetically to endorse it. In any case, though social process theories have a certain popular vogue, because of their messianic and prophetic implications, they are regarded as poor relations by academic historians and social scientists, who preen themselves on their scientific emancipation from the apocalyptic tendencies of their forbears. Consequently I have limited my sketch of sociological theory to social statics.

PSYCHOLOGY OF THE INDIVIDUAL

Much the same story can be told of psychology. There are numbers of large scale theories of human development and personality. Some of these, like Freud's, are based on stages of erotogenous concentration, which, in conjunction with an elastic range of events taken as producing fixation at one of the stages, accounts for later-life miserliness or profligacy, frigidity or nymphomania, and perhaps even the choice of one's wife or model of car. Others borrow the terminology and form of physical theories which, in the case of someone like Lewin, attempts to reduce the study of personality to a study of geometrical relationships, much as this sort of reduction has taken place in mechanics. But Lewin's topological and vectorial representations are not theories, but models of what a theory ought to look like if it is to conform to the pattern set for scientific theory by Einstein. Psychologists object to Lewin's formulae on the ground that they fail to predict or disclose new information, and this is quite correct. But the same point might be put by saying that his views never come to grips with questions about human behaviour at all, but afford comments only on what a theory ought to be like if it is to count as a scientific theory of personality or human behaviour. Freud's oral, anal and genital stages come closer to what we can observe in human development and have, perhaps, something to say when stripped of the vaguely mechanical language in which they are clothed. But here we will see that the metaphors by which Freud stated his position are essential to its survival, and make his theory a rather special case which will require consideration in its proper place.

All of this, then, is merely introductory. Its aim is to provide the background against which a more numerous body of academic psychologists have staked out their scientific claims, and congratulated themselves that they are not as their poor and speculative brothers, but 'hard' scientists. The question is whether they can fulfil their scientific programme without being reduced to methodological sterility, as in theories like Lewin's, or maintain some bearing on what can be observed of human doings without exceeding the bounds of their self-imposed scientific regimen. We shall need to answer this question by reviewing a number of methodological devices the psychologist supposes he must use to meet these aims.

A good deal of argument goes on in psychology between those who maintain that, ideally at least, psychological laws will be nomothetic and those who maintain that they must be idiographic. Sometimes this issue is clouded by a closely related controversy, in which a distinction is drawn between deterministic and probabilistic laws. So far as I can understand or summarize the different battles in this war, it would appear that nomothetic and idiographic laws are both deterministic. Perhaps it may be possible to combine the two dichotomies in the following way.

(1) A nomothetic theory is general in form. Its consequences describe or predict the events which follow if certain conditions obtain. Such a theory is deterministic in that, given the initial conditions, the consequences described must happen. The relationship between gravitational theory and the description of the acceleration of a falling body, or again, between the law of free fall and the fall of any body in a given gravitational field, would presumably be instances.

(2) A probabilistic theory is also general in form, but its consequences do not record the occurrence of events, but the probability of their occurrence. The laws of elementary particle physics and the prediction from them of the likelihood of an energy jump is a standard example.

(3) An idiographic theory is also law-like. But unlike a nomothetic theory, both the law and its consequences refer to specific events and specific objects. Kepler's laws of planetary motion is the standard instance.

Let us leave nomothetic and probabilistic models of theory formation aside until the next section and deal first with idiographic models. There is good reason for the demand for idiographic theories. In psychology one is supposed to be dealing with people, and explaining what they do. There are, says Gordon Allport, in *Becoming*,

many areas of psychology where individuality is of no concern. What is wanted is knowledge about averages, about the generalized human mind, or about types of people. But when we are interested in guiding, or predicting John's behaviour, or in understanding the Johnian quality of John, we need to transcend the limitations of a psychology of species, and develop a more adequate psychology of personal growth.[7]

[7] Gordon Allport, *Becoming* (Yale University Press Paperbound, 1960), p. 23.

The psychologist, then, takes on as his task the prediction of the next action of John. It is as if psychology has failed, or partially failed, if it succeeds only in framing statistical likelihoods that this or that type of person will do this or that sort of action in this or that situation. But, the argument goes on, to explain in any creditable way means to subsume the actions or events to be explained under laws. The wedding of this aim and this procedure requires laws for individuals, or at least laws which, in conjunction with initial conditions describing particular individuals, enable the psychologist to draw conclusions in the form of description and predictions of the behaviour of this or that individual. So Kepler's laws, as I have said, come to serve as the idiographic psychologist's ideal, for these laws do have the virtue of describing, and far in advance at that, the actual behaviour of specific, *named* bodies. Now Kepler's laws are rather unique in this respect, and so are apt to be misleading as models of appropriate scientific pursuits. It is perhaps idle to attempt to show that the psychologist's aim is *logically* misconceived in this respect. But the odds are certainly against him. In order to derive consequences about John's behaviour in the next minute, hour, or year from the laws of personality, the initial conditions which afford the bridge from laws to consequences must be extraordinarily complicated, for people and their separate histories are extraordinarily complex. Thus, if knowing John is knowing all about him, our knowledge will be so detailed and varied that we must have recourse in making our predictions, not to statistical regularities associating the situation with a wide range of uniform behaviour, but to an assessment of John as a person. Our very concept of personality will arise via assessment, and denote the composite picture of John or Mary pieced together by means of long study and observation. The psychoanalyst, to make use of one of Meehl's excellent examples,[8] explains a woman's hallucinations of a raven on her pillow as a need to test her husband's love. He cannot have recourse to statistical formulations of the association of avian hallucination and a desire to test a husband's love. And the ways in which one could state general principles would be so general as to be vacuous. He must, because it is just *this* hallucination and *this* person which concern him, resort to other techniques which could be fairly characterized as hunches. Freud glorifies this notion as the 'resonance' of the analyst's unconscious with the patient's.[9] What he is saying might better be put in the language

[8] Paul Meehl, *Clinical and Statistical Prediction* (University of Minnesota Press, 1954), pp. 49–50.
[9] Sigmund Freud, *Collected Papers* (The Hogarth Press and Institute of Psychoanalysis, 1924), Vol. II, p. 328.

of assessment: that kind of inference lacking formalized steps which can be rehearsed at will. And being unable to reproduce them, we are unable to elevate this collection of more or less informed hunches to the level of a method to be practised by any qualified member of a profession. It is not that there is no place for hunches, for understanding others, for assessment; these are indeed the tools we have at our disposal for the kinds of judgments we are inclined to make about individuals. We surely also want to admit that some people have a 'gift' for this sort of thing. Psychoanalysts like Freud and Sullivan, and perhaps others like Reik or Stekel, demonstrate constantly in their dealings with patients the ability to 'size-up' and predict the patients' behaviour.

But, as Meehl notes, there can be no genuine logic to such predictions or assessments, except in the actuarial analysis of their results. Psycho-analysts' claims might then be tested in the following manner. If any one is trained by special people in a special manner he will have signifi-cantly greater success in predicting individual behaviour than anyone else. There are, of course, no statistics of this sort except the dubious reports of analysts in congratulating themselves on their successes. The statistics that are available would lead one to suppose that training and theory have very little to do with the successful issue of prediction. In short the successes have more to do with the kind of individual making the predictions than with the method or theory they employ in making them.

In the *Psychopathology of Everyday Life*, Freud provides many examples of his flair in making shrewd guesses about the problems troubling people, from their mistakes and lapses of memory. In one case, for example, 'a young man of academic education' attempts to quote the line from Vergil: 'Exoriare aliquis nostris ex ossibus ultor', but cannot supply the word 'aliquis'. On being asked for everything that came to his mind, the young man produced the following associations: a-liquis, reliques, liquidation, liquidity, fluid; and then: 'of Simon of Trent, whose relics I saw two years ago in a church in Trent', of the work of *Kleinpaul*, of an article entitled 'What St. Augustine said concerning Women', of a gentleman he had met who was 'an original type', and whose name was Benedict. At this point Freud interpolates: '. . . you give a grouping of saints and church fathers: St. Simon, St. Augustine, and St. Benedict . . . *Origenes* . . . and Paul in the name Kleinpaul.'

The man now thinks of St. Januarius and his blood miracle, a reference to the supposed liquefaction of the saint's blood, kept in a phial in a church in Naples, and of an occasion on which the miracle failed to take place on time. While soldiers waited for the liquefaction, the young man remembers, Garibaldi hinted to the priest that the miracle *should* take place. All of this leads the young man to 'an intimate matter' which he is reluctant to impart, but eventually says: 'I suddenly thought of a woman from whom I could easily get a message that would be very annoying to us both.'

Freud: 'That she missed her courses?'

The young man is appropriately astonished, but Freud notes, 'You prepared me for it long enough. Just think of the *saints of the calendar, the liquefying of the blood on a certain day, the excitement if the event does not take place,* and *the distinct threat that the miracle must take place. . . .'* And so Freud triumphantly concludes, 'Indeed, you have elaborated the miracle of St. Januarius into a clever allusion to the courses of the woman'.[10]

What can be gathered from this case? First, it is obvious that there is something to the interpretation. It has the virtues of logical consistency (provided one accepts the punning ground rules) and it appears to be borne out by the evidence. Though it may seem extraordinary or repellent that mistakes and omissions may have this meaning, it would appear difficult to doubt Freud's interpretation, for the man's testimony bears out the remarkable inferences. But the manner of inference is obscure, and for that reason is apt to be called intuitive; the process of inference cannot be described. But if the inferential process cannot be described, it is no longer possible to decide whether an analyst is correctly using it. The tests of his insights are the results in particular cases. In place of a method which could be correctly or incorrectly applied, one is forced to depend wholly on the person making the inferences, and he is evaluated wholly in terms of his successes.

The force of these objections can be brought home more clearly by contrasting the previous case with another drawn from the same work (on pp. 35–38 of the *Basic Works*), which along with the *aliquis* case, Freud regards as an example of his skill, method and theory. But here the inferences are far-fetched and the punning connexions strained. Freud had been trying to recall the name Signorelli, but produced instead the names of two other artists, Botticelli and Boltraffio. The occasion of his lapse of memory was a conversation in which Freud and a travelling companion had been discussing, just prior to the difficulty over the name, the fatalistic attitude of Turks living in Bosnia and Herzegovina toward death. A colleague, Freud reported, says of them that 'when one is

10 *The Basic Works of Sigmund Freud*, edited and translated by A. A. Brill (Random House: Modern Library, 1938), pp. 41–44.

compelled to inform them that there is no help for the patient, they answer: "*Sir* (Herr), what can I say? I know that if he could be saved, you would save him".'

At this juncture Freud says that he was about to call attention to a further characteristic of Turks living in Bosnia and Herzegovina, that they 'value sexual pleasure above all else', one of his colleague's patients telling him: 'For you know, Sir (Herr), if that ceases, life no longer has any charm.' Freud blocked this thought, he tells us, because of its associations with the theme of 'Death and Sexuality'. He was much affected at the time by a message he had received while staying at *Trafoi*, telling of a patient who had committed suicide 'on account of an incurable sexual disturbance'.

We are now invited to draw a punning connexion between *Bos*nia and the two obtruding names, *Bol*traffio and *Bo*tticelli, between Trafoi and Bol*traffio*, and between *Signor*elli, *Herze*govina and the conversational references to 'Sir' in 'Sir, what can I say . . .' and 'For you know, sir . . .'.

Now the practice of punning is, in its humble way, a skill. One may be good at it (Freud perhaps), or hopelessly bad. Furthermore, one man may fall into punning habits while another man's chain of thoughts may operate on rather different principles. Thus it may be supposed that Freud has told us something about his own thinking habits, and has given in addition samples of his virtuosity in carrying off puns in a more or less dashing or felicitous manner. But it is not clear that a talent for puns will bear the theoretical load that Freud wishes to put upon it. Of course, the reason given for forgetting is not the mere capacity to weave a chain of words or thoughts out of punning connexions, but the fact that the puns lead ultimately to unpleasant recollections, thus showing why some member of the set of pun-linked terms has been forgotten through repression. The odd thing in the present case is that it is not clear why one name (Signorelli) could not be recalled, while others (Botticelli and Boltraffio), connected with the same force by the punning inferences to the objectionable thoughts, should obtrude themselves. What is left is the demonstration of a somewhat dubious punning skill in a case that is supposed instead to lay the foundations for a general theory of forgetting. In the *aliquis* case we are prone to marvel at a turn of mind that can ferret out human problems and preoccupations from the slender evidence of a forgotten word. But in the *Signorelli* case we are more apt to marvel at the capacity to link up a fact, already known, with a chain of ingenious puns. But in both cases we are struck by a unique performance, rather than a process of inference from statable premises and by replicable methods

It is no wonder that we marvel at successful performances of this sort. when we could have no inkling of how the thing could be done at all.

Psychoanalysts seem to be aware of their personal virtues, for their works bristle with just such astounding inferential successes, astounding just in the sense that the method by which they have been reached cannot be stated. Meehl (p. 51) quotes a case from Theodore Reik, who, in *Listening with the Third Ear*, relates the following analytic episode. A female patient tells him that she had been to the dentist, where after an injection of novacaine, a wisdom tooth was pulled. Now the spot is hurting again. All at once 'she pointed to my bookcase in the corner and said, "There's a book standing on its head". Without the slightest hesitation (Reik reports) I said, "But why did you not tell me that you had had an abortion?" ' Now here is a marvel of prophetic acumen which, like that of the detective in crime fiction, may gain in magic through the suppression of details which, had their auditors and readers been in the know, would not have seemed so marvellous. But even allowing Reik his striking guess, his achievement must still be seen as a reflection of extensive experience with patients and a flair for punning inferences. Theories about the relation of abortions to the use of certain kinds of symbols and concern over things upside down are obviously too cumbersome to employ, and much too hedged about with qualifications to stand as significant theories. These predictions are, like most of our ordinary life assessments and predictions of human action, *ad hoc*. For even if a successful theory of paralogical behaviour could be devised, it would not help in working with the special case.

The enormous difference between the basis for predictions and the theory introduced to support them can be best seen in the contrast between the earlier and later descriptions and diagnoses of patients' troubles in the work of Freud. Within the *Psychopathology* itself some of the cases, like the *aliquis* case, appear to be reports of that case alone, untroubled by theoretical considerations, while others are interpretations forced by the demand that rules of interpretation hold for all possible cases. The long case with which the *Psychopathology* begins is an instance. The punning inferences which lead through the names Botticelli, Signorelli, Boltraffio, Herzegovina, and Trafoi to thoughts of death and sexuality are demanded by theoretical considerations, and the consequences reached by their means refer to vague thoughts and feelings rather than to the specific but forgotten or suppressed events, which make of the *aliquis* case such a *tour de force*. And this leads eventually, as in the Little Hans case, to an inattention to the particular circumstances of the patient. The boy's words and actions are noted only so far as they can be forced into the theory of Oedipus fixation. The boy, in fact, plays this game in a quite intelligent fashion with Freud, construing his own behaviour in the light of what he is expected to say. The typical response of Hans is: 'If he thinks it, it is good all the same, because you can write it to the Professor.'[11]

In the earlier Freud, of the *Psychopathology*, *The Interpretations of Dreams* and *Studies on Hysteria*, one sees a collection of often brilliant but *ad hoc* insights. Naturally, one supposes, there are other cases, not reported, in which the divinations went astray. Analysts are not prone to report their failures. In the successful cases, too, it is possible to see general patterns, tendencies and circumstances, in which people make slips, dream, or adopt strange habits and beliefs. But these themes do not as yet constitute anything so pretentious as a theory from which the observed slips, dreams and practices follow. That is, they do not afford a reliable basis for prediction, though they may serve as *prima facie* rules of interpretation. For the basis for prediction is still a study of the individual, so detailed as to defeat the application of laws stating uniform connexions of some kinds of experience with some kinds of behaviour.

In the later Freud, the themes that emerge as common patterns in earlier divinations acquire theoretical standing. This change is required if psychoanalytic procedure is to live up to its scientific claims. So, for the hunches growing out of and tested in particular interviews, he substitutes laws of paralogical processes. These laws have the virtue of mechanical applicability; they can be learned in some unambiguous way by pupils of the analytic method. But applied in this spirit they defeat the kind of divining procedure, the pursuit of hunches, the shrewd guess, that gives point to the psychiatric interview. When an analyst attempts to convey what he has learned about the examination of patients, as Harry Stack Sullivan does in *The Psychiatric Interview*,[12] for example, it is clear that he cannot tell the novice the exact circumstances in which a rule can be invoked, or an interpretation made. He can tell him that certain rules and certain cues are helpful, if applied with due care (and how is this to be defined?) to the case before him, but there is nothing here that has the clarity of rules governing experiments in physics or biology. Individual actions are the consequences of a whole history and all the complexities of the situation in which they occur. To invoke general laws presupposes a simple and general relation holding between limited numbers of

---

[11] *Collected Papers* III, p. 215. There are two excellent critiques of the Little Hans case, the first by H. J. Eysenck, in the Spring 1961 issue of *Inquiry*, the second in Philip Rieff's study, *Freud: The Mind of the Moralist* (Viking Press, 1959). The upshot of both critiques is that Freud has over-explained the case, and has been joined in this enterprise by the very clever boy.
[12] Harry Stack Sullivan, *The Psychiatric Interview* (Norton, 1954).

variables, ignoring the differentia of individual cases. Consequently, if I wish to predict whether a given arrow from a given bow is going to hit its target, I will rely on my impression of the archer, and not on calculations which will include the wind velocity, the physical properties of bow and arrow, muscle, nerve and bone, and innumerable other properties which might, some years hence, fall into place in an enormously complicated formula from which I could predict precisely the outcome which occurred years before. Nor is a computer the answer here, for the problem is a matter of stating the exact nature of the relation among the many variables, and getting the values for them, and not merely calculating the consequences of the specific assortment of values. The difficulties have to do with programming, not using, the computer. We might say of the arrow thudding in the target that there are laws governing this occurrence. But we should not be able to say that the laws allow us to predict the precise consequence of any particular, but complex, situation.

The *clinical* use of psychiatric theory has the same disadvantages. If it is used as a way of predicting and explaining every remark, dream, or gesture, it blots out the idiosyncratic features of the case which in fact allow perspicacious description and prediction of particular actions or particular individuals on particular occasions. Laws of the paralogical process may, of course, relate to the actions of an individual. And so, to the clinician, theory may provide the rough outlines, the limits, of his approach. But employed in this spirit psychiatric theory consists of rules of thumb to be tentatively applied and, if useless, discarded. As rules of thumb, they cannot be used as determinants of what happens, but only as surmises that might make what happens intelligible, or as instructions to look out for certain things. The status of the theory itself is another matter which will concern us later. But it must be in this entirely flexible way that it applies to the clinical work.

If a baseball player wishes to improve his batting average, he does not go to the physicist whose laws govern what happens when a bat hits a ball, or to the physiologist, whose expertise entitles him to say something about the movements of his muscles as responses to the stimuli acting upon his eye. He goes instead to the batting coach who, though entirely ignorant of these theories, has the long observation and practice which enables him to diagnose the batter's particular difficulties. It is like this in clinical practice: experience and detail enable some psychiatrists, some writers, some husbands, some mothers to have something perspicacious to say about particular cases. Idiographic theorists are unhappy with this situation, just because it is both successful and *ad hoc*; it is not governed adequately by laws and criteria which would give it status as scientific knowledge. If their attempt to supply the theory for these disparate observations fails, as I think it must, then, perhaps, one ought to look more carefully at the epistemology which has led them to suppose that such a demand is a requisite for any knowledge claim.

PSYCHOLOGY: GENERAL THEORY

Many psychologists would endorse this demotion of idiographic theories. They wish, like the sociologists, to operate along lines more like those of physics, and so consider it their aim to devise nomothetic or probabilistic theories. This impulse to pattern their inquiries after the manner of physics leads psychologists to suppose that the object of their inquiries is observable and measurable behaviour, the results of which can then be formulated into laws stating relationships between two or more such variables, or between some of them and features of the environment. According to some this is enough. There is no need for a further stage at which the psychologist tries to explain the observed regularities or functional dependencies. Skinner, for example, sees the explanation of behaviour, if I understand him aright, as arising in another context which is no concern of the psychologist. Others would be inclined to say that when regularities are established behaviour has been explained; explanation is no more than a description sophisticated enough to juggle more than one variable at a time. Still others find that regularities afford the basis for theories which in turn will explain why people act as they do. Let us consider the last of these first.

To do so is to bring in a new pair of terms from the psychologist's arsenal of methodological terms, 'hypothetical construct' and 'intervening variable'. I shall follow the policy of shortening these expressions to, simply, construct and variable. 'Hypothetical' is redundant, and 'intervening' has a connotation which needs to be avoided in understanding their use of the term. The terms seem to have been introduced into psychology by Tolman, but I shall be following the sense given them in an article by MacCorquodale and Meehl.[13] Both concepts add something to what is directly observed. Constructs are conjectures as to the sort of mechanism that might explain why an observed response attends a given stimulus. Variables are mathematical facilitations of inferences, especially predictions, without ontological implications. In physics, the parallelogram of forces might be construed as involving only variables; the particle theory of light would be regarded as a construct.

[13] 'On a Distinction between hypothetical constructs and intervening variables', *Psychological Review*, 55 (1948), pp. 95–107.

The role of the variable is not difficult to understand. It might be supposed, for example, that a direct relation holds between number of trials and speed of solution of a maze. When the experimental evidence does not support such a surmise, one turns to rather more complicated mathematical techniques. As long ago as 1885 Ebbinghaus was introducing logarithmic equations in place of simple proportionality. In the same spirit, Hull's complicated formula relating 'habit strength' to trials, $sHr = M(1-e^{-kt})$, introduces the base of natural logarithms (e) as a constant enabling the law to fit the observed data.[14] It has no empirical or theoretical meaning in itself. Psychologists seem to be in agreement that variables can be introduced at will, if they facilitate a more generalized description or prediction. Nothing beyond pragmatic advantage hinges on the employment of such techniques. Consequently they have no explanatory significance, and do not raise particular problems for us. The construct is another kettle of fish. In standard sorts of experiments it is found that rewards, punishments, trials, and so on, correlate with learning speed. Now two attitudes toward such correlations could be taken. A thoroughgoing behaviourist might insist that the whole story is to be found in these correlations. So Thorndike's law of effect, according to which an organism tends to repeat actions that lead to pleasurable consequences, could be reformulated in terms of reinforcement, according to which the consequences which count as reinforcing are just those which show up in correlation with learning and other behaviour tendencies. If Skinner's reformulation does not ring true it is perhaps because we know, at the start of an investigation, the sorts of consequences which would count as reinforcing, and it is odd to think of a rigorous operational redefinition of concepts and an experimental test of reinforcement hypotheses leading to such platitudinous conclusions.

I shall return in a moment to strict behaviourism. For the present, I wish to consider the views of those who regard the correlations of responses with stimuli (however considered) as the basis for the elaboration of theoretical links joining them. Sometimes, perhaps, links of this kind are felt to be necessary as a result of a mentalistic prejudice. A complete account of behaviour must surely show the mediation of thoughts and intentions, motives and desires, sensations and perceptions, between external stimuli and observed behaviour. Tolman's generous allowance of mentalistic variables would be an instance. Such theories wish to assign a place to a concept like motive, for example, which both redefines

[14] Taken from E. R. Hilgard, *Theories of Learning* (Appleton-Century Crofts, 1956), p. 372. The other variables are: M = upper limit of habit strength, t = trials, k = constant expressing learning rate.

the term in the language of physical occurrence and still allows it the force of a 'mental' concept. I shall postpone treatment of this use of such concepts, partly because R. S. Peters, in *The Concept of Motivation*, and many other recent philosophers, have argued the case for the logical impropriety of such theories with great effect, and partly because it will suffice to see them against a different interpretation of mentalistic concepts later on (Chapter VI). In any case, I do not believe that the mentalistic howler is committed as often by psychologists as Cartesian myth-hunters among philosophers pretend. The drift toward constructs has more to do with the attempt to avoid platitudes in the formulation of S-R connexions than with fixation on a Cartesian model of thinking. The typical laws of learning, for example, are strikingly like observations any one of us could have made without benefit of research. Animal trainers and parents take for granted in their day to day dealings with animals and children that behaviour can be altered or conditioned by rewards and punishments. It is built into the concept of pleasure that people will repeat actions with pleasurable consequences; we should regard them as peculiar if they did not. Thorndike's law of effect is only a more pompous rendering of this platitude. We are also quite aware of the value of repetition, recency, association and all the other devices that psychologists supposedly have shown to relate to the learning process. In another day these were perhaps thought of as mnemonic devices, techniques facilitating learning in this and that case, though not to be interpreted as laws determining behaviour. And so psychologists have tried to suggest that their measures of habit strength, reinforcement, motive, and all the rest are not simply descriptions of clockable behaviour, which are discovered to have precisely the relation to learning that we already knew, but that they are indirect measures of other elements in the organism, elements which, in day to day psychologizing, ordinary men would never have stumbled upon. Such a concept is drive, another, as psychologists have appropriated the term, is motive. It is this desire for explanatory novelty, seconded by writings in the philosophy of science, that play up the role of theoretical constructs in scientific explanation, which accounts, I believe, for the prevalence of such constructs in psychology. The question is whether they do the job for which they are intended, i.e., whether they explain behaviour.

In some contexts, notably Freudian theory, psychologists of learning are rightly suspicious of the concept of drive. Their objection is that libido or psychic energy is put forward as a quantitative notion, yet remains essentially non-measurable. In contrast, they point with pride to their own experimental measurements, which have converted drive from a shadowy and occult force into an indirectly measurable concept. It is like, they say, the contrast between the Epicurean and the modern atom.

But there are difficulties. Atoms, electrons and other particles are described in a language common to observed movements as well, that is, velocity, direction of movement, position and spin. If drive is identified with what is measured, hours of food-deprivation for example, it is not quite clear why it is called a construct. If it is assumed to be an unknown quantity that increases with length of deprivation, its explanatory role is wholly redundant. For the construct only restates in a language of occult events what we observe when we see that an organism tries harder to get something it has been deprived of longer. If it is clear why adding to the time of deprivation increases or intensifies a certain behaviour, B, then it is clear by the same token why increasing drive or habit strength or motive affects B. If it is not clear why increased deprivation affects B, then neither is it clear why increased drive affects B. For all we know about drive is what is measured by time of deprivation. The alternative to redundancy is to suppose that by drive is meant more than what is measured. The 'more' in this case (which psychologists sometimes refer to as 'surplus meaning') is apparently the explanatory power which, in ordinary life, accompanies such commonplace observations as, men eat more voraciously when they are very hungry. If it is this surplus that explains, it is surely not something established by painstaking experimental procedures. It would be odd for the psychologist to claim that now, for the first time, we know that people eat because they are hungry, or pursue women because of sexual cravings, or a fast buck because of a desire to get rich quick. The horns of the dilemma of the drive construct are redundancy and platitude.

Concepts like effort, strength of feeling and desire, and thought are the currency of ordinary speech, explaining actions in piecemeal ways, without benefit of theory. They take us back to our initial observations, that most of our accounting of human action is *ad hoc*, but still sufficient. The grounds for their sufficiency needs still to be traced, but it is not the sort of thing that can be supported by the theories of psychologists. These theories are, by implication, causal chain theories. Deprivation produces a need, which gives rise to a drive, which pumps up the bodily machine to action. There are two ways of analysing the intervening terms. One way leads to an identification of need with deprivation, that is, we see as observers that the deprivation will have certain consequences unless something is done. The drive, in turn, is identified with the action, that is, with the propensity to behave in a given manner. If this road is taken, it is up to the psychologist to show that the connexion of deprivation (or other numerically describable features of the situation) and action is (*a*) law-like and (*b*) extends our account of human behaviour. The other way leads to an identification of need and drive with physiological states. The first of these alternatives is behaviourism, in at least one sense of that term, the second reduces psychology to physiology.

Now behaviourism is in a sense the basis for a physiological science. It is a method for describing the movements that people and animals make without the usual ties of our descriptions to purposive explanation. Instead of talking about a person reaching out for a cup of coffee or a rat struggling towards its reward, behaviourism provides a way of talking about the movements of bodily parts through space together with the varying repetitions and speeds of such movements. These in turn can be connected with carefully measured and introduced (or withheld) items in the environment, like the amount of food, the time intervals of feeding, or the intensity, duration and frequency of shocks. This neutral description opens up a new view of human and animal behaviour; it sees it as preceding and following other events. This is of use if an older and a self-explanatory way of describing the behaviour muddles the issue. Talk about actions, purposes, desires, motives is no more amenable to the physiological account of behaviour than terms like hard, soft, fast and slow, green and brown are to a Galilean description of motion. The quantitative description of behaviour thus serves as a basis for rather more precisely worded inferences as to complicated neural processes than would be possible on an ordinary description of a man's movements. So Hebb, noting that the lapse in time between a stimulus and a response is uniformly greater than that required for the actual transmission of nervous signals, surmises that something like a holding mechanism, familiar from telephone exchanges, keeps the message going, as it were, without immediately discharging it into the appropriate afferent nerves.[15] The holding mechanism is a construct indeed, and a genuine one. It is of a logical piece with the disparate kinds of events it is supposed to connect and explain, and while it may not be observable in practice, it is not unobservable in principle. At least it is conceivable that some independent evidence of such neural structure and action might be forthcoming.

In this sense, then, behavioural psychology is a method for exploring the physiological structures that constitute the surmised links between stimuli and behaviour. It is not, in that sense, a body of laws or theory in its own right, but the procedure and the evidence that can become relevant to, and united in, physiological theory.

[15] D. O. Hebb, *Textbook of Psychology* (W. B. Saunders, 1958), pp. 55–58.

Psychologists commonly eschew physiologizing, however; some because they hold that there are genuine psychological constructs like motive and drive, others because they feel that physiological knowledge and method of inquiry is insufficient to predict and explain human action adequately. These two views are often held together, but as we have already seen the danger of redundancy or platitude inherent in the supposition that there are constructs which avoid both common sense and physiology, we can confine our attention to the second of these claims. Sometimes these objections are empirical; physiological inquiry is in its infancy, and highly speculative, and it is not reasonable to expect that current knowledge and techniques can provide an adequate physiological explanation of S-R connexions. But in such circumstances it might be supposed that we ought, as psychologists, to busy ourselves with a physiological investigation and, until we improve our methods and enlarge our discoveries, refrain from talk about explanatory constructs. Many psychologists, however, reject physiology on logical grounds. Even admitting a more adequate conception of what is going on in the nervous system, it is argued that this information and the method of acquiring it will be much too complicated to be of service in accounting for specific human actions. Hebb, who is a chief exponent of the physiological tendency within psychology, provides these people with their best illustration. Interpreting or predicting gross and particular behaviour by means of neural processes would be like interpreting, describing and predicting a storm through a description of individual raindrops.[16]

These reservations go back to the psychologist's idiographic hopes. The psychologist talks a great deal about general laws which will enable him to predict, but he seems ultimately dissatisfied with any kind of prediction except that which will, in Allport's way of talking, tell him what John will do next. He is also principally concerned with control, and here too he has in mind what he can do with a specific individual. A theory will satisfy him only if it will tell him exactly what to do in order to turn out a particular kind of person or promote a particular action. The odds do not favour this aim, except, of course, that in ordinary life we have a reasonable degree of success in such prediction. But this kind of prediction, as we have seen is essentially a business of assessment based on long acquaintance with a particular individual, and is not the short-circuited method provided by the application of general laws.

In any case, the psychologist's hope is vitiated by the ambiguity of his use of the term behaviour. It is quite possible to isolate from the normal activities of human beings and animals types of muscular movement,

[16] D. O. Hebb, *Textbook*, p. 262.

and to connect these with actual or hypothetical neural events, and these in turn to classes of stimuli, for example, light frequencies or electric shocks. This way of cutting up behaviour into units recommends itself to psychologists because of its 'scientific' rigour. Unfortunately these units do not add up in any way to the objects of the psychologist's interest. This unit of interest is, in the psychologist's jargon, *molar*, that is, a division of behaviour into practices, habits, and actions identified by the fact that a given stretch of movements can be seen as purposive, meaningful or intentional. Physiological description of human or animal behaviour, on the other hand, is *molecular*, of which the elements are the spatio-temporal properties of behaviour. Psychologists sometimes talk as if their choice of a molar or molecular analysis is purely a matter of how finely you want to cut the units. But there is no reason to suppose that a number of molecular units add up to a molar unit or that a particular molar unit subdivides neatly into so-and-so many molecular units. They are different ways of cutting up behaviour into identifiable units of investigation; they may very well overlap and so fail to contribute to each other's purposes. Molecular subdivisions of behaviour provide precise descriptions, for they are, by definition, measurable units of behaviour; but this does not make them more precise units of the type formerly provided by molar units. Part of the muddle here is to be found in the supposition that when in ordinary life we talk about actions we are referring in a vague way to what psychologists, with notions like speed of response or muscular movement, are talking about in a precise way. As the rest of this book will be concerned in one way or another with a reinterpretation of the concept of action we may for the moment pass by this particular confusion.

All of this leaves intact a kind of analysis of behaviour which, as it were, is half-way between the molar concept of action and the molecular concept of muscular movement, an analysis which is best seen in concepts like speed of response, number of trials, and hours of deprivation. The possibility of constructing a graph by computing, say, numbers of trials against numbers of errors, or extinction responses against the number of reinforcements, gives a mathematical means of forecasting learning behaviour (provided it is properly interpreted) and so meets at least some of the conditions of a scientific theory, mathematical formulation and prediction. The mathematical description does not provide an explanation of learning, though, if significant, the curves present some interesting puzzles worth explaining. The curious fact about psychological research is that so much argument goes on with respect to the proper shape of the curves. There is, in other words, basic disagreement on the evidence, and not merely on the proper way of explaining it. This is perhaps not too surprising. Different experimenters use different subjects, and the rates of learning and extinction might be thought to reflect differences in the subjects not accounted for in the experimenter's variables. All the various curves and the mathematical formulae designed to express them may be correct for the particular range of subjects, but the total range of response may be so wide that a generalized formula for these different curves is totally useless. If, for example, some bodies in a gravitational field were to move in circles around the centre of mass, others in ellipses, others in ovoids and still others in negatively curved lines it would be possible to construct mathematical formulae for each of the cases, and, perhaps, a formula which would average out the different movements. But the generalized formula would be of no use in describing or predicting any particular case. It is surely not that sort of generalization that the scientist hankers after. The parameters must provide limits which give the formula a significant probability. Skinner's studies of individual cases reflect the anxiety of one who supposes that his generalizations ought to have pertinence to cases; thus his investigations allow the extrapolation of curves which will predict the next trial, but always of a particular rat or pigeon.[17] To suppose that a science of psychology will be a compendium of mathematical formulae for individual cases is to defeat the very point of scientific organization. This I suppose is why so many psychologists have found Skinner's results so anaemic, even if in his procedures, Skinner has avoided the pitfalls of constructs or common sense explanations. His procedure leads back to the difficulties of idiographic theory.

But with a difference. Skinner's plan seems to be to replace the normal human and animal environment with laboratory conditions. He conceives of psychology as a piece of human engineering. He wishes to demonstrate that, with adequate controls, any desired kind of behaviour can be produced in a subject. We all know this in a general way, and Skinner is the first to admit that his views are built on quite ordinary conceptions of the function of reinforcement in everyday life. In ordinary life, however, we take these principles of teaching and, if you will, conditioning, as techniques that might do the job desired, not as laws that explain the manifold behaviour of human or animal populations. What Skinner has added to these commonplaces, that pleasurable experiences are likely to be repeated, that rewards promote learning, that punishment (which of course he disavows as a method) may block the formation of bad habits, is a technique for making more certain that a reward will

[17] In the ensuing remarks, I am relying particularly on *Cumulative Record* (Appleton-Century Crofts, 1961), a collection of B. F. Skinner's papers.

have the desired effect. The experimental environment makes it possible to control and induce behaviour in a way not paralleled in normal environments. The regularities of stimulus–response connections in the laboratory can not then be extrapolated as more accurate measurements of what must also hold for the world at large. They are artificially produced, and represent what human or animal nature can be like under such artificial circumstances. Both the conditioning psychologist and the bureaucratic sociologist are engaged in the practical endeavour, based on some of the potentialities of their human subjects, of constructing an environment which will produce the desired response, or the desired conformity. But if the experimental situation is taken as providing the key test for a general theory of behaviour, these techniques will be interpreted instead as laws of human nature and of society, as the only ways that human and animal subjects behave. Thus experiment seems to produce what we have never had before, explanatory laws of behaviour.

Psychology's successes are essentially successes in the mechanics of control, and not in the explanation of normal human action. Both in psychology and sociology successful methods for controlling particular kinds of behaviour are confused with general laws explaining human behaviour. The conditioned animal thus becomes, not the special case of what can happen in an artificially controlled environment, but the paradigm case for human behaviour generally, and the social conformist becomes, not the specialized product achieved by the cunning employment of specialized techniques of social control but the inevitable result of the interplay of social forces and individual motives.

As theory, then, psychology avoids the redundancy-platitude dilemma only by changing the human environment. It is an enormous step from the rules applicable to these artificial situations to laws of human nature. When these rules are extended to apply to the general condition of human existence they result in the typical tautologies or platitudes that we found also to be characteristic of sociological theories. Toward the end of his survey of learning theories, for example, Hilgard formulates a series of propositions which he feels psychologists might advance without fear of disagreement.[18] Some of these are clearly tautological. For example, his first proposition tells us that 'brighter people can learn things less bright ones cannot learn'. It is nowhere made clear how we could identify the brighter person save in his ability to learn more than his duller brother. Or again, number two tells us that 'a motivated learner acquires what he learns more readily than one who is not motivated'. The tests of motivation are so intimately bound up with

[18] *Theories of Learning*, pp. 486–7.

successful, avid, or persistent performance that it is difficult to understand this statement in any sense other than that a person who learns readily learns readily.

Others among Hilgard's statements are just as clearly platitudinous, in the sense that our use of certain kinds of concepts commits us to these propositions without further research. Thus number three: 'motivation that is too intense (especially pain, fear and anxiety) may be accompanied by distracting emotional states, so that excessive motivation may be less effective than moderate motivation for learning some kinds of tasks, especially those involving difficult discriminations'. A person bothered by great pain is not likely to attend to a task very well. So, he goes on to say, learning under control of reward is usually preferable to learning under control of punishment, a statement which is often taken to reflect a new break-through in learning theory. But a moment's reflection will lead us to see that it is rather difficult to think of pain, anxiety and punishment except as distracting. We know the distracting and obstructing effects of pain on learning or any activity, in knowing what we mean by pain.

A number of Hilgard's items relate to the old formula, practice makes perfect. Any concert pianist, athlete or student must know that (number 11) 'there is no substitute for repetitive practice in the overlearning of skills . . . or in the memorization of unrelated facts that have to be automatized', or (12) that 'information about the nature of a good performance, knowledge of his own mistakes, and knowledge of successful results, aid learning', or (13) 'transfer to new tasks will be better if, in learning, the learner can discover relationships for himself, and if he has experience during learning of applying the principles within a variety of tasks', or (14) that 'spaced or distributed recalls are advantageous in fixing material that is to be long retained'. We all do these things in trying to learn a subject-matter or acquire a skill. We must practice; we must know, approximately at least, what is aimed at if we are to know if we have achieved it. It helps to figure things out for oneself, or to be able to apply something learned already to a new subject-matter, or to go at a subject, especially involving long memorization, in spurts, going away from it and coming back. It would be difficult to reach any kind of goal in life without such procedures. It is difficult to imagine why refined techniques of experimental inquiry should labour to bring forth such mice. It is the same with the platitudes in which Hilgard points to the importance of realistic goal-setting, the advantage of balance of successes over failures, or active participation of the learner. Realistic goal-setting is, in the first place, part of what we mean by getting a balance of successes, and I take it that if one consistently fails it is not long before one gives up a task. The importance of active participation has been debated in schools of education as if there were an issue to be decided. The learn-by-doing thesis is not a profoundly new discovery about human learning, but the observation that learning is, after all, a species of doing.

Finally, number eight, Hilgard's catch-all: 'The personal history of the individual, for example, his reaction to authority, may hamper or enhance his ability to learn from a given teacher.' This is less a generalization than a repository for an indefinitely large cluster of particular statements about the relationships between students and teachers. The generalization does not here support the particular assertions but merely summarizes those well known though *ad hoc* cases in which we find it difficult to attend to a certain manner of lecturing, or cannot be bothered to respond to a certain style of exhortation.

In short, something is wrong with a science that lists such propositions as items to its credit. These statements suggest instead how tautology is embraced in order to secure general truth, platitude to avoid irrelevance. If the psychologist's statements have substance, it is as policies for achieving certain aims, which may or may not be undertaken, and hence may or may not come to characterize the way in which humans learn or acquire other habits. Explanation of human action still resides, for all the efforts of psychologists, in the *ad hoc* pronouncements which we make with confidence about the motives and intentions, desires and anxieties, the anticipated pleasures and the felt pains which account for this or that human action. It is possible to imagine the laborious analysis of behaviour into measurable units serving as the structure and the evidence for physiological hypotheses. But psychology as a science with its own explanatory laws, falls in a no-man's land between physiology and the *ad hoc* deliverances of every-day life.

CHAPTER THREE

INTERACTION

IN THE last chapter I tried to show that redundancy and platitude are the consequences of typical attempts to apply wholesale the techniques of the natural sciences to explanation of human behaviour. This suggests that something might be radically wrong with the conception of explanation borrowed from physics and the philosophy of science, that is, the view that to explain an occurrence is to bring it under a law, and to explain a law is to bring it under another law.[1] The law may be a generalization that embraces a great number of particular instances; thus the fragility of glass might be cited in explaining the shattering of a certain glass. Or it might be a mathematical formula, the values of whose variables arrived at by measurement provide descriptions of a great number of occurrences or predictions of a great number of future occurrences.

If this account is taken as orthodox, something must be done about vast numbers of explanations offered in ordinary life of human actions. For these apparently *ad hoc* appeals to this or that purpose, desire, or interest do not appear to be supported by anything like genuine laws. One way out of the difficulty is to take the view that psychology and the other sciences of human behaviour are late comers on the scene of human discovery. We simply don't know enough about behaviour to offer proper explanations. This view, like most philosophical revelations, has an air of paradox. Surely we do know perfectly well why someone is walking down the street when he tells us, or we discover, that he is going to the store to buy groceries. At the same time it is equally paradoxical to suppose that these quite confident assertions are really supported by law-like statements after all. For example, in *The Structure of Science* Nagel wishes to give an explanation of Cassius' plotting against Caesar in probabilistic terms, thus bringing it within the favoured conception of explanation. 'In ancient Rome (he says, pp. 22–23) the relative frequency (or probability) was high (e.g., greater than one-half) that an individual belonging to the upper strata of society and possessed by great hatred of

---

[1] John Hospers, 'What is Explanation?' in Antony Flew, *Essays in Conceptual Analysis* (Macmillan, 1956), pp. 94–119. The literature supporting this position is very extensive. Cf. e.g. R. B. Braithwaite, *Scientific Explanation* (Cambridge University Press, 1955); Ernest Nagel, *The Structure of Science* (Harcourt Brace, 1961); Carl Hempel and Paul Oppenheim, 'The Logic of Explanation', *Philosophy of Science*, Vol. 15 (1948), reprinted in H. Feigl and M. Brodbeck (eds.), *Readings in the Philosophy of Science* (Appleton-Century Crofts, 1953), pp. 319 ff.

tyranny would plot the death of men who were in a position to secure
tyrannical power. Cassius was such a Roman and Caesar such a potential
tyrant. Hence, though it does not follow that Cassius plotted the death
of Caesar, it is highly probable that he did so.' Or, another example,
from Hempel's paper on 'The Function of General Laws in History'[2]:
the migration of the dustbowl farmers to California is to be explained
by reference to hypotheses which lead us to expect that the events in
question will and do occur. Drought and sandstorm render a farming
existence precarious, California offers better living conditions, and
'populations will tend to migrate toward regions which offer better
living conditions'. In these examples, the generalizations can be pro-
nounced with less authority than the account of the cases which they are
designed to support. We know about Cassius' republicanism and his
ambitions, and about the starvation and frantic hopes of the dustbowlers.
But the tendency statements are little more than arbitrary generalizations
of the single cases, made up just so that no explanation could escape the
generality net. At best they are merely summaries of explanations
accepted for individual cases; they are not generalizations which, by the
manner in which they embrace instances, explain them. In short, I see no
reason to abandon Aristotle's rule that the *explicans* must be better known
than the *explicandum* simply in order to accommodate all cases to the
favoured model of explanation.

Still, the generality thesis is a strong one. The test of any explanation,
on this view, is its scope; the number of instances which can be seen to
follow from it is a clear and objective way of assigning plus marks. To
admit *ad hoc* explanations, on the other hand, is to allow instances of
proper explanations which do not meet any particular standard. It is thus
not uncommon to find those defending non-scientific or non-general
explanation resorting to such vague and subjective notions as 'making
sense' or 'intelligibility' or the extravagant devices of putting oneself in
another's place and reliving his life. If this is the alternative, it would
seem to reduce explanation to feelings of satisfaction with one course of
events as against another, or one account rather than another. Nevertheless, the germ of a correct account of much of our explanation of human
behaviour is to be found in such views, though it will take a good deal
of work to purge them of their subjectivist excesses.

The problem, then, is this. The generality view of explanation has to
its credit straightforward criteria for assessing explanation candidates—
scope, and its special instance, prediction. *Ad hoc* explanations have to

---

[2] Reprinted in H. Feigl and W. Sellars, *Philosophical Analysis* (Appleton–Century Crofts,
1949), pp. 459 ff., and Patrick Gardiner, *Theories of History* (Free Press, 1959), pp. 344 ff.

their credit relevance to cases at hand, which, after all, is what typically interests us when we talk about explaining human behaviour. To apply generalization to these accounts is only to summarize cases which we are quite sure of severally and individually.

We might begin to extricate ourselves from this dilemma by considering the case which lies at the heart of physical explanation, that is, the use of 'cause' in which one event is explained by citing another event temporally prior to it. It is usually supposed that this case illustrates most clearly the generalization thesis in explanation. If a blow causes a man to fall it is because blows of a certain force generally are followed by toppling men. If we accept this account grudgingly, we only need to be reminded that the alternative is an appeal to ghostly forces or hidden springs, unobservable and undescribable, and that is enough to lead us to embrace the Humean thesis.

These, I suggest, are not the alternatives. A further way out is to see that explanatory terms are frequently given a use, not by rule or criterion, but by paradigm. The movements of colliding billard balls is what we mean by causal interaction. Collision verbs reflect this. When we talk about hitting and striking, breaking and scratching, moulding and tearing, we are not (normally) making inferences about the probable consequences of certain kinds of events, we are describing something we observe as a whole. I see one car collide with another, I see one boxer knock another down, I see a player hit a ball with a bat. Doubtless, if nature did not exhibit these uniformities we should not have had a use for such concepts. This, I think, is the gist of Hume's psychological account of the causal relation. But when I explain a case of causal interaction it is not in a normal sense an inference from general sequences at all, but a statement of what I have observed. To treat an instance of collision as a special case of a generalization, is to generalize as artificially as it appeared to be in the case of Cassius plotting the death of Caesar. I do not first become convinced that A's are uniformally followed by B's and then come to be convinced that A caused B in the case happening before my eyes. I am first of all quite sure that what I saw was car A smashing into car B and crumpling its fender. I see, if you like, a continuous sequence of events, which, taken as a whole, can be described as a collision. It would be very odd to maintain that I do not observe the interaction, but only the cars, and that I infer the relation between the car and the crumpled fender. Observed collision, in short, provides a paradigm of causal interaction. We may be said to see, not merely *what* happens in such cases, but *why* it happens.

Hume is led to the generality view of causal ascriptions because of his interest in certain subsidiary cases which do not match the paradigm, particularly cases of mind–body connexion and action at a distance. Let us confine our attention for the moment to the second of these, since the first will occupy us later on.

Why should action at a distance be a problem? If collision is the paradigm of causal explanation (in one of its senses) it is easy to see why. Gravitational attraction requires that one body act upon another in a way not observed, for the conditions of observing the relation could only be met by supposing that the bodies are connected by intervening links. Continuity is lacking. Newton conjectured that the planets may have been hurled into their orbits by the hand of God; and this is perhaps a conjecture of natural as well as theistic piety. It reflects a respect for the standard case of observed interaction. At other times he imposed on his investigations the well-known reservation, *hypotheses non fingo*, claiming only to describe planetary motions in such a way as to embrace in this description falling apples, water climbing the sides of rotating buckets, and oscillating pendulums as well. An explanation of such movements would seem to imply for him reference to the unobserved links which bring objects with regularly accelerating speeds to the ground, or which swing the planets around the sun in elliptical paths. On this conjecture, summarized in the concept of lines of force, the universe would be indeed a machine, in the quite literal sense that it operates by means of inter-connected, interlocking parts.

Hume disposes of the conjectured links of this system, but wishes to preserve the explanatory power that seems to reside in the gravitational theory. He is thus led to reject the interaction paradigm and substitute for it the criterion of observed regularities. He solves the puzzle of action at a distance, and incidentally mind–body interaction, by denying that cause means anything more than a condensed summary of repeatedly observed sequences. But if his bar to the admission of unobserved and occult forces is applied, it becomes quite unnecessary to employ his concept of cause with respect to gravitation at all. Force becomes a way of talking in condensed form about a regular connection of mass and acceleration. We can then describe the orbit or the acceleration or the mass of a body, given values for the other variables, and preserve the explanatory significance of these equations by resorting to the hypothetico-deductive model according to which a law explains just because a wide variety of phenomena can be described by its means. On the other hand, it becomes paradoxical to reduce cases of observed interaction to the generality form. His theory of causation thus makes the term unnecessary or inapplicable.

Hume wanted a criterion by which to judge causal explanations without appeal to empirically undecidable beliefs. To say, 'I saw A hit B' has an air of finality out of all proportion to our ability to defend it. Frequency was a form of evidence that could meet a statable criterion. But of course the sigh of relief had to be temporary. Disposing of causal judgments would only result in raising a host of similar questions about other claims to observe something. Hume is thus led to a theory about the foundations of empirical knowledge, according to which, what is observed can properly be said to be neither defeasible nor challengeable. Observations are of simple impressions, which gain their incorrigibility from their mental residence (the later sense-datum doctrine) or their unanalysability (the later atomistic doctrine). Hume is like all classical empiricists in this respect from Locke to Russell and the positivists. Beginning with the incontestable thesis that knowledge of the world depends upon observation, he wished to devise a theory of what is observed that would free the basis of empirical knowledge from any doubt or challenge. That is, there must be some class of things or qualities which provides the ultimate basis of evidence, and thus requires a clear-cut distinction between what is observed and what is inferred, between evidence and theory. Observations, after all, form the evidence for theories; a theory-infected observation would be a *petitio principii*. In theories, moreover, resides the explanatory force of an account of events. Since they are based on numerous and potentially unending observations an explanation must be general in form.

Now the distinction between observation and theory is context-bound.[3] The trajectory of a ball, from the moment it collides with a bat until it is caught, may count as an observation within the context of a theory stating relations among forces, velocities, trajectories and the like. In this context the motion of the ball is one observed event, the bat striking the ball another. This refinement in the units of observation, however, has nothing to do with establishing that the ball was driven to the edge of the field by the swing of the bat. This is justified by observing the entire sequence. It is not necessary to break up this sequence into smaller units of observation in order to be quite sure that the swing of the bat caused the ball to follow its trajectory; this refinement has to do with an entirely different story that needs to be told about the mathematical

---

[3] Cf. Stephen Toulmin, *The Uses of Argument* (Cambridge University Press, 1958), in which are distinguished field-invariant and field-dependent arguments, the latter of which can be used to make this kind of point.

properties of trajectories, masses and velocities. This new story, in turn, reveals new features of the world to be explained, especially when it is discovered that all balls follow trajectories of the same general mathematical form. But it does not confirm now and at last that the ball really was hit with the bat. We can still say with propriety that we *saw* it happen; the physicist has introduced a way of describing these events which are irrelevant to the purposes of sportsmen and spectators, though relevant to the discovery of events and relations among them of interest to physicists. It would thus be misleading to suggest that the physicist had got down to the level of what is really observed, such as logical atoms or sense-data, and so has provided the basis for explaining events hitherto roughly accounted for by a much less precise use of observation. What counts as the proper object of observation, then, does not constitute a particular class of things, meeting special criteria, but varies with the interest of the onlooker. The notion of a special and universal class of observables thus seems to misconstrue the way in which that concept functions in providing evidence, both in science and in everyday life.

The villain of the piece turns out to be the doctrine of incorrigibility. In their search for ultimate observables classical empiricists were led by the question: have I now got something which would provide the incontestable basis for any knowledge claim? So they were driven to the equally unpalatable extremes of unanalysability or a mental location of the objects of immediate acquaintance. The first of these we have seen to be incoherent, for the unanalysability is provided, not at the beginning of a venture, but after having determined its nature. The second leads to the well-known difficulties of the doctrine of sense-data, the chief of which is that we buy certainty at the price of significance. Since observations are introduced to defend propositions about the world, it defeats the purpose to suppose that they are private, even though, in their privacy they attain by attenuation, the cherished incorrigibility. If this objection does not suffice, it is perhaps not out of line to pass on the duty of exposing the logical difficulties and peculiarities of the sense-datum view to more competent hands, for example, Austin's lectures *Sense and Sensibilia*.

In any case, if observations could be held to be crucial without maintaining that they are incorrigible we should be a long way toward relocating the defence of empirical knowledge on firmer ground. Once again, perhaps, the simple case gives the answer. A man could be mistaken in saying that a player hit the ball, yet his grounds for claiming that the ball was hit is the attention he pays to the events on the field. To conjoin these statements, however, is not disastrous to the view that knowledge depends upon observation. Indeed, the empirical thesis, as it is usually understood, depends upon the possibility that any statement may be false. The demand that all statements be defended by observation should be taken to mean that any statement needs to be defended by employing certain procedures which can be defined without recourse to the consequences that generally follow upon their employment. Unless we so define observation, the whole point of the empiricist's polemic against the *a priori* goes by the board. We leave it up to observation, implying that we cannot know beforehand what is going to be observed. The man who, in defence of his assertion, says, 'I saw it' is, in one sense, always right. He has made the proper kind of defence. But of course he may not have seen it at all. In the same way a man who moves his bishop diagonally is doing the right sort of thing, though by such a move he may forfeit his queen and lose the game.

So far from requiring incorrigible objects, atoms or sense-data as grounds for empirical knowledge, it appears that we would have to jettison them in order to retain our standing as fair-playing empiricists. Otherwise, it is as if we want to play the game but first be sure of winning. Empirical knowledge is a game which it must be possible to lose. And this is the virtue of its victories.[4]

At the same time the more elastic use of observation does not admit any metaphysical hypothesis or woolly surmise. There are many requirements that need to be met for descriptive or theoretical adequacy. But these requirements are dictated by the kind of case and the questions asked about it. Notions like precision and accuracy are not univocal. We cannot always decide whether a player stepped outside a foul line with the kind of precision with which we can determine the dimensions of the playing field. So long as it is clear within a context what would count as evidence, and so long as witnesses claim to have made the appropriate observations, we have done all we can in the possibly humble

---

[4] These comments may appear to bear a relation to Karl Popper's remarks about falsifiability, in, among other places, *The Logic of Scientific Discovery* (Basic Books, 1959). Popper, however, introduced the notion of falsifiability in treating logical problems of the status of laws, i.e. general statements. Since they do not appear to be verifiable, they run the danger of expulsion from the positivist's *élite* circle of meaningful propositions. I am concerned rather with the special and somewhat ambivalent role played by such statements as 'I see . . .' in that they serve both to indicate that appropriate procedures have been undertaken and to describe the results of these undertakings. It is perhaps this confusion that leads to the supposition that what is seen is incorrigible. This is why I introduced the comparison to the chessplayer. For *he* can always say, I made the proper move, and yet it didn't work out.

It might also be added that Popper on occasion, e.g. in the recent volume, *Conjectures and Refutations* (Routledge and Kegan Paul, 1956), puts his falsifiability doctrine to a different and rather important polemical use. It becomes a way of criticizing large-scale theories like those of Freud and Marx, who, in the formulation of their laws, protect themselves from possibly discouraging evidence by accommodating them to any possible evidence. This procedure, of course, while guaranteeing their irrefutability also deprives them of empirical significance. In this sense the point is much closer to my own.

job of setting this or that epistemological record straight. The difficulties, especially for the behavioural sciences, arise when it is supposed that a common epistemology obtains for all inquiries. For then the tendency is to make use of those samples of human knowledge that most readily accommodate themselves to explicit criteria (like scope or generality), and impose them willy-nilly on more recalcitrant materials. In this way physics becomes the paradigm for explanation.

If the demands of classical empiricism can be seen as both unnecessary and extraordinary, the commonly accepted gap between observation and theory upon which the generality theory is based, disappears. Suppose for example, that a man goes through a door operated by a treadle concealed under a mat. The door opens and, somewhat surprised, he repeats the experiment. These are the conditions, one might say, for the Humean view, that knowledge is wholly based on inferences from uniformities. Or, to put the view in the mouth of a psychologist, and thus show the relevance of the argument to our target: 'If we are not to forget the teachings of Hume and John Stuart Mill we must realize that there is nothing observed but concomitant variation—of greater or less relative frequency—and that all analysis of causal textures rests upon this foundation.'[5] But notice that the occasion of the surprise is the absence of observable links. He repeats the process because he is really not sure that there *is* a relation between his footsteps, the treadle and the door. Perhaps because it really doesn't matter, or because it would really be so difficult, not to say illegal, to rip up the treadle and expose the works, he is content with the uniformity. He is capable at this juncture of adequately describing and predicting what happens and will happen when he steps on the treadle. But his explanation at this juncture is likely to be the vacuous: 'something connects them'. This is not a trivial kind of vacuity, however, for it indicates that the sort of events that would explain the occurrence are in the form of connecting links. If he rips up the floor and sees the machinery and observes its operation, his vacuous hypothesis is converted to observed fact, that is, he observes the treadle opening the door. The appeal to regularity is second best, suggesting that something or other (perhaps of a very familiar type) might be happening unseen; but when the unseen is revealed it is what is observed that explains.

What satisfies the man here, and so explains, is, *pace* Hospers, seeing the familiar in the unfamiliar. But Hospers is right in rejecting this formula for the nature of explanation if it means simply adjusting our view of the strange to the customary. The familiar which guides the concept of

⁵ Egon Brunswik, 'The Probability Point of View', in Melvin H. Marx, *Psychological Theory* (Macmillan, 1951), p. 202.

explanation has here the force of the paradigm. When we have exposed the mechanical links joining the treadle to the door, and seen them operate, we have exhibited a standard case of causal interaction. One billiard ball colliding with and moving another, one gear meshing with another, are cases that exemplify the meaning of causal interaction. We should have had no occasion to elevate the case in this way to paradigm status if nature were not reasonably uniform. If balls sometimes disappeared or disintegrated or went straight up out of sight when struck by others we should no doubt have taken a very different, perhaps a statistical, view of the universe, and this would have affected our concept of explanation. Thus Hume's insistence on regularity is a precondition of our use of causal language. But it is not what we mean by causal explanation. The meaning is tied to standard cases of what we observe when we see bodies colliding, or processes operating through a continuum, or parts interlocking. These explanations are *ad hoc* in that what is crucial to their support is seeing something happen, and not inferring connexions based on regularly observed discrete occurrences.

A subsidiary class of this sort of explanation is what Max Black calls 'making something happen'.[6] This class differs from collision in that it involves human intervention. Otherwise, it shares the *ad hoc* features of that class. Cutting, striking, moulding, pulling and pushing are paradigm cases of manipulations, causing or making something happen. If we are able to describe the actions of ourselves and others by phrases like 'cutting the bread', 'kneading the dough', or 'pushing the baby-carriage' we explain what is happening in our description of the action. Appeal to the general relation between the exercise of our muscles and transformations in our environment is thus redundant, and cannot be stated in an unqualified enough form or with the force sufficient to guarantee application to the particular case.

Hume and his successors, down to contemporary philosophers of science, have thought wholly in terms of explanations that would abide by explicit criteria. The only criterion available to them appeared to be generality and thus all explanation seemed to be the business of bringing a case under a law. To make this thesis hold they have had to allow many cases in which appeal to generality is redundant. Their choice of a criterion was itself governed by paradigmatic considerations, however; which they found, or looked for, in physical science. With respect to issues of certainty, precision, accuracy and predictability, the paradigm was perhaps well chosen. But with respect to the meaning of explanation

[6] Max Black, 'Making Something Happen', in Sidney Hook, ed. *Determinism and Freedom* (Collier Books, 1961), pp. 31 ff.

it is not clear that physics in any way approximates a standard case of understanding why things happen.

Indeed, much of physics could be interpreted as a way of bringing discoveries of the functional dependence of one kind of event on others discontinuous with it within recognizable reach of paradigms of collision and manipulation. No one, perhaps, would regard the formula $S = v_0 t + \frac{1}{2} a t^2$ as explaining the acceleration of falling objects. The hypothetical notion of a steadily increased tug on the body as it nears the centre of mass of a system, or the constant tugs on the planets which at every moment deflect them by so much from the straight lines they would otherwise follow, are attempts to picture regularly recurring and discrete phenomena on the models of collision and effort. It may be that scientists have rejected such comparisons, and substituted the notion of logical scope of theories for observed interaction as the proper object of their discipline. It may even be that this conception has introduced a secondary notion of explanation. In that case, though a good deal of what goes on in the world cannot be accommodated to paradigms of observed interaction, it follows only that a different sort of procedure is required for the strange cases, and not that the generalizing technique is proper to any kind of explanation. And, as a precautionary note, it must be remembered that the interaction picture in mechanics, though it appals operationalists and positivists, was the picture that governed Newton's search for generalizations. Successes in physical science do not appear to meet the philosopher's exacting criteria; and so it is not surprising if slavish devotion to these criteria as guides to research should result in sterile parodies of scientific theory.

The thesis that we can see, not merely the discrete and hypothetical elements of visual experience, but objects and relations among them as well, has momentous consequences for the so-called behavioural sciences. Psychologists and sociologists have based their case, at least implicitly and often quite explicitly, on an atomistic epistemology, which lends itself readily to the view that by some consistently applied and repeated effort we build up the content of the world and explanations of it out of pristine and incorrigible pieces of sense-experience. What is observed, on such a view, tells us nothing about the nature of the thing observed or its connexions with other observed items; knowledge of the world is based on inferences from such inert and mute data, inferences which are only possible by means of statistical sampling, repeated observation, and the formation of hypotheses from which data, both old and new, will follow. The view is given further currency by the supposition that only general and precise criteria for what counts as a datum will preserve empirical knowledge from the taint of the *a priori*. I have tried to suggest, first, that what counts as a datum or evidence is governed by contexts; the attempt to define it generally leads to the incoherence of atomistic or sense-datum theories. Second, the admission of objects and inter-actions to the status of observables does not contain the dire threat to empirical knowledge feared by classical empiricists. For the use of object and interaction terms is governed by the paradigm by which we learn such terms and the contexts appropriate to their employment.

CHAPTER FOUR

APPRAISAL AND DESCRIPTION

THE OBJECT of the preceding chapter was to suggest, by attacking the citadel of causal explanation of physical events, that all is not well with the generality theory of explanation. This is in part a softening-up move; if the thesis is not secure at home, its claims over foreign territory must be even more precarious. But, polemics aside, it is important to recognize that often we do see why things happen without benefit of laws, models, or generalizations. Numbers of philosophers reject the extension of the generality model to human affairs while holding to a Humean orthodoxy with respect to causal statements. In order to deny that accounts of human action are or could be causal, they are led to invoke an often suspicious distinction between reasons and causes. The distinction seems to be demanded because the generality thesis is taken to be correct with respect to our use of cause, but paradoxical when applied to human actions. We do not normally invoke laws in order to understand what we do. It surely is correct to say that my mood is the cause of my anger, or that what someone said was the cause of my mood, just in the sense that had these events not occurred, my responses would not have occurred. Yet we do not want to say that we know the causes of our moods in the way we know that one sort of occurrence is regularly associated with another. If we find that we do not need to invoke generalizations to support causal explanations, we will not be forced to adopt cumbersome theories by which such explanations are relieved of causal status.

None the less, much of what we do in explaining human conduct does not exhibit the causal form in either the interaction or the regularity sense. When we appeal to desires, pleasures, emotions, motives, purposes and reasons we are offering what I shall call moral explanations. I shall develop this theme in a general way in the present chapter and apply it to particular concepts in those that follow.

When people talk of morality they generally have in mind questions of substance—what to do, what is right, how to patch up inconsistencies in one's moral code, and so on. The only way to go about this is to begin with moral premises, principles, aims, or sentiments. So it seems that morality has to do with rightness, or establishing the rightness, of actions. It is to be contrasted to *im*morality, perhaps *a*morality, but not *non*-morality. The result is that rationality has been identified with conclusions reached or actions undertaken rather than with a method of arriving at conclusions or deciding to act. Conclusions or actions are rational only if they are right. If they are wrong, it is supposed that the person acting or making a claim is succumbing to desires, interpreted as quasi-physical or Humean internal impressions, as events which could be linked causally to actions or speech. As a result, insufficient attention is paid to the possibility that rational action, and morality itself, might be defined or characterized in terms of procedures as against the consequences that match or fail to match particular moral standards. On the procedural view, a man whose actions are guided by his assessments, and his understanding of his own and others' actions by the grounds he finds for those actions in the situation of the actor, is looking at behaviour morally. So long as he describes his own and others' conduct as doing something well or poorly, effectively or clumsily, appropriately or mistakenly, he is a moral agent or observer. It may be that the grounds he discovers as the end products of his diagnoses shock or offend various moral sensibilities; but this is relatively unimportant. The point is, he thinks in terms of grounds. He acts or describes action, not by seeking temporal antecedents or functional dependencies, but by deciding that the situation *entitles* a man to act in the way he did or is likely to do.

The typical language we use to convey such a way of looking at behaviour is the language of motive. The phrase 'having a motive' does not imply that a person did, is now doing, will do, or has a disposition to do the act for which he has the motive. It implies rather that the situation in which the person finds himself would justify him acting in a certain way. The typical son of crime fiction, cut out of his father's will, has a motive for doing away with dear old dad; the girl a motive for getting even with her jilting lover; the dishonest bank clerk a motive for fixing the books.

A number of things can be said about our use of motive. First, when we ascribe motives to agents it is not at all like what we do when we speak of antecedent circumstances as the cause of events. Motives do not necessitate actions. Second, motive explanations are often *post hoc*; they follow upon the acts explained, without having to be known in advance of the acts to which they are applied. Third, ascriptions of motive are not inferences or hypotheses designed to account for observed tendencies in behaviour. There is an element of generality in our ascription of motives, but this generality is not of a statistical or nomothetic form justified by the instances accumulated in its support or the deductions made from it. The generality in this case is rather in the form of a moral principle or aim which is seen to bear on the situation. Rules and aims apply to actions *prima facie*; they are neither moral absolutes in the manner hankered after by Kant, nor deterministic in the way taken to be characteristic of physical laws. But they can, when the action and the situation match the principle or aim, be decisive. They are principles of justification, of excuse, or entitlement, though I hope to use these terms without the implication that I am endorsing the actions that come under them. I understand the son's rationale for killing the father who disinherits him. I can admit his provocation without benefit of studies of the actions of his age, sex, or social group or an elaborate plumbing of his past, simply because I understand that sort of situation to be provoking. At the same time, I may deplore the measures he takes. When I ascribe to him motives of anger, indignation, despair or monetary interest, I am offering a moral explanation.

A view common to writers of ethics and philosophers of science stands in the way of accepting this thesis. Describing and reporting, so goes this view, is one thing; assessing, evaluating and judging quite another. By psychologists and social scientists this view is expressed in the slogan, science must be value-free; among writers of ethics in the slogan, value cannot be deduced from fact.

Now it would be absurd to deny some of the arguments and examples that fortify this thesis. We want to prune the historian's account of his Whig or Tory biases and discount as misleading the missionary's colourful descriptions of native licentiousness. Similarly, we want to block the moves from the facts of evolution to the moral endorsement of later stages of it, or from successful to right. If we begin with cases which clearly exhibit the corruption of facts by moral attitudes or the irrelevance of the facts to a moral thesis, it soon seems possible to generalize this No Trespass into a permanent boundary between values and facts.

The gulf is widened if an attempt is made to define rigorously what counts as fact, the sort of attempt upon which we have cast some doubts in the previous chapter. For the essence of that attempt is to provide criteria for a fact or datum entirely free of context. I have argued that it is only context that nourishes our conception of facts, observations, or data. It thus remains possible that what we call facts may in some cases arise within a moral or appraising context, that moral conceptions provide a way of looking at the world and so describing and explaining it. This will be my thesis with regard to desire and need, pleasure and pain, motive and reason. But let us first turn to cases that do not involve us in the additional business of explanation; that is, cases in which an appraising term only describes.

One application of this notion is to the theory of perception. Smells and tastes are normally described by means of evaluative or commending terms like sweet and sour, acrid and bitter, and the other senses too occasionally admit of such descriptions, for example, soft and hard, piercing and dulcet, bright and dim, and so on. It may be, though I throw it in as an aside, that much of the temptation that arises in philosophy to call what we sense subjective arises from the fact that we recognize and identify sense-qualities by means of such appraising terms, which are notoriously subject to context, so that we are unable to describe sensations with confidence for someone else, or even, perhaps, for ourselves in other circumstances. Thus colour properties are eminently objective, because they are freed of evaluative contexts at least much of the time. There is a story here of interest to epistemologists, but our theme takes us in another direction.

In a superficial sense, the view I am advocating here has been frequently held by behavioural scientists. Our concerns with human agents, it is argued, are moral concerns. In his *Textbook of Psychology*, for example, Hebb claims social conflict and mental disorder as the chief objects of the psychologist's interests and the rationale of his investigations. Social order and mental health are thus values directing psychological inquiry. This is not quite what I have in mind. Medicine, too, is concerned with values like survival and health. But its nomenclature is physical and value-neutral. For the value concept of illness has been restricted to cases that can be defined in terms of disease organisms, fever and toxic conditions, and so identified and described without benefit of our attitudes toward them. It may seem conceivable that Hebb's concern with mental illness and social conflict—from gang wars and criminal behaviour to international conflict—could be translated into a concern with disease entities or conditions, for example peculiarities in blood composition, so that bio-psychologists could be poised with the appropriate hypodermic to restore normal functioning.

The trouble is, the concept of mental illness does not accommodate itself to this translation. Suppose, for example, that the blood theory prohibited the application of the medical concept of illness to hysterics or obsessives, or even to that particular kind of babbling insanity found in back ward patients. Would we say, nothing wrong with them after all? The difficulty of accepting such a consequence reflects the intractably moral use of the term 'mental illness'. Our use of the term does not indicate a vague attempt to get at an as yet poorly recognized physical reality, which psychiatrists will supposedly some day apprehend, but a sense of something having gone wrong with an individual's performance in one or many of life's roles. Whatever the underlying physical basis, we need a term to denote these failures to achieve standard human performances. And there is no *a priori* reason to suppose that the physical correlates coincide with our social and, in this larger sense, moral needs.

The disturbances of mental illness, like their counterparts characterizing delinquent, criminal, business or political behaviour, are social problems. They do not match, necessarily, matters of physical disability. They are singled out for notice because they are unconventional, and depart in some way or another from a model of action that supposedly contributes to a properly conducted social order. Since the conception of social propriety is highly variable, what counts as mental illness, and all the rest, is also bound to vary. Consequently it is impossible to give sense to the hope that these variables will correlate with physical constants.

We need to recognize, then, that in observing and diagnosing human problems what is observed is productive and destructive, industrious and lazy, brave and cowardly behaviour. These are value judgments, to be sure, but they are also descriptive. Such labels are perhaps at the mercy of more capricious application than are those that seem to qualify as descriptions under positivistic restrictions. For they do serve as epithets, and the temptation to use them without careful attention to the standards of their use can easily lead one to suppose that they cannot, in any case, be applied with propriety.

Consider an interchange in which one colleague says to another, 'You're a coward, or you'd tell Jones that he doesn't have the ability to work toward a degree'. And the man answers, 'I'm not a coward, I'm only sensitive to the feelings of others'. Is one saying foul and the other fair, and that's the end of it? Of course it is a case of foul and fair; but there is a matter of fact here which is very much bound up with calling foul and fair. A spectator might, without taking sides, see something in the actions of the man which would lead him to say, 'Yes; coward' or 'No, it isn't cowardice, it is a reluctance to hurt others, for look: here he was brave, and here and again here'. There are many possibilities of describing the action, all of which would involve using terms with such pejorative or laudatory possibilities, yet using them in ways which we would say illuminate or accurately describe a man or a situation. If we deprive ourselves of words because of their possible use to form attitudes or incite actions, we deprive ourselves also of what is often the relevant description. The man or situation is not seen and then appraised, or appraised and then seen in distortion; it is seen morally. Value and fact merge.

For reasons of precision, ease of manipulation or success in forecast, we may wish to substitute physical, value-neutral terms of description for moral concepts. But we are then redefining our point of view, we are seeing the world differently, and we cannot suppose with complacency that the new precision will do what we were trying to do with the old and alarmingly vague vocabulary. It would be unreasonable to expect chemical categories of mental disorder to preserve the kinds of distinction currently enshrined under such labels as paranoid or schizophrenic, hysteric or compulsive. Paranoia depends on the notion of current or rational inferences which the paranoid transgresses, schizophrenia on standards of correctness in perception or propriety in mood. Even if there were a rough identity of reference, we should be misled in speaking of blood chemistry as the cause of errors, for it would be irrelevant to appeal to causes as grounds for correctness. To speak of paranoia and schizophrenia in the way that these terms contrast with proper ways of thinking, feeling, or acting is to use them in an appraising sense, and it then muddles the case to suppose that we are really all along talking about events in a physical setting. This must not be construed, as it is by some psychiatrists, as immunizing psychopathological behaviour from physiological or medical inquiry. It is only to suggest that if we look at this behaviour from a physiological or medical point of view, we must discard the psychiatrist's terms along with the method of appraisal, for these are not independent of one another.

Perhaps these remarks are best illustrated by the psychologists' use of the concept of intelligence. Since the development of intelligence tests, psychologists have wondered what they measure. Do the scores really measure intelligence, or do they simply reflect how well an individual can do on a certain test? The question is peculiar because it suggests that something lies within, not disclosed directly by performances of this or that kind but, it is to be hoped, validly inferable from these performances. Perhaps we could ask instead, do the test scores provide a reliable index to a range of performances? Do they indicate, for example, academic performance? But psychologists labour under the need to mechanize. And as they have mechanized motives and needs into drives, so they have somehow wished to treat tests as the signs of occurrences, enduring patterns or episodes which determine a man's capabilities. We do, of course, use terms like intelligence in an explanatory way—we say a man is capable of thinking cogently about relativity theory and quantum mechanics because he is bright or intelligent—and this seems to afford a basis for the psychologist's way of discussing the matter. And we do find, with the psychologist, 'surplus' meaning in the concept of intelligence, that is, meaning over and above the actual behaviour of the subject in answering questions or solving problems in a certain time. Such discomfort is quite proper, for intelligent behaviour is not 'pure' behaviour in the sense that pigeon-pressing-bar or rat-turning-right might be described as instances of unsullied observed reactions. But surplus meaning cannot be assigned to ghostly entities either. Intelligence is not something of which the behaviour is symptomatic, something inferred from behaviour, but is exhibited in the behaviour, providing that one is looking at the given action, whether it be problem solving, similarity noting, inference making, or block building, from the point of view of paradigms of that kind of behaviour. These are paradigms of what it is to solve a problem or to be especially imaginative, in short, what it is to do something well or properly. To speak of a man as intelligent is thus to describe much of his behaviour as matching canons of correct procedure. It is at once to describe and to assess an agent's performance.

We shall see that statements ascribing desire, need, self-interest and anxiety to human agents, and role and status, function and habit to social forms and processes, arise in the context of moral appraisal. They have to do with the rules and conventions by which various kinds of human action are identified and assessed. It is the tendency among behavioural scientists to think of value as a subtle and dangerous obstacle to the business of objective description of human action. So these scientists feel that if they set their values to one side, articulate them, and isolate them in a preface all will be well.[1] But values do not enter descriptions of human affairs as disruptive influences; rather, they allow us to describe human behaviour in terms of action. Inasmuch as the units of examination of human behaviour are actions, they cannot be observed, identified, or isolated except through categories of assessment and appraisal. There are not two stages, an identification of properties and qualities in nature and then an assessment of them, stages which then could become the business of different experts. There is only one stage, the delineation and description of occurrences in value terms. We describe people as more or less intelligent. The various refinements of tests and measures simply make more explicit (if they are successful) what we are doing in our ordinary and rather more vague appraisals. If there are disputes between the advocates of different tests, it is not because one test is a better index of

---

[1] Cf. e.g. Edward Tolman's preface to *Drives Toward War* (Appleton-Century Crofts, 1942).

some further property, the shadowy thing which really is intelligence. It may be an empirical dispute as to whether one or another test affords the most likely index to some further performance of interest to the parties to this dispute. Perhaps the further interest is classroom performance or ability in a particular profession. This presumably is to be settled by matching test scores against some rating of that further performance. But more frequently and more likely the dispute is over what tasks, what performances, what abilities are to be prized. Perhaps one party is thinking of speed in calculation, another individual initiative, another care and accuracy, another breadth of knowledge, and so on indefinitely. Intelligence, as a word functioning in appraisal contexts, must clearly reflect a variety of conditions, circumstances and criteria. And what counts as intelligent action must thus cover, as Wittgenstein would say, a family of cases, joined, not by some common characteristic to be seen in the action or the actor, but by the attitude taken by the observer towards this action, that is, seeing the action as meeting some criteria of excellence. But what will count as fulfilling the criteria, hence what will count as intelligent action, will vary from criterion to criterion and context to context. Consequently it would be quixotic to suppose that one could locate, test and describe action in such a way that a general theory of intelligent behaviour and of rational conduct might emerge. For what counts as intelligent in one context might clearly be quite inappropri ate in another.

There is a remarkable passage in John Collier's *His Monkey Wife* in which the incredible chimpanzee is complaining about psychological tests of her intelligence which consist of the one-box-on-another-to-reach-a-banana sort typical of Kohler's laboratory. Of course, she says, they don't tell anything about her intelligence. In the first place, perhaps she doesn't want the banana, and besides, what does that sort of thing tell about the deep and inscrutable thoughts of a chimpanzee? So psychologists fixed on speed of response may insult a subject who thinks of intelligent action as a matter of care or originality. This subject in turn will find his supporters among other psychologists who sponsor a different view of intelligence. The debate is not a matter to be settled by research; indeed, in a sense it is often not a matter to be settled at all, except to recognize that different performances are prized by different observers. The point is, a question about intelligence could not arise unless some performances were prized; it thus becomes pointless to try to set aside our preferences in order to decide what intelligence really is. Appraisal is the means for identifying the object of inquiry, so far as this is concerned, not with muscular movements and nervous impulses but with actions, that is, performances. Actions are movements that can be done well or ill, and appraised as achievements or failures. Lacking these terms of appraisal we are no longer in a position to identify performances.

What we say about intelligence is a matter of importance for the psychology of cognition, which is, after all, a study of intelligent performances. To seek ways of following the normal routes of scientific inquiry and explanation in order to understand why a person is engaged in a performance is gratuitous. Unless the performer is in a position to understand what he does, he cannot perform. It would be like explaining the moves of a mathematician by recourse to generalizations on what this and other mathematicians do in this or that circumstance. But the mathematician takes the next step because it is the next step in his proof, a matter to be justified by appeal to the rules of inference, the definitions and axioms with which he operates, and not by appeal to what he generally does. The same could be applied to many normal human tasks, at least those involving discrimination, inference and judgment, the kinds of performance of concern to the psychologist of cognition. Such a psychologist might claim, of course, that his concern is not with the strategy of cognition (though this is the claim of a standard volume on the subject[2]) but with the connection of successful performances to other factors, like manner of learning, emotional state, or environmental circumstances. This raises further questions and invokes new concepts, but the new questions and concepts are no longer precisely within the field of cognition and spill over into personality and learning theory.

Cognition theorists, on the other hand, claim at least as their distinct province the analysis of the kinds of behaviour that count as intelligent performances, and the development of simplified models of strategies for dealing with them. These are essentially philosophical tasks, for the simplified models are, like logical theories, ways of stating precisely the criteria for what counts as a proper or intelligent performance. The explanation of a part of a performance is given in the conception of what the performance is, for example, solving a mathematical problem, working one's way out of a maze, or choosing optimum advantage among alternative courses of action. To be able to perform is thus to explain one's action. A psychology of cognition does not, in this sense, contribute anything to our understanding of performances. It may clarify the nature of the performance, but this is a task which, as I have said, is philosophical

---

[2] J. S. Bruner, J. J. Goodnow and G. A. Austin, *A Study of Thinking* (John Wiley, 1956).

and not empirical. If, in short, intelligence is defined in terms of certain sorts of behaviour, it clearly does not explain that behaviour. If it is identified with test scores, it does not explain further behaviour, for test scores serve only as indices to further performances. So whatever the status and contributions of a psychology of cognition, it does not constitute an explanatory theory of human action.

We do speak of intelligence as the reason for a performance, however. But we do so in particular contexts, in which the force of the appeal has much to do with what is being denied. We are saying, for example, that passing the exam was *not* due to accident, or knowing the questions beforehand, or the coaching he got. We are saying, in effect, that the performance is to his credit. This too is a description, for it enables us to make numbers of inferences about the conditions under which the performance was undertaken. But it is a favoured description, that is, one involving and provided by the sense in which intelligence is a word of appraisal.

This is the matter of importance in everything that follows. We do not apprehend a world of facts, sense-data, or physical objects, describable wholly in terms of spatio-temporal or sensed properties, and then, according to our values, call out 'good' and 'bad', 'fair' and 'foul' to every discrete item as it passes our ken. Sometimes we identify and describe items in our experience by means of terms of appraisal. The reports of occurrences that issue from the application of these concepts I shall call moral descriptions. The possibility of offering moral descriptions of action, that is, statements which can count as descriptively true or false though governed by appraising conceptions, is of the utmost importance to everything that follows. For I shall be arguing that much of what we offer by way of explaining human action is moral explanation. The objection might then be raised, to be sure, the concepts you analyse bear the stamp of moral explanation, but it is this that argues most forcefully for the view that some other way of treating human nature is imperative, if we are to advance accounts of behaviour that have factual content. It is thus necessary to show that moral explanations have factual content, that they describe features of human experience which will be intelligible to any user of a common tongue. In a term like intelligence, or others like courage and cowardice, the kind of logic at play not only hints at this thesis but requires it. For these terms, in virtue of their appraising function, allow us to describe what people do and are likely to do in ways which would be quite out of reach without them. Those who contend that moral explanations are vitiated because they lack empirical content must then explain our use of terms like intelligence by denying either their descriptive or their evaluative powers. Such separation, I have urged, deprives these terms of either use; so a *prima facie* case is made at least for the possibility and propriety of moral explanations. It will turn out that the value–fact dichotomy, like so many of the philosopher's most popular legacies, does not carry a degree of conviction equal to the tasks it is usually called on to perform.

CHAPTER FIVE

DESIRE

THERE ARE a number of terms which appear to play a dual role with respect to human actions. Such terms as liking, preference, desire, pleasure and pain, love and hate, anger and fear are employed to explain actions. But they are also used in ways that suggest that they are names for states of the organism or of experience. It is tempting to combine the two senses and argue that, since the terms do explain and appear to name occurrences, the explanations we offer by their means are standard sorts of causal connexions. Desires and the rest thus become internal episodes which cause human and perhaps animal organisms to react in certain ways.

There are difficulties that stand in the way of merging these two senses of terms like desire. In the first place, as internal episodes, they are private and lack the guarantees for which psychologists hanker; that is, they cannot be operationally defined. If, to remedy this defect, desire concepts are defined operationally by 'unpacking' them (as Ryle would say) into descriptions of tendencies or patterns of behaviour, they lose their explanatory significance. That a man persists in a line of conduct may be explained by citing his strong desire, but not if desire means only the tendency or pattern of behaviour in which he persists.

In the second place, even if we allow that internal occurrences always accompany our use of concepts like desire, liking and pleasure, it is not clear that it is by virtue of such episodes that we identify or recognize instances of desire. For all we know, the feelings of desire may vary from person to person or episode to episode, whereas the terms themselves are applied with at least some degree of constancy.

Third, there are formidable arguments, advanced by Wittgenstein and others, against supposing that these terms refer to episodes at all. And finally, most of these terms, in their explanatory uses, depend upon future occurrences, the objects of desire or pleasure.

Theories about desire and its cognates often become hopelessly confused because it is assumed that desire concepts belong to a common logical family. And this may be the case, for certain purposes. They all contrast in some way with physical events in at least one favoured sense of that term. But this similarity is apt to blind us to differences of major importance for our purposes. I shall treat these concepts, then, in piecemeal fashion, even at the risk of repetition as I move from case to case.

LIKINGS

To begin with 'liking'. This term is of special interest because of its role in positivist and emotivist theories of ethics. That these theories rely so heavily on terms like 'preference' and 'liking' in analysing moral statements may suggest that such terms are already packed with moral significance. The typical move in such theories, however, is to replace moral with empirical questions by means of the concept 'liking'. Thus Ayer, a number of years after *Language, Truth and Logic*, still wishes to say that the question 'why people respond favourably to certain facts and unfavourably to others is a question for the sociologist'.[1] Moral statements contain a non-factual component, an act of commendation or disapproval or an expression of preference, and a factual report, describing the feelings or attitudes that one notes in oneself in contemplating an object or an action. The typical formula for such a report is, of course, 'I like *x*'.

The emotive theory draws its support from the inconclusiveness of moral arguments. Since it is difficult to get agreement as to what counts for or against moral judgments, it seems plausible to suppose that there are no proper moral arguments. If there is real disagreement, the only recourse is to fists and guns, which is taken by emotivists to mean that the disagreement arises from facts of nature which psychologists and sociologists ought to be able to explain some day, and perhaps control. Moral disagreements are not subject to rational resolution.

Notice, however, that it is taken for granted that moral disagreement could always be explained by disclosing the relevant attitudes. No further evidence is brought forward showing that moral beliefs, decisions and quarrels are the regular and law-like consequences of antecedent conditions. The rest of the story is left to the psychologist and sociologist. The philosopher's job is only to assign the tasks to others. Only two alternatives are allowed: either ethics is itself a science, in which case events can be brought under laws, or moral actions are the object of some other scientific investigation. It is clearly not the first, otherwise we should at least not differ over fundamentals; so it must be the latter. Since moral claims are intimately connected with attitudes of approval and disapproval, liking and disliking, preference and avoidance, it is these feelings and habits that appear to afford the proper empirical study of morality.

This thesis bristles with so many difficulties that it is hard to know where to begin criticism of it. Perhaps it would be best to see first what

---

[1] A. J. Ayer, 'Analysis of Moral Judgments', in *Philosophical Essays* (Macmillan, 1959), p. 238.

will not be criticized. The reservations against the emotivist theory do nothing to alter or blunt the criticism of traditional ethics, so far as those theories were concerned to provide the ultimate principles of all action. It is one thing to see, as Kant saw, that moral defence always embodies an appeal to principles, quite another to devise a principle against which all action is to be tested. We are all familiar with the vacuity that lies at the end of that road. Similarly, the popularity of certain goals (pleasure?) does not convert them into criteria for the rightness or wrongness of moral action or into the evidence for moral judgments, though an appeal to goals is also a standard gambit in moral argument. The appeal to principles, goals and the consequences of action are all familiar patterns of moral reasoning, but they are also the sources of moral disagreement, so that moral debate looks as if it is always inconclusive. It is this feature which lends strength to the emotive or any subjectivist theory.

But we are in danger of assuming too much if we then conclude that moral judgments and actions are nothing more than the effects of ante-cedent conditions, and thus non-rational in character. Even if our appeal to principles and goals in order to decide or persuade is inconclusive, it is none the less rational, in contrast to acting impulsively or being forced, goaded or compelled. Perhaps from the stern eminence of physics, statements like 'x is good' and 'I like x' do not seem to have a worthy cognitive content, for they are not accompanied by successful prediction or control and do not lead to the formulation of laws. But it does not follow that likings and moral decisions just happen or that they are to be explained, like natural events, by appeal to antecedent conditions forming the province of a special science like psychology or sociology. To say 'I like x', or 'I like x better than y', is less a report of immediate fact than it is an appraisal, based often on criteria, or in some way related to grounds for judgment. One of the tests to decide whether a man really likes Bach is that he listens to Bach's music in preference to that of other composers. But very commonly a further test is relevant. He might defend or amplify his liking by describing the characteristics of Bach's music. And he can do this well or poorly, accurately or inaccurately. A poor or inaccurate description is likely to lead us to say, he doesn't really like Bach, but only claims to for inappropriate reasons. In short, it is relevant to ask, 'Why do you like x?' not anticipating an answer that will tell stories about early life or neurological condition, but that will set forth the defences for one's judgment.

There is a tendency, of course, to use the locution less as a defence than as an apology. The record collector who is shamed by his friend's collection of the works of Anton Webern says, 'I just *like* Tchaikovski'. This argumentative dodge occurs with such frequency that it is natural to suppose that liking is less a judgment of appraisal than it is the ultimate and capricious basis for choices and habits. The theory that reduces moral and aesthetic judgments to matters of taste rests upon this ambivalence in the use of liking concepts. But that theory is itself ambivalent. Does it mean that moral and aesthetic judgments are decisions of taste, a view that is vacuously true, or that they are the utterances standing in the place of any adequate reason, which is surely false? Many 'likings' are the results of practice, learning and discrimination. I do not mean that likings so arrived at are 'better' than the more ingenuous claims; merely that they exhibit a very different form than do 'mere' expressions of taste. In both the analysed and the ingenuous cases, however, 'I like it' functions in argument. In the analysed case, the expression of liking or preference is the conclusion of an argument, and acquires its significance from the possibility of adducing grounds for one's choices. In the ingenuous case, 'I like it' is parasitic on the analysed case. For we should find no need for the apologetic use save in contrast to the argumentative use. It is the stall of embarrassment, and tells us that there are no grounds, or that one cannot think of any grounds, but one nevertheless chooses it, and does so on the supposition that there might be grounds, if only one was intelligent or informed or had time enough to provide them.

'Liking' also serves as a name for preferences, that is, for actions generally taken or goals frequently pursued. That a man likes Singing Strings, therefore, is shown by his well-worn records of sentimental light classics, and the shiny, unplayed B minor Mass gives the lie to his statement that, of course, he likes Bach very much. Here the statement that I like x or he likes x is a report of tendencies to do certain things or make certain choices. And this, as in so many similar cases, makes us think that we are always reporting facts in our use of such locutions. But in the sense that the locution describes or reports, it describes or reports behaviour to be explained or justified, and is not itself explanatory.

I see no reason to allow a further sense in which likings name feelings. The common judgment of liking or preference may be accompanied by a wide range of feeling states, and it thus is difficult to see how a particular feeling could be the source of judgments of tastes. Feelings can, indeed, become special objects upon which the judgment of liking or choice is exercised. But we may postpone treatment of this use until we are in a position to gather together other instances sharing this feature. So let us turn now to a further concept of this general family.

DESIRE

Surely with respect to desire, someone will say, one finds a causal account of behaviour. Desires prod and stimulate; a person can be moved and overcome by his desires. These common locutions lead very readily to technical derivations, refinements, and expansions of them, like drive and libido. More of these in a moment.

First, notice that to say I did it because I wanted to is vacuous. If it explains it is in virtue of a context in which one may not have expected just that action or may have suspected that it was done under duress. The explanatory appeal to desire is designed to show that something or other really wasn't the case without explaining why the action in question was undertaken. A man who gives most of his earnings to charities may say 'I wanted to' in order to dispel the notion that he was easing a guilty conscience or avoiding payment of income tax. But if, out of the blue, a man responds to the question, 'why are you doing x?' with 'because I want to' the answer is likely to be, 'Of course you want to, otherwise you wouldn't be doing it. But why (specifically) are you doing it?'

This suggests that 'I want to' is vacuous as an explanation. In contrast, I want it is not. Here the action is explained by indicating the goal toward which it leads. In this sense desire joins the purposive family of concepts which will be taken up in the next chapter.

The ambiguity in the term desire is further complicated by the way in which we might be said to recognize or identify desires. The push-pull school would appear to be committed to the view that desire names a class of events which enter into causal relations with other events characteristic of human and animal organisms. Desire events may then be said to be the effects of stimuli and the causes of action. This is surely a very natural way of speaking. A woman going about her shopping, sees a hat in a shop window, and is overwhelmed by a desire to have it. She hesitates, thinks of her bank account, but finally cannot resist, rushes into the shop and buys it. Some modern philosophers have been anxious to avoid the use of causal language in contexts like this, for they have assumed that causal talk implies that a person knows that he is tempted by attending to past regularities in his behaviour. In our case the woman knows that seeing the hat causes her desire, and the desire her actions, because in the past seeing hats in shop windows has generally led to these consequences. And this interpretation is nothing short of absurd. But in one sense the relation hat–desire–purchase is surely a straightforward instance of a causal relation. For it is quite correct to say that, had the woman not seen the hat, she would not have felt the temptation nor bought the hat. The contrary–to–fact conditional exposes the logic, at least, of causal talk. The problem lies, not in the extension of such talk to cases of arousing desires, but in the regularity thesis of causation. An account of the causes of desire may, then, be exempt from the model of moral explanation which I am, in a general way, urging in this chapter. But it does not follow that it becomes, then, a reasonable object of scientific scrutiny, for it is not the kind of relationship which requires the special techniques of experimentation and generalization in order to establish. And this holds whether desire is identified with internal occurrences or patterns of behaviour.

Identifying a concept with internal occurrences leads to a tendency to allow the concept to spill over on both sides of its reputed causal links. On the one hand, it comes to be identified with the objects of desire, and, on the other, with the actions which indicate pursuit or striving. It is clearly not used, except redundantly, in the latter sense when it is supposed that desire explains one's actions. One does not attribute one's actions to desire when desire is identified with what one is doing. When desire is identified with its object or stimulus, on the other hand, it seems to be a condensed form of the causal ascription we have just considered. And here we are thinking, if the internal term is dropped, of the object—the hat in the window—as the cause of the action. Here desire becomes the general name for a kind of explanation; it is not appealed to as the explaining occurrence or hypothesis.

But desire is used as the explaining occurrence, and this seems to lead straight back to the internal-event view. This view, however, is vitiated by a fatal flaw; a flaw, by the way, which makes for difficulties also with the identification of desire with the stimulus event. Recognizing a desire involves more than identifying a particular object (the hat) or bodily feeling or sensation. It is recognizing that an object or an action stands in a certain relation to oneself. There are a number of possibilities here.

1. The object, if embraced, consumed, or in some way used dissipates pain or tension. In this sense the concept of desire is parasitic on the concept of need, and we may safely postpone what else must be said about it until we take up that concept.

2. The object, if used in some way, prolongs or intensifies certain feelings. The same side-tracking is possible as in (1), though here a pair of subsidiary observations are pertinent. First, our inclination to treat (1) though not (2) as the standard formula for need, betrays the tendency to regard need as a quasi-moral concept. In (2) you have what you need; what you want now are luxuries. More of this in a moment. Second, both (1) and (2) depend on reference to feelings and bodily states. It is thus tempting to identify desire with the feeling or bodily state itself,

for example, hunger pangs, parched throat, tension in various muscles, 'hollowness' in the chest, or, in the case of (2), taste, smell, and other sensations. Doubt is often cast on the occurrence of such states or events because of a reluctance to discriminate between the desire and the thing or feeling desired. There are not, to paraphrase Ryle's view, two events, the desire and the feeling toward which it is addressed or with which it is conjoined, but simply the occurrence of the feelings as desired. If it is plausible to admit that we recognize some occurrences as valued, in the manner suggested in the previous chapter, then this case presents no special difficulties. To recognize and identify a bodily state as one of tension *is* to see it as requiring release, and to recognize a bodily state as warm or sweet or exciting is to see it as something to be preserved. Thus it is possible to maintain that desire names events, so long as it is not maintained that it is an event over and above the tension or the sweetness. Desires are the kinds of events recognized as to be prized or avoided. They enter, in a crucial way, into the moral way of looking at the world.

3. Desire thus borrows its significance from the desirable. This view, which is developed with great cogency and skill by Melden in his monograph, *Free Action*,[2] is hard to swallow only because it seems to rest on highly attenuated cases of desire, in which judgment is made as to what is worthy of pursuit or acquisition by examining a case to see whether it meets explicit criteria. For example, one might speak of desiring one wine more than another if a course in wine-tasting had shown the way to making observations and discriminations of a very refined kind by means of precisely worded criteria governing the taste and the bouquet of wine. It is not as plausible to suppose that the lady's desire for the hat in the shop window is determined by the criteria she might use if appraising hats in a fashion show. The difference here seems to be between immediate reaction and deliberative evaluation. And this distinction soon comes to mark a gulf between actions prompted by urges and those suggested by judgment, or between desire and the desirable. To make a case for Melden's view, that desire gains its significance from the desirable, something must be done to bridge this gulf. It must be admitted that there are attenuated cases in which a conscious appraisal dominates and others in which the reactions are spontaneous, but both cases depend upon seeing an object as desirable. The hat is seen as desirable, the wine judged so. And this is like the difference between seeing and inferring objects, or relations among them. There are cases which display desirability, and others which need to be tested for it. In both cases, an explanation of an action as due to desire is a moral explanation, for the

2 J. A. Melden, *Free Action* (Routledge and Kegan Paul, 1961).

desirability of the object, directly seen or inferred by invoking criteria, is the grounds for the action.

It does not need to be repeated, I hope, that this sense of moral does not imply approval or consent to the action, but refers only to a particular strategy of explanation. Appeals to desires involve the same sorts of strategies as appeals to the kinds of reasons we do approve of, a fact which was noted, if in a paradoxical way, by ethical egoists. The difficulty in ethics has been that rational action has been identified with approved action, and this, furthermore, with particular kinds of virtues like self-sacrifice, humility and abstinence. Thus acting on desire has seemed quite different from acting on principle, and it becomes possible to talk about being overcome by desires. One is never overcome by the desire to do good, or to fast, or humiliate oneself, but one is often and regrettably overcome by the desire to kill or maim, seduce or rob, or speak an unkind word. Thus, properly speaking, there is no desire, but only reason, to be good, and desires represent the urges and proddings of the flesh. Christian ethics permeate modern psychology, for the Christian, like the psychologist, regards desires as particular kinds of events determining action.

It is not surprising, perhaps, that the concept of desire has come to be identified with its most dramatic instances, and since these instances come most frequently under moral proscription, it is easy to suppose that reason and desire form a dichotomy. If we can stand apart from our moral convictions for a moment, however, it is possible to see that our appeals to desire and to principles in explaining our actions are explanations of the same type, that is, justifying explanations. We speak of the intensity of desire as the reason for acting in certain ways, which along traditional lines suggests a physical force precipitating action. This is the sense in which we say we are overcome by desires. But this language is, in fact, embarrassing to the proponents of the desire-as-cause view. For it suggests that desires or urges have, as it were, built-in causal status. They have the kind of occult force which Hume was at such pains to exorcize from the language of science. Most proponents of the desire-as-cause view have followed Hume here. In following him they have had to embrace the equally unpalatable views that desires are events having causal significance because of the regularity of their connection with behaviour, and that desires are hidden events used by psychologists as constructs to explain behaviour. To suppose that they are occult powers is excluded for obvious reasons; one sees, so the view goes, events, not causes. To suppose that we know them to be causes either by appeal to regularities or by con-structing hypotheses clearly does not match at all the way in which we know that desires lead us to act. We know without research that desires account for actions.

The expression 'overcome by desire' provides the cue. For this is an expression which depends on terms of moral reference. We are overcome by desires, not in the way that we are knocked down by a wave at the seashore, but because we end up doing something which conflicts with something we feel we ought to do. We are thus apt to say, 'I ought to do x, but I want to do y.' But this is a conflict which occurs typically *within* moral reasoning. A person may see an end as desirable, but a principle as blocking its achievement. A man may feel a duty towards his wife and a longing for his mistress. It may be that one of these considerations should carry more weight than the other, and sometimes it does. When it fails to, we accuse the man of moral weakness, for we need some kind of redress to actions we regard as reprehensible. But this does not disguise or remove the fact that in both cases he is judging something to be sufficiently desirable to warrant the action in spite of its conflict with other considerations. In both cases, the connexion between circumstance and action, whether of principle, desire or craving, is a rationally drawn connexion; the circumstances provide the ground for acting. Once again, whether or not this is called a causal relation is a matter of indifference, unless causes are identified with regularity of connexion or observed interaction. Here at least the connexion is drawn by seeing the circumstances, the desire, the principle, the goal, as the grounds for acting. Desire is a species of acting on principle. We suppose very naturally that if we put the comfort of others above our own we are acting morally. But we are, even if acting immorally, engaged in the same kind of procedure in putting our own comfort above that of others. Indeed, in that happy case where our own comfort does not conflict with that of others, we might be inclined to regard someone less as a moral hero than as quite irrational if he failed to see wherein his comfort lay and acted upon it. If it does conflict, we should say perhaps that his action is wrong, unfortunate or misguided, but his actions are still undertaken in accordance with an assessment as to what is desirable in the situation.

One obstacle to accepting this view, then, is morality itself, which finds it necessary to protect itself from at least some socially destructive grounds for acting. The other is the tendency to identify desires with those particularly dramatic bodily sensations which happen, frequently enough, to characterize certain patterns of action. And so we are led to think of these sensations as the events which precipitate the actions. But these sensations, too, are grounds for action, for we are aware of them *as*

pleasurable or painful, further concepts which belong, as I will suggest
shortly, to the moral point of view. It is a warranting relation that binds
them to the actions that often follow from them. One alternative to this
interpretation is to fall back on occult powers, which are unpalatable to
just those philosophers and psychologists who argue most strenuously for
the causal status of desire-events. The only other alternative is to mis-
represent the way in which we know that our actions are prompted by
desires, by continuing to hold the regularity analysis of causation.

Need

We can now turn to the sense of desire which depends upon the
concept need. It may clear the air to begin with the obvious occasions
on which we employ the concept in daily life. The psychologist, of
course, is not limited by such uses, but a comparison of the technical
with the ordinary uses may reveal ways in which the technical use
depends for its explanatory force on the ordinary use. We say: what is
needed here is a two-by-four, a high-protein diet, the facts, a sense of
public responsibility. An employee needs a raise; an employer needs to
cut costs. A need in any of these cases is whatever is instrumental to
achieving an end, meeting a demand, perpetuating a condition, or
satisfying a principle.

Two matters deserve notice. First, there are many actions that are
explicitly undertaken on the understanding that something can be
achieved or dispelled, augmented or diminished, by so acting. A special
investigation of needs in this sense would be redundant; they are not the
hypothetical constructs which stand at the end of an investigation of
patterns in human behaviour, but the reasons for particular actions.
Second, when the need is established, as for survival, food, health or a
birth certificate, the means of satisfying it may very well be in the domain
of an expert, whether a merchant, doctor, lawyer or banker. Sometimes
experts may be more than purveyors of means; they may be in a position
to tell the layman what he needs, as the dentist may inform me of a
need for calcium or fluorine in my teeth. But it is not clear how a psychologist can establish what my needs in general are. For 'need' is another
of our context-bound terms; it applies and explains within some commonly accepted rules or goals. Supposedly the psychologist examines,
on the other hand, needs which can be generalized for human or animal
subjects quite apart from contexts. He succeeds in making this plausible
only to the extent to which he is able to treat needs as hidden causes,
whose discovery is made possible by his special techniques.

Three senses can be noted in the psychologist's use of need. The first two of these senses are subject to the above criticism. When food, water and sex are taken to be needs, for example, need is used in the sense of conditions for survival, whether for the individual or the species. Now the need for survival may be omnipresent and the desire for it may be 'strong', and this seems to afford the basis for the push-pull model that tempts psychologists. We do know of exceptions, certainly, which in itself is not particularly important. But strength of need seems capable only of being interpreted as that which takes precedence over other aims. It has, as it were, moral strength, for if it comes to a matter of survival numbers of other aims and principles may bow out or defer their claim upon action. While it is a mundane observation that food and water are necessary for survival, it is not particularly a psychological (causal) but a moral rationale that gives to survival its particular prominence.

If this is true of the first sense of need, it is even more clearly true of the second. For here the same conditions hold as in the first sense, only more broadly interpreted. This is the sense in which it is not mere survival that is at stake, but quality of survival. A person on occasion needs to eat a steak dinner or play a game of chess. Here the concept of need clearly depends upon our being able to discriminate things of more or less value to us.

The third sense identifies need with homeostatic processes of physiological nature, in which certain kinds of activities restore an independently defined equilibrium. This is clearly a new and technical appropriation of the concept, but it may be the most serious contender for the role of general theory of behaviour. It can, however, be ignored here for the moment, since most psychological theories of need have been advanced through ignorance or deliberate avoidance of physiological processes and concepts. If the notion of homeostasis is introduced, it is in a metaphorical sense, given meaning through the approval that one bestows on certain stages in behaviour sequences or cycles. It would miss the point, however, to dismiss such knowledge as mere appraisal; that a person lacks something is important knowledge for him in guiding his conduct and for us in gauging what he is most likely to do. It might be thought that 'lack' here could be translated into the neutral term, 'absence'. But that a person lacks food is not to say at all the same thing as that a mushroom lacks chlorophyll or the moon an atmosphere. The lack which declares a need is the absence of something wanted, or something contributing to a goal, an element that would complete, complement or cap an activity or project. Thus need is tied to desire, in the sense that the identification of desires depends upon the appraisal of a situation in terms of what is desirable. Need accounts are a common part of our ordinary and evaluative description of human activities. They cannot serve as bases for a general theory, purporting to show how a wide range of behaviour follows from laws stated in terms of a small number of needs. Within contexts and in cases it is a commonplace to observe that people eat (if they can) when hungry, drink when thirsty, and make love when the opportunity arises. The psychologist casts such observations in a theoretical form which makes it appear as if it is a laboratory discovery of human characteristics heretofore overlooked because, in our ordinary lives, we have failed to employ the proper techniques of experimentation, prediction and hypothesis formation. When the concept of need does its work, it does so in evaluating contexts which we must be quite generally capable of employing if we are to act at all. As employed by psychologists anxious to avoid evaluation, it loses that significance, and becomes as we have already seen, an idling expression, introduced to explain the relationship between stimuli and responses, but failing to add anything to what is described. Failing as an evaluative term, need comes to function for the psychologist as a specious cause, whose significance is totally exhausted in a description of the stimuli conditions. The connexion between empty stomachs and particular kinds of motor activities strikes us as obvious, because we constantly set this relationship in the context in which an empty stomach is seen as grounds for food-getting actions. If the psychologist took this road it would trivialize his experiments, so he is forced to a strictly behaviouristic account in which all terms disappear except those required to describe stimulus conditions and muscular responses. If, however, he is reluctant to give up the explanatory shadow of need, he must invoke it as a mysterious intervening link between the stimulus and the response. It is quite clear that no meaning is really assigned to need by treating it as a construct, but only so far as it has been identified with stimulus conditions. Nor is behaviourism above suspicion. We know the relation between empty stomachs and food-getting actions without benefit of the experimental research designed to reveal it. We don't describe empty stomachs neutrally, but as conditions of hunger, which are apprehended as the grounds for food-getting behaviour.

We are tempted to think of needs, like desires, as causes because of the sensations commonly felt in various parts of the body at times when one diagnoses one's condition as a state of need. Hunger pangs, parched throats and erotic tensions are describable events that have a certain location and last a certain time. And we are then apt to say, these are the causes of our action in search of food, drink or sexual release. But these sensations, like those associated with desires, are viewed and described as more or less intense, which in this context means that they count as more or less important and worthy of attention. That is, they are described in terms of evaluation and assessment. Moreover, it does not become incorrect to speak of needs if characteristic bodily sensations are lacking. The sorts of needs that psychologists are prone to demote as secondary are just as clearly instances of need; we can with just as much assurance point out that actions are due to them as we can with actions due to so-called primary needs. A man may decide to go to college because he needs a larger income, or join the church because he needs peace of mind. There are, perhaps, no assignable sensations that one could speak of intelligibly here, but the explanatory pattern is not therefore disrupted.

The absence of sensations in many cases may account for their demotion by psychologists to secondary status, for without the hint of internal processes or events much of the causal aura is lost. But another reason is that secondary needs are context-bound, and do not afford the basis for large-scale generalizations, as is, or seems to be, the case with primary needs. It would be silly to deny that most people will put their survival above almost everything else; so the pompous formulae, man needs food and drink, look like laws of human behaviour. They are sound generalizations, no doubt; however, the issue is not generalizability, but the importance of generalization in the business of explaining. On this score generalization is irrelevant. We are not appealing to what men generally do, in explaining a man's actions as an attempt to stay alive. We are seeing, rather, how in a given context his actions are marked by just such strategies which the principle of survival would warrant or justify.

Both desire and need are marked by a further characteristic, they serve as exhortations. So the politician says to his constituents, 'What this country needs is a tax cut'. When the economist talks about needs of a part of the economy or the whole, he appears to be using need in much this sense. Ricardo and Malthus talk about the workers' needs, which in their case is defined as subsistence—whatever is required to enable the worker to get on the job in the morning and last till the whistle blows at night. The disagreements that arose in projecting and planning wages and prices on such theories has a good deal to do with this conception of need. Nowadays, it would probably be interpreted as including a balanced diet, a home, a car and a television set. What will count as needs for the economist will thus depend in great measure on what society tends to view as the rights of individuals and what they are entitled to.

On the erroneous supposition that the appeal to need was a piece of unwarranted psychologizing, some economists have tried to define need in terms of demand. But the picture is clear here only for a highly simplified economy, a small group of producers in which goods are exchanged on the basis of what each needs to satisfy his wants. In this Utopian dream, wants are roughly equivalent, or the bounty of nature is such that no amount of goods that one member trades off in any way affects his material well-being. But needs grow in complexity with the complexity of the situation. Limited resources create a situation in which A no longer accepts B's claim as an honest expression of need. For A has only so much to trade, and he requires an abundance of other commodities. So the question of A's and B's needs cannot be judged simply by the course of the bargaining. Both parties start from need-claims in excess of their expectations, and the nature of the bargain that is finally struck reflects a compromise arrived at in different ways in different cases by different traders. To introduce demand as a measure of need leads to highly paradoxical consequences. For if any actual measure of demand is taken as expressing need, the inference can always be made that needs are being satisfied. If a depressed labour class has managed to bargain for subsistence living, its need is for subsistence living, for that is the measure of its purchases. There is no difficulty about this if it is understood that need is used only in the sense in which it is measured by demand, but criteria of assessment and justification which provide us with the original concept of need are not so easily discarded. Thus in classical economics an investigation of supply and demand provides the basis not only for predicting and explaining economic behaviour, but for justifying a particular economic system. Purchases at a given time are taken as a level of the appropriate pattern of production and consumption, and economists are led to say that one party is demanding too much or another getting too little, as if these actions are somehow violations of laws of nature. If they are natural laws, there is no point in speaking of their violation. The fact that 'conservative' economists argue against interference with the natural order of events shows clearly that the kind of laws involved are not quasi-psychological or sociological generalizations, but beliefs as to the proper distribution of goods and exercise of economic authority. Shorn of this alleged descriptive character, classical economics becomes a moral theory. Its laws are cast in terms of an envisaged equilibrium, and the facts enter as the means for achieving or perpetuating it. But does the notion of equilibrium record a circumstance definable without recourse to the ethical or quasi-ethical use of terms like need?

First, what is meant by equilibrium? The earth-moon system is an equilibrium in that it maintains a relatively static pattern of motion. However, in this sense, it is the system as a whole which is an equilibrium, not some particular state of it. It is often alleged that students of trade cycles reject the equilibrium view. But what they reject is the moral sense of equilibrium characteristic of classical economic theory, substituting for it a study of equilibrium in the sense of finding regular patterns of fluctuation in the economy.

In a second sense, a certain state of a system is spoken of as an equilibrium. A gas or liquid at a certain temperature might be said to be in equilibrium when its particles are at rest with respect to one another. Water in the ocean is in equilibrium as against water running downhill. Here equilibrium refers to a static phase of a system. The notions of rest and least effort, introduced into a description of nature because of our interest in maintaining or producing such states, can be given objective and measurable significance. But when we describe nature this way we are apt to suppose that nature seeks these goals, or tends in this direction. But this is talk about our method of description, not about the world.

An economic equilibrium may appear to be a still further variety, namely, an ideal state in which (1) everything that is produced is consumed or (2) income covers expenditures or (3) economic transactions are at an optimum. Equilibrium here relies on one or both of the earlier uses. A balance of trade, of production/consumption, import/export, salary/expenditure looks like the kind of measure that could be decided objectively. And this is, of course, true so long as one talks about what is produced and what is consumed, exported and imported, earned and spent. But economists have interpreted such calculable balances as equilibria in a further sense, that between economic transactions and economic needs. The great virtue of Keynes's theory is its denial that the latter is entailed by the former. (In a more restricted way, the physiocrats realized that a favourable balance of trade did not entail economic prosperity, by noticing that it represented as much a drain on goods as a saving of money.) The economic situation that answers to needs is the desirable situation, not in fact, but by definition. Whether or not any of the mentioned balances provides that equilibrium is a question of fact, not of definition. It is Keynes's view that a classical balance of production and consumption does not necessarily contribute to a healthy or prosperous economy, that is, to full employment, but the matter of chief concern is not the question of fact, but that of logic. In classical economics, and in Marxist theory, too, it is supposed that the solution to the balance problem guarantees economic prosperity; the connection is analytic. But the prosperity problem is not decided by an appeal to the various balances alone, but by whatever conditions and intentions are imposed on the notion of prosperity. It is conceivable that everything produced is consumed, yet the bulk of the population remain in abject poverty; indeed, Malthus and Ricardo seem to have thought of this as the inevitable and proper consequence of the laws of economic equilibrium. If we reject this economic picture, it is because we have altered our conception of the good society, and not because we have made new discoveries about economic processes. We have, say, recast our conception of the equilibrium in terms of full employment, profit distribution, or a specified standard of living or minimum wage. Our concept of need has altered, and takes more into account than the national balance sheet (mercantilism), more than the profit accruing from the complete sale of goods (classical economics), more than the distribution of profit among the producers (Marxism), more, perhaps, than full employment.

I do not wish to defend this or that economic policy, but only to point out that, with the exception of the purely statistical studies of the business cycle, the volume and velocity of the movement of credit, money, and products, economics as a theory is a moral theory. Nor does this discredit it. We require a clear statement of the aims of the economy in order to make pertinent inquiries into the physical possibilities of the economic situation, enabling us to decide how altering one circumstance will affect others. Difficulties arise only when a concept like need, after having saturated the study of the economy with moral considerations, is then trotted forth as an innocent and discoverable fact, which then makes us prone to take special interests as if they reflected inevitable laws of nature.

Take, for example, the view one hears so much of nowadays that man is by nature a profit-seeking animal. This view is stated as a law of human nature, which can then be employed to explain all the variety of human actions. It is derived from Adam Smith but, if its role there is examined with care, its essentially polemical nature will emerge. The search for profit is essential to Smith's exhortation to let the economy govern itself. The assumption is that men, left to themselves, will, in fact, act so as to maximize profit, and thus contribute to the general good (wealth) of the community as a whole. We may set aside the obvious difficulties that arise when one considers that profit for one might mean loss for others; we are concerned rather with the status of the profit-seeking-animal hypothesis. In the first place, it is clear that it does not hold for all societies or all times and places. It belongs rather among the conventions subscribed to by particular men in particular cultures. And, in a sense, Adam Smith had much to do with articulating the moral view that makes the pursuit of profit a *sine qua non* of human activity. The point is, we know what men will do for profit, and we can expect a person involved in a bargaining position to buy as cheaply as he can and sell as dearly as he can, because those are the conventions under which he operates in the market-place. We have not divined some hitherto hidden truth about human nature to which we must bow, but have noted the conventions common to certain institutions and practices, which we can and do work to alter. Once again, the special flavour of an explanation like, a man does something for profit, is the moral flavour. We expect a man to behave in certain ways in economic situations, not because it is inevitable that he do so, but because, if he didn't, we would think of him as a poor business man or a lunatic. Profit-seeking is not a causal law, but a paradigm of activity in specialized situations. Persons entering into such situations are expected to match the paradigm if they can, because that is the thing to do. But it does not disrupt the place of the paradigm to discover, even most of the time, that economic behaviour does not quite match up to it. As a causal law, profit-seeking would entitle us to infer the future behaviour of economic agents; if discrepancies turn up, so much the worse for the law. But, as a rule of practice, we are entitled rather to moral expectations; when discrepancies turn up, so much the worse for the merchant.

If there is any value-free use of need, it would seem to be connected with Hebb's use of the term homeostasis, a term often rather irresponsibly bandied about by psychologists and sociologists. Hebb gives it a strict mechanical sense. A machine that is capable of maintaining itself at a certain level of response, a certain speed or in specifically planned adjustment may be said to be a homeostatic system. Hebb succeeds in applying the concept, at least hypothetically, to the human organism. Thus we need only postulate a state of the organism as the point of departure for any description of it, and note how the organism operates to restore this state. Postulation here is perhaps too strong; it may be that the so-called 'normal' state is defined wholly by the kinds of properties it exhibits most of the time. Theoretically, and some day perhaps practically, one could tell the physiological story in terms of mechanisms like feed-back which involve none of the value considerations normally associated with need. Hebb, in a sense, has not redefined need so much as eliminated its importance. In any event, it would be a mistake to assume that, because physiologists have discovered the mechanisms at work on those occasions in which we also speak of hunger, thirst and sexual need, we now fully understand where formerly we only surmised, why we eat, drink and seek sexual gratification. Ordinary life accounts—eating because hungry, drinking because thirsty, or nervous or frustrated—are not rough approximations to a physiological account, but stories of an entirely different sort employing a radically different vocabulary. They do the job they are tailor-made to do, and there is no vagueness, mystery or guesswork about it. When we say that a man, voraciously consuming a heaping plate of meat, vegetables and potatoes needed a square meal, our remark is not a surmise which requires the fortification of laboratory work or technical information to verify. For this account has no bearing on nerve pathways, glandular secretions or the other elements of the physiological story.

Physiological theory, however, remains as a possible and potentially informative account of the mechanisms that make the human organism operate as it does. It parallels, but is independent of, reason-giving and justifying accounts. Non-physiological psychology, on the other hand, is in some difficulties on this score. In Hull's theory, for example, need enters as a postulated stimulus to account for empirically noted deviations from the observed S-R patterns.[3] S-R is regarded as strengthened whenever S and R occur together and a need-stimulus, N, decreases at the same time. But to postulate need as stimulus defeats the whole point of an empirical psychology. The stimulus must be that aspect of the situation which is governed and manipulated by the investigator. So the whole point of the exhaustive attempts to define discrimination in terms of behaviour is to make sure the stimulus is a public object. A person or animal discriminates on this view, not between two or more internal feelings, urges or sense-data, but between two or more objects presented by the experimenter. If need is allowed as a stimulus, then the class of stimuli includes, beyond public and manipulable objects, putative internal occurrences which do not meet the criteria of public confirmation and experimental manipulation. But the point of S-R methodology was presumably to meet these criteria. The failure of the strict S-R account to produce regularity laws of any significance might perhaps warrant the search for or postulation of 'intervening variables' or 'hypothetical constructs' of a physiological nature. But to relapse into a mentalistic and introspective language is to deprive the system of its causal-mechanical character. To introduce need, then, is not to introduce a stimulus of any kind, either observable or hypothetical, but is to seek an account of behaviour informed by a conception of values, reasons and principles for action. As such it cannot possibly conform to a hypothetico-deductive or a causal model of explanation. More important, it is in looking at behaviour as satisfying needs and wants that need-explanations are

[3] Cf. Hebb, *Organization of Behaviour* (John Wiley, 1949).

generated. Consequently, if we can correctly assign a need, we have already explained the action to which we have assigned it. There is no further or more fruitful research to be done.

PLEASURE AND PAIN

That something is pleasant explains why a man pursues or does it, at the moment or persistently; that it is painful explains why he avoids it. Very good. But these commonplaces are often transformed by philosophers and psychologists into rather different theories according to which pleasure-seeking and pain-avoiding become the mainsprings of human action. We can eliminate, I think, any form of such a theory.

1. The object of a man's action is always some pleasure, the impetus is his desire for it. Desire for pleasure is like desire for anything. We need add nothing to our earlier comments in order to show that this theory is plausible because desire (and pleasure) is a ground for acting. Beyond this we can appeal to the formidable arguments advanced by Bishop Butler against hedonistic and egoistic theories of human nature. Feelings of pleasure are consequences of achievement, and cannot then be regarded as the objects of human striving. Unless one pursues and obtains something other than pleasure, it is not clear how gratification can be obtained.

2. Sometimes pleasure is used as a general name for what men do in fact pursue. It would then be tautologically true to say that a man pursues what he pursues. If it is not tautologous, the general term is an ellipsis for the hosts of individual objects and activities which might be cited as the reasons for a person's acting. Thus I smoke because I like to roll a cigar about in my mouth and enjoy the rich, cool smoke.

Pleasure, in this sense, is not a particular ingredient in the things enjoyed. It is the smoke, the cigar itself, that are enjoyed. Sometimes the things generally enjoyed cease to be enjoyed; the wrapper starts to unravel and deposit rag ends of tobacco in my mouth, the smoke towards the end is hot and bitter. The thing itself has changed; it is not that something is going on, much as before, and only the pleasure has evaporated. This I take to be Ryle's point in *The Concept of Mind* and in *Dilemmas.*[4] The pleasure is not a separate ingredient that could be contemplated and described; it is rather seeing or judging the ingredients of the viewed, heard, tasted, felt or smelled as pleasant. If pleasure explains here, it is because of its evaluative role. In seeing an object or action as pleasant, one sees it as grounds for acting.

[4] Gilbert Ryle, *The Concept of Mind* (Hutchinson, 1949), Chapter IV, Section 6; *Dilemmas* (Cambridge University Press, 1954), Chapter IV.

3. Pleasure is sometimes identified with certain classes of feelings, such as euphoria or ecstasy, calm or contentment. Some activities, we find, contribute to the occurrence or maintenance of such feelings, and so we pursue them. This interpretation rescues hedonism from redundancy. For we now say: whatever objects or actions a person pursues, he does so for this special kind of consequence.

4. This view may be examined together with its less optimistic counterpart, that pleasure is to be identified with the absence of pain. Human action on this view is always an attempt to reduce or avoid painful sensations, like burns, throbs and tensions. The interesting thing to be noticed about the lists of pleasurable and painful feelings is that it would be logically contradictory to suppose that the feeling labelled as euphoric or contented might be painful or neutral. Once we apply these labels we have chosen to regard the experience as pleasant, just as our descriptions of colours as clashing, sounds as discordant, tastes and smells as nauseating, lead us to see, hear, taste or smell them as painful.

But there are two sides to this observation. On the one side, it is true, it is impossible to separate the pleasure from the feeling, taste or smell, and this seems to give some comfort to the Ryleian view that when I get pleasure out of gardening or puffing on a pipe there are not two things, the pleasure and the gardening or puffing, but only the enjoyed gardening or smoking. But it would be difficult to say that concepts like pleasure and pain have their use only in appraising activities like gardening or smoking, or objects like Picasso paintings or glasses of beer, for surely these terms describe our reactions to activities and objects. Thus, it might be argued, we do have grounds for speaking of pleasure events. On the other side, however, the events themselves are sights and sounds, flavours and odours, and particular bodily feelings. Our pleasure-pain vocabulary is utilized to describe colours or shapes, flavours or odours, in an evaluative way. If it is sometimes difficult to separate the pleasure or pain from the other properties of the event or feeling, save by such appraising terms. In more attenuated cases, it is easy to see that adding the label 'pleasant' or 'displeasing' to the event or activity in view is a matter of judging what is viewed, and not discovering some new property of it.

In this sense, we do things for pleasure and avoid things because of pain, because these are grounds for pursuing or shunning. In this sense, pleasure is by definition something worthy of pursuit and pain something worthy of being avoided. This has seemed alarming because of the persistent Puritan view that pleasure is bad. It takes little philosophy to realize that the Puritan has identified pleasure with the performance of certain kinds of activity, but it takes a much greater effort to shake off the pejorative burden of the term. There is a tendency to identify pleasure with impulses of a socially disruptive nature or with personally offensive actions. Some pleasant activities have untoward consequences, and yet these activities are frequently those which appear most intrinsically desirable in themselves. And this has led philosophers to set a gulf between pleasure concepts and moral concepts, the one describing how men are, the other prescribing what men should do. This dichotomy forces us to treat pleasures as the names for special occurrences, in themselves morally neutral and capable of being judged good or bad, depending on whether they meet or fail to meet moral standards. And this is embarrassing, for it is impossible to single out and describe pleasure events without describing the other properties of objects and actions as prized. We have already favourably described circumstances in calling them pleasant, and so it is a logical gaffe to force together 'pleasure' and 'bad'. What seems to allow this conjunction is the complexity of moral situations. What may, on one occasion, appear good, in the sense of object or action worthy of pursuit may, on another, turn out to involve consequences which would be looked on as neither good nor pleasant. And this argues that ascribing pleasure to objects and actions is a business to be undertaken with care and attention to the details of the situation. The language of pleasure is an aspect of the language of moral perception, but is not thereby exempt from criticism from rules and principles of wider scope, any more than a statement of what one sees is exempt from the accumulation of knowledge as to what generally happens or what others find to be the case. The urge, which leads philosophers to find in some observations the incorrigible bases for our knowledge of the world, prompts us in ethics to deny a moral status to anything which cannot be the incontrovertible and universal criterion of moral worth. Such has been the fate of both desire and pleasure.

So traditional ethical theories and empiricist metaphysics combine to play havoc with the concept of pleasure. But the everyday use of the concept pain has much to do with it also. For surely pains are events, the sorts of occurrences which we cannot escape or overlook. And surely such occurrences cause men and animals to recoil, run, and generally exhibit avoidance behaviour. Pleasure is the opposite of pain, and so the analogous account is forced on that term.

Numbers of philosophers have argued in ways suggesting that pleasure and pain are not opposites. But this, I think, will not do. It will not do, for example, to say that pains are antecedent to the actions explained by their occurrence, while pleasures are the consequences of them, even if this should turn out to be true for the great run of cases. For a pain can be anticipated and so produce an action, and pleasure can be experienced, perhaps at random or at the first tentative exploration, and so lead to actions furthering it. It may seem more to the point to say that, while pleasures subdivide into qualities of things enjoyed, pains subdivide into qualities of pains. They are not qualities of objects, but of persons feeling them, and this seems grounds for saying that pleasure and pain do not belong to the same genus. But beyond these differences, pains, like pleasures, are not described by means of the neutral properties of objects or situations, like colours, sizes or shapes, but by means of attitudes. The terms by which pains are described all imply avoidance, just as the descriptions of pleasures imply acceptance or pursuit. Thus the general rule, avoid pain, like the general rule, pursue pleasure, is vacuously true. What is not vacuously true is the connexion between particular things, activities and sensations and avoidance behaviour. Thus we might ask, what establishes the connection between boiling water flowing over the fingers and the sensations and actions that follow it? The question might suggest the Humean answer, repeated experience. But the familiar adage, once bitten, twice shy, indicates a different answer, that something is known directly from the single case.

What can we say about this? Sufficient argument has been offered, I trust, to reject the Humean answer, that I remove my hand now because in the past I have removed my hand. But this leaves available only the view that in experiencing something as painful we apprehend it as something to be avoided. It is lucky for us we do, and this may afford the basis for a very different kind of explanation according to which we appeal to the survival of the fittest to explain why we react immediately to stimuli as painful and so to be avoided. But when we apprehend the stimulus as painful, there is no further story to be told about the connexion between it and avoidance behaviour. For we view the stimulus as something to be avoided.

This view might seem to be incompatible with the alleged facts of masochism. But the motto here is: 'I will endure', not, 'it is painful and therefore to be embraced.' The experience must at least be identified as one which ought to be avoided but, for some reason or other—a desire for punishment, or a wish to play the hero—comes under a rule or inclination of greater importance to the individual. It is not self-contradictory to pursue what one identifies as painful, or avoid what one identifies as pleasant, for pain and pleasure are not to be identified with what is avoided or pursued, but that for which there are good reasons for avoidance or pursuit.

and do deplore violent reactions, and admire those that are calm
⋯ained. Because 'rational' and 'reasonable' are honorific labels, it
⋯d to restrain their application to the kinds of actions and responses
⋯ we approve. Thus 'emotional' comes to be identified with the
⋯ur of which we disapprove, and 'rational' with the behaviour we
⋯. The man who turns the other cheek may merit our applause,
⋯man who returns the blow may deserve our blame, but we under-
⋯at both responses are among the wide range of actions or gestures
⋯ed by the situation. One is not causally determined, and the other
⋯d simply because we approve or admire one more than the other.
⋯ond objection is that emotions name feelings which arise because
⋯ituations in which their possessors find themselves, and lead to the
⋯f behaviour we generally call emotional. The strength of this
⋯s much to do with the prominence of bodily sensations in at least
⋯f the emotions. In fear one sweats, has palpitations, feels clammy,
⋯ak at the knees. In anger, one may report stifling or choking
⋯ns. These cases suggest the James–Lange theory of the emotions,
⋯ng to which an emotion is an awareness of bodily processes. Most
⋯emotions which we manage to distinguish without too much
⋯ty would be impossible to distinguish on this basis, however.
⋯different emotional states are described in almost identical feeling
⋯ Anger is sometimes described as a pressure in the chest, but so also
⋯, sorrow, elation, despair, and half a dozen other refinements of
⋯motional states. We might, none the less, speak of the feelings which
⋯ to enter into descriptions of the emotions as causing us to act in
⋯ ways. Flight, a scream, lashing out with fist or words might be
⋯ted to those leaden, tightening, or constricting feelings at the base
⋯breast bone. But when this is done, it appears that actions are
⋯ted to these feelings in the sense that painful or pleasant sensations
⋯e regarded as the reasons for acting. They serve as grounds or at
⋯s excuses for acting in certain ways, and differ from factors in the
⋯nment only in being privy to the actor. If we call these feelings by
⋯mes for emotions we do not thereby subscribe to a causal inter-
⋯ion of the relation of emotions to actions; accounting here still has
⋯ason-for-acting form. In any case, we do not identify an emotion
⋯erence to such a feeling, but, as Aristotle supposes in De Anima, by
⋯ropriate object.

⋯hird difficulty with our thesis is the wide variation of emotional
⋯iour. One man's eye twitches at an insult, another man's mouth
⋯rs, a third man resorts to blows, a fourth drums on the table, a fifth
⋯rfectly still with only the slightest swelling perceptible in the veins

As general laws of human behaviour, inexorably determining human
conduct, pain-avoidance and pleasure-pursuit are inadequate candidates.
But they fail also as general rules of conduct. We may see an action or
object as pleasant or painful and so decide how to act toward it. But the
decision is tentative and *prima facie*, for it is always possible that the
context will lead us to avoid that particular pleasure or embrace that
particular pain. None the less, seeing something as pleasant or painful is
to see it as constituting grounds for pursuit or avoidance. And this is the
sense in which these terms come to explain human conduct. Such
explanations could not pretend to general or theoretical status. For once
we say, 'All men pursue pleasure', we lose contact with the variety of
objects and situations which men find or judge to be worthy of pursuit,
and our thesis becomes vacuous. The same holds for the moral thesis:
'pursue pleasure!' for this will result in a chaos of conflicting aims and
judgments. To say of an object or situation that it is pleasing or painful
is to say that it provides grounds for acting. In no sense does it say that it
is the cause of action. And finally, though it serves as grounds for acting,
it does not exclude other considerations suggesting or dictating different
lines of conduct. Pleasure and pain explain morally, and they explain in
context.

THE EMOTIONS

If pleasure and pain are evaluative ways of looking at objects and
qualities, surely the emotions are as well. Fear and anger, joy and sorrow,
love and hate, disgust and enthusiasm are terms which enter naturally
into morally charged descriptions. But we also speak of the emotions as
caused by stimuli and as the causes of behaviour. So it seems possible
that a psychological science might investigate them.

But there are preliminary difficulties standing in the way of either a
psychological or a philosophical theory of the emotions. Emotion labels
are applied in various ways. Sometimes, as in love and hate, they are
distinguished by their characteristic pro or con attitudes. In such cases
approval and disapproval, preference and aversion become standard
criteria for distinguishing emotions. In other cases, they seem to be distinguished according to their intensity, and so dislike is distinguished from
hate and apprehension from fear. We are also inclined to say at times that
a person acts emotionally and at other times that he feels emotions.

This last way of talking seems to allow the possibility that we can
never know whether another person is angry. A person may behave
emotionally while not feeling the corresponding emotion, and feel the
emotion while resisting the impulse to express it in the appropriate

behaviour. We are apt to think that behaviour is the only avenue to acquaintance with another's emotional state, and since these inferences are hedged round with so many qualifications, it seems unlikely that we can speak of our knowledge of the emotions of others at all. Is he cautious or afraid, is he really angry with me, does she love me, are agonizing and unanswerable questions.

This view has been taken to task by Austin,[5] who suggests that actions like running away or throwing things are not symptoms but expressions of fear or anger. The problem for Austin arises because he assumes that we do know (sometimes) that a person is angry or afraid. Since our evidence is the person's behaviour, that behaviour must be connected in a more intimate way with our use of emotion terms than is the relation of symptom to inner event. And it does resolve the issue as to how we know whether another person is angry or afraid (assuming that we do know) to say that being angry means throwing things, trembling lips, and red faces, and that fear means running away, chattering teeth, and knocking knees. For these are surely the sorts of occurrences we can witness and so claim to know about.

But Austin's solution is itself attended by a pair of difficulties. First, we can only say, apparently, that a man is angry when he throws things. But we all know he could be putting it on, or that, on other occasions, he can smile and stroke the cat and yet be furious. Second, we must suppose that the question of knowing about an emotional state arises only in the case of other people. It becomes senseless to say that I know that I am angry, for I cannot be said, without fear of absurdity, to read off my emotional state from my own behaviour. One does not decide that one is angry by observing oneself throwing things and then reporting this fact by saying, 'I am angry'.

Austin attempts to dispose of this difficulty by suggesting that 'I am angry' is not a report of an occurrence, whether of internal events or behaviour, but is itself a performance. Like throwing things, the state-ment, 'I am angry', evinces or declares anger. Thus, the absurdity of describing my emotional state from observation of my own behaviour is avoided. That situation could not arise, since I am not describing my anger in saying I am angry, I am being angry.

But a man may still feign anger or disguise his anger, and surely there must be something absent in the case of feigning and present in the case of disguising, which is being feigned or disguised. There are, in Austin's way of talking, felicitous and infelicitous employments of expressions of

emotion and, more generally, of performative utte
extend Austin's analysis and say that a man is not entit
situations which are not provoking, to appear fearful
are not dangerous or threatening, or to express joy a
relations, or sorrow at the success of one's friends.
which we speak of someone being angry or afraid is
behaviour is appropriate to the situation in which h
see the world as containing objects and situations wh
string of oaths, laughter or tears. Knowing that som
afraid is, in the standard case, seeing him exhibit the
with anger or fear in a situation justifying that b
oneself to be angry or afraid, or in other ways acting
is occasioned by one's judgment of the situation,
provoking or threatening.[6]

In the *standard* case, then, there can be no questio
causes of an emotion. If a man did not know he h
hammer he would not be swearing and throwing
ledge, clearly enough, is not of the regularity patter
swore and threw things when hitting thumb with
occasions that he knows why he is doing so nov
provoking situation, to which swearing, at least, i
Seeing it as a provoking situation is to see it as justify
ate range of responses. In short, emotion is not
philosophers and psychologists, an irrational eru
pimples and rashes, we seek the physical causes, l
response to standard situations of provocation.

Various difficulties stand in the way of endorsing
view that emotions are passions, forces to which w
sive behaviour that we use. They well up and
deliberation or judgment, and often in spite of it
supported by contrasting emotional behaviour wit
are allegedly not emotional. But it turns out th
within the general rubric of emotion. When we
sobriety instead of hysteria and intemperance, whe
lip instead of succumbing to a trembling lower o
acting unemotionally. But emotional and unem
in the sense that they both refer to characteristic
expressions in response to situations seen as justifyi

[5] J. L. Austin, 'Other Minds', *Philosophical Papers* (Oxford University Press, 1961), pp. 44 ff. Cf. in the same volume, 'Pretending' and 'Performative Utterances'.

[6] I refrain from belabouring this point, partly because it has b
to desire and pleasure, and thus should need no further explic
thesis has been treated cogently and in detail by Errol Bedfor
Society Proceedings, LVII (1956–7), pp. 281–304.

of his neck. We have no difficulty in accommodating our account of an emotion to any of these, but the extreme flexibility of the range makes it hard to believe that emotional behaviour is a convention for expressing attitudes in appropriate situations. For a gesture, movement, or speech can count as conventional only if limits have been set to its form, so that it can be pretty generally recognized for what it is. With emotional displays, however, gestures and bodily movements are often quite idiosyncratic and cannot count as conventions. Even worse, much of typical emotional display, particularly of so-called 'primary' emotions like fear and rage, can hardly be called learned behaviour in the sense that imitation and instruction leads to the perfection of the appropriate gestures. Yet surely conventions have to be learned. The arched back, spitting, and hair standing on end are surely signs of *something* in a cat, but are they conventional signs? The same problem arises with many of the basic acts of embrace or recoil which can be observed, surely, in the youngest and most untutored human infant.

This difficulty suggests a biological answer, an attempt to account, as Darwin did, for the variety of gestures in animals and men, by examining them for their survival value, and so bring this whole question within evolutionary and genetic theory. On this explanation the role of emotions in explaining behaviour simply does not arise. A man may throw things because he is angry, he may also throw things because the movement of repulsion has become part of the genetic equipment of the organism through the process of natural selection. These two accounts converge on the same event or class of events, but they are not incompatible. The biological answer may be stated without any reference to the emotions as such. It refers only to the role that a given gesture might play in the survival of the organism. The question is not, why is the cat afraid, but why does it arch its back and bristle its tail in certain situations. If we lapse into the language of emotion here, it is because the situation in which the cat indulges in this behaviour is seen as dangerous or threatening. Of course, it works both ways. Eventually we may decide that the animal faces a dangerous situation, of which we are not aware, because it arches its back and bristles its tail. The biological story tempts us to suppose that we are explaining by means of emotions, or explaining the emotions, but this is not quite the case. It is a puzzling thing that different speakers have selected different groups of sounds out of which to form their languages. I do not have any idea what sort of theory might be advanced to explain this variety, but an answer to it is not an answer to the question why a speaker on a particular occasion or type of occasion uses the words he does. For now we have shifted our attention from the antecedent conditions which led to the choice of certain sounds to the reasons why he said and meant certain things. Similarly, we can speculate on the antecedents of visceral responses to certain dangerous situations, but this is no answer to the question, why is he afraid? That question consists in exhibiting the circumstances in the environment which constitute threats or dangers. And this is true of the animal as much as the man. We do not have to imagine that we are divining internal agitations, as Ryle likes to call them, in diagnosing an animal's fear or rage. We are able to speak for the animal, because we see the situation in which he finds himself as provoking or fearful. We do the same with humans. A man's behaviour may suggest that he is afraid, but it is the context that makes us sure of this. And, in being sure, we also explain his behaviour. This explanation is not something over and above the best evidence we have that he is angry or afraid. Knowing that he is afraid is, in the fullest sense, to know why the situation leads him to act the way he does. The psychologist presumably starts with the description of behaviour given as a case of anger or fear, lust or protectiveness, sorrow or joy, and then wishes to raise the question, why do men in general, or this subject in particular, respond in this way? The question, so far as it is a question about emotion, is idle. In knowing that it is a case of anger or other emotion, he already knows why the behaviour is indulged. The explanation does not stand in need of any further research. If a question does arise as to why this kind of action is performed, which is not answered by a description in terms of the relevant emotion, it appears to be a biological question.

If we speak of emotional behaviour as conventional, then, it is in virtue of knowledge we have about the contexts of actions. Seeing a rattlesnake coiled in the path, we are in a better position to say that a man is giving way to fear, than we are, seeing only his odd and fixed expression or his sudden pallor. Of course, if his behaviour failed to show marked change, if he continued to whistle merrily and stepped considerately around the coiled horror, we should say that he isn't afraid. To say that a person is afraid, then, is to see the situation as dangerous or threatening and to see as well that his behaviour does alter somewhat dramatically in the encounter. But it is the situation appraised as threatening that leads us to speak of the reaction as an expression of recoil to it, to see it as *bespeaking* fear, and not merely as a consequence of something within.

This analysis allows us also to resolve some of the doubtful cases in which we say that a person is angry or afraid. There are, surely, cases beyond doubt, where, for example, the man screams with horror at the rattlesnake and faints dead away. The situation is too generally taken to be threatening, and the action too generally and convincingly expressive of fear to know any more what we might be asking for in demanding further evidence. But there are many cases where a situation is appraised as frightening by one and harmless by another, and others in which we can't really be quite sure that actions express fear. So mother bites her nails and says, 'Doesn't Johnny realize what will happen if he goes down the hill so fast?', or a soldier watches his tough sergeant with the bullets whistling all around and thinks: 'Isn't he afraid . . . ? Isn't, perhaps, that way he has of putting his finger in his collar, or gripping and ungripping the stock of his rifle . . .?' And, of course, even more obscure cases, where we doubt really whether we could quite say it's a threatening situation, or where the alteration in behaviour is so minute as hardly to count. These are the borderlines on which sceptical philosophers batten. We may, indeed, have irresolvable doubts in such cases, but this is because they are not as clear as standard cases. They may even outnumber the clear cases. But this is not to deny that there are cases in which we can quite appropriately say that a person is afraid, nor is it to suggest that we must always remain in the dark because of our lack of acquaintance with inner goings-on. It is not such events which, even in our own favoured case, leads us to say we are afraid, but our appraisal of the situation in which we find ourselves.

The upshot is that our talk about and ascription of emotions is talk and ascription to cases in particular contexts. The torturing doubts arise and, with them, the supposed advantage of experimental techniques in psychology, because we try to generalize, to say what must count as ultimate evidence that a man—any man—is angry or afraid. And then, of course, we come up against the innumerable troubling cases—how can he handle that snake? or fail to weep at Little Nell? We are undoubtedly in agreement in viewing the world as containing at least some threatening, provoking, enticing, or sorrowful circumstances. And we are in fair accord in our ways of evincing these attitudes and judgments. But so much of our emotion talk, while clear enough when we confine ourselves to contexts, becomes hopelessly vague and inapplicable when generalized for an entire range of behaviour. To decide out of context whether a twitching eyelid means fear or anger is quite impossible. But to decide whether the twitching lid of Jones-nagged-by-wife is anger is perhaps not as difficult. Scepticism appears irresolvable only so long as we insist on a general criterion for the application of emotion words to behaviour.

A final difficulty is the most important, for it suggests the need for a general theory of human behaviour as a way of improving on our *ad hoc* talk about emotions. Suppose we admit that the above account has survived the perils of the previous objections, and so come to see that our ascription of emotion words to behaviour is in virtue of aspects of the situation which warrant the behaviour. Still, it might be argued, there are many cases in which we should be quite ready to speak of emotional behaviour, but explicitly deny the rationale. So enters psychiatry, with mania and depression, neurotic fears and anxieties, choleric anger and the rest. If the rationale is lost, we must have recourse to some other way (perhaps causal) to account for this behaviour.

We might forestall this move away from a reason-giving account by observing that the assigning of an emotion to behaviour *sans* rationale is parasitic upon the case in which we do assign the emotion to behaviour with reason and in context. Some behaviour, through its association with contexts seen as threatening, provoking or exciting, comes to have the significance of a style of fear, anger or joy. It is difficult to imagine such behaviour except as expressions of such attitudes in response to such situations. And so we wonder what can make a person afraid or depressed when there is nothing in the obvious environment which would warrant such behaviour, and probe until we discover (perhaps) a rather unique view of the environment which does, then, make the behaviour intelligible. This has much to do, no doubt, with the psychiatrist's recourse to hallucination and delusion to account for nameless fears. It is a way of picturing the patient's world so that his emotional outbursts do seem to be warranted. What is not warranted is the patient's interpretation of his situation. And in long talk with the patient, if he will talk, some of this conjecture may be converted to fact, and a process of re-education begun.

But the psychiatrist frequently does something else. Behaviour is sometimes called anxious even though neither the situation nor the action suggests what we would normally call anxious. A mother may peer out of the window, walk the floor and wring her hands, and this is standard anxious behaviour. She and those who observe her may know that her son is overdue from his tuba lesson, that he has to cross a busy street, that he can't see the intersection very well because he staggers under the burden of the gigantic instrument. The knowledge of the context may lead us to describe her behaviour as anxious, though this behaviour is itself somewhat ambiguous—perhaps she is talking a trifle fast, or a trifle loud, or turning her wedding ring. Or the behaviour may be paradigmatic, though we don't know, at the moment, what in the situation prompts the behaviour. But now we are asked to admit cases in which neither the situation nor the behaviour is paradigmatic. The man who plunges into his work, or the miser into his pot of gold, the Don Juan who pursues every female with whom he comes in contact, are often alleged to be acting from anxiety. In this way of talking, anxiety becomes the way to a general theory of human behaviour, and must be treated as if it were a kind of tension, permanently characteristic of the organism, and capable, under various kinds of circumstances, of being stretched or slackened.

This picturesque view is a substitute among many 'neo-Freudian' psychiatrists for the Freudian view. It is as if a harmonic has been substituted for a hydraulic metaphor. But both metaphors betray their dependence upon a conception of an appropriate, and so an inappropriate, quantity of tension or pressure. What alerts the psychiatrist to the actions of the zealous business man, the gloating miser, or the frantic Don Juan is that his behaviour is rather too much. Interest in business cannot justify the total immersion in work; money does not have the kind of intrinsic value assigned to it by the miser; the Don Juan's affairs are much too frequent, and directed toward women of widely varying charms, to be justified by sexual attraction. There is something extraordinary about these cases, in the sense that the behaviour is beyond the bounds of normal warrants. That the conduct in question reflects a departure from the normal level of activity suggests an account in terms of emotion. For one of the ways in which an emotional state is diagnosed is by the departure in the style of behaviour from earlier conduct of the individual or from conduct common to most people in his situation. If we look at behaviour in this way, a form of explaining comes naturally to mind: his activity is his way of working off or forgetting or submerging his fears, his anxieties. But filling the form with content depends upon showing that circumstances do justify or warrant this behaviour.

The psychiatrist in these circumstances has extended the grounds permitting us to call a person anxious or afraid, by extending the context that we would ordinarily think of as relating to specific actions. A man in his thirties finds the warrant (and the excuse) for his impotence in the child of two witnessing his parents in coitus; so goes the Freudian story. In a sense, the neo-Freudian story is more tenuous, because it is more general. A man's frantic devotion to business is a consequence of his anxiety. But why should he be anxious? This is never as clearly spelled out, because it is assumed, by writers like Horney and Sullivan, that anxiety is a driving force, just as it was assumed by Freud that the libido moved the creaking psyche. In the particular case, perhaps, we come to see that the patient looks at the world as a rather alarming place, and so his excessive attention to business and his ulcers. But, in such a case, the psychiatrist has entered the lists of moral argument with the patient. He is not

diagnosing a quasi-physical tension which needs to be exorcised or dispelled; he is getting the person to see that his rationale for his conduct is
not sufficient to support that line of conduct.

Brought forward so nakedly, this moral exhortation might strike the
patient as something worth discussing with all the tentativeness that such
moral talk implies, but not as something to be embraced as a discovery as
to how human nature or the human mind works. It appears as a discovery
because it is clothed in the metaphor of psychic energy or tension, dammed
or screwed up to intolerable pitch, and finding its way out finally in
neurotic, or psychotic, or just plain not-quite-right behaviour. Suppose
the analyst were to say: 'Well, you saw your parents having intercourse,
and that entitles you to be jumpy today. Of course, many people have
popped into parents' bedrooms at untoward times and now live as happily
as the mortal lot will allow. But as we are looking, not for causes, but
excuses, this will do. . . .' But, of course, it won't do at all. The wizardry
by which moral suasion is converted to causal necessity is a requirement
of the polemic of psychotherapy, in order to convince the patient of the
truth of the diagnosis. The trauma of the two-year-old becomes an
excuse for the adult, not because we can quite happily accept this event
as belonging to the sort of situation which does justify emotional behaviour,
but because the hydraulic or harmonic metaphors convince the patient
that his behaviour is determined by these circumstances. For we all, in
some way or another, share the prejudice that determinism relieves us of
responsibility. Yet our grounds for connecting the event and the behaviour
are along the normal lines by which emotional behaviour is connected
with situations. The latter warrant the former. Without this connexion
we should not be entitled to speak of the behaviour as an instance of an
emotion, whether anxiety, fear, or any other member of that catalogue
(for example, 'he loves his mother'). So the mechanisms, whether of the
unconscious survival of traumatic memories or the screwed up strings of
anxiety, are applied to cases which logically resist the application of such
metaphors. For the metaphors are designed to convert what are first
identified as rational responses to situations to consequences of causal
agency. The tactical body of therapy does not fit the clothing of this kind
of theory.

But if we reject the causal thesis, what remains is the moral aim—
getting a person to adopt a less, or possibly a more, severe attitude and
interpretation of his past actions and his environment. But now, more
often than not, psychoanalysis gives the appearance of a salvation ethic,
in which, according to the Menningers, for example, any kind of unhappi-
ness is worth eradicating, even if the result is bland social conformity or

a Polyannic indifference to one's own or one's neighbours' situation. It is often, in fact, a rather shabby moral position that is being offered, and, if compared with its moral competitors, is not apt to command the assent given on the assumption that analysis has uncovered psychological truths.

In fine, the psychiatrist's extension of the concept emotion is not so much the result of pressure exerted by discovery of new facts as the result of stretching the normal grounds we should be prepared to regard as warranting or excusing action. Thus, the last objection to my thesis turns out to be less a difficulty than a defence. For the alleged science in which emotion terms seem to find a prominent place is precisely the study which turns upon an awareness of conduct as appropriate or inappropriate. And thus we see emotions as identified, not by the inference of feelings from symptoms, by means of defective analogy with one's own case, but by the alterations in behaviour in contexts which seem to justify or excuse these alterations. Thus, to identify an emotion is also to identify its 'cause', that is, to identify the grounds for the display. The upshot is that desires, emotions, pleasures and pains have been improperly described and catalogued if they are placed in a class over against the rational component of the soul. Desires and emotions, pleasures and pains, are identified in ourselves and others, in the light of what we regard or infer or see as desirable, appropriate, or entailed by the situations in which we find ourselves. As a consequence, such terms explain actions, not by showing the regular connexion or the observed interaction of inner events with outward actions, but by seeing the situation as entitling the action. And this, as we shall now see, provides a formula for an account of what has more traditionally been thought of as reasons for acting.

CHAPTER SIX

REASONS

DESCARTES AND subsequent philosophers make a customary distinction between reason and the passions. They join ranks with contemporary psychologists in supposing that the latter afford typical instances of causal explanation. I have argued that in itself there is nothing wrong with this until the concept of cause is identified with a special technique of investigation, so that an explanation in terms of feelings, emotions, or desires seems to require the procedures and the evidence supplied by an empirical science of psychology. Members of this family of concepts might be said to be used in causal explanations, in the sense that, had there not been a feeling, or a desirable consequence, or a situation warranting certain kinds of action, the action would not have taken place. But we understand the relation of the action to feelings, consequences or situations in our identification of them as feelings of pleasure, desires for objects, and grounds for emotions. There is no further discovery or technique for forming hypotheses required in order to draw the connection expressed in such forms as: Had I not hit my thumb with the hammer, I would not have offended your feminine ears, or, Had I not thought how good a glass of beer would taste, I would have been home earlier.

In seeing this, however, it is possible to see as well that the distinction between the passions and reason is not an easy and perhaps not an intelligible one to draw. Acting on emotion or desire is not at all clearly marked off from acting from motives or on purpose, or from intending to act. Even the most rational of moves, that taken in a mathematical proof, say, is explainable by the same pattern that we have seen to be characteristic of explanations in terms of desires and emotions. The mathematician explains his move, or the chess player his, by appealing to rules of inference, the nature of the problem, the rules of the game or the disposition of the pieces that justify or perhaps strictly entail his moves. The use of desire is governed less strictly by rule and relevant circumstance than the use of motive or intention, which in turn is not governed as strictly as the moves in logic or a game of chess. And so our ascriptions of explanations of actions are apt to be made more tentatively in the first cases than the second, and in the second than in the last. Since they are not quite decisive, it looks as if further evidence ought to be forthcoming. But if the provision of warrants is the kind of strategy required to explain these cases, the decisiveness and scope of our entitling formulae will vary with the degree of uniformity and explicit convention characteristic of the kind of action to be explained. Thus we must be satisfied, sometimes, with less precise and more tentative explanations, for we lack the kind of agreement as to what counts as desirable, pleasant, provoking or threatening that we have with respect to appropriate moves in a scientific laboratory, on a mathematician's blackboard or a chess player's chequered squares.

I do not, then, in marking off reasons from desires by beginning a fresh chapter, make a hard and fast distinction between them. It is possible, even, to speak of reasons as causes of behaviour, for we shall see that motives, intentions and purposes are, like desires and emotions, causal in a sense that does not require a special science to establish. I shall begin with motive, a term of special interest to the psychologist, and then continue with concepts like intention and purpose, which the psychologist rejects as old-fashioned and pre-scientific ways of talking, largely because they are less amenable to his techniques.

MOTIVE

In a casual way (Chapter Four) we have seen that motives are ascribed to individuals in the context of situations entitling them to act. Often, people do not exercise their license, but when they do are we not entitled to say that the situation caused the action? The old man and his cantankerous ways and bloated bank account goaded his son into killing him. There is nothing wrong with putting the case this way unless it is implied that behind such a statement lies the authority of a generalization about cantankerous fathers and quick-tempered offspring. In short, we need to free the concept of cause of its theoretical entanglements.

This is perhaps the easier of the two tasks that face us. It is possible to say that, had the father not been so cantankerous as to cut the erring son out of his will, the son would not have shot him. And surely this is a typical formula of causal ascription: no B without A. But we need not and cannot support this assertion by showing that, if A is not present, B will not occur, or that whenever A occurs B will follow. The range of reasons for parricide are too wide to admit any sense to the first of these procedures, and the temperament of sons too various to suppose that cantankerous fathers who cut relatives out of their wills always or 90 or 50 per cent of the time come to a violent end. Being cut out of a will by an irascible parent is grounds for murder, though these grounds may not be exercised. But when the grounds are present, when, to clinch the case, the erring son is drowning in debt, we have no compunction in citing the motive, or, if you like, finding the cause of his action in these circumstances. Whatever our choice of terms, the situation can become impressive enough to allow us to claim that it explains the conduct by providing grounds for it. The more complete and consistent the pattern, the more likely it is that we will speak of the situation as providing *the* motive for the action. Given a degree of complexity and inconsistency in the environment, we are more apt to say, *a* motive. And so on, down to the point at which we can conjecture motives, but not assign them. It is in part this frequent opacity of motive in ordinary examination of human doings that leads philosophers and psychologists to suppose that a new technique is needed to divine motives or a more rigorous criterion to limit the candidates to motive ascription. But the remarks offered with respect to desire explanations apply equally here. Motive is the kind of concept that is bound to have doubtful and indeterminate applications. Our conjecture as to motive is not in the absence of evidence we might possess but don't, but is a review of a range of possibilities where behaviour just is ambiguous. The fact is, we act ourselves and observe others acting on mixed motives, tenuous motives, conflicting motives. We often find it difficult to assign a motive just because we find little in the situation which could justify our actions and face the scrutiny of objective appraisal. Suppose a thief said, 'Before I got caught I thought I knew why I stole'. There was a time when the situation in which he found himself seemed to afford him grounds: he was poor, or poorer than most, society was based on obvious inequities, he had his rights. Getting caught led him to construe the situation rather differently. Not that the same considerations no longer obtained; he now saw his act in a context including wider dimensions, new facts, which somehow disrupted the simple warrant, I am poor, therefore I steal.

It is cases like these, with the progressive opacity of the entitling relation that characterizes them, that add fuel to the fires of simplistic or scientific reformulations. An example of the first is Ryle's well-known reduction of motives to dispositions to act. There are numerous objections to this view which seem to be overwhelming. Among them we need consider only two. The first is that it makes it impossible to suppose that a person ever acts on a motive only once.[1] Yet this is a very common and successful case of motive-ascription, which is easily handled on the supposition that attributing a motive to someone (including oneself) is seeing a situation as providing grounds for an action. The second difficulty is that on Ryle's account motive cannot, except redundantly, feature in an explanation of action. For if his account is correct, to say that a person commits

[1] Cf. G. E. M. Anscombe, *Intention* (Blackwell, 1958) p. 21.

MOTIVE   97

an act because of a certain motive is only to say that he generally commits
the act, and to explain why he generally commits the act is simply to say
that he generally commits the act. But it is quite normal to appeal to
motives as a reason for doing a repeated act, as, say, when the unhappy
husband continually gets drunk because of nagging at home. The nagging
is his motive, and it is his motive, as much the first or any single time as
it is for the whole collection of melancholy occasions.

The scientific reformulation is provided by psychologists, particularly
personality theorists. They have given a curious twist to the term motive.
First, of course, they wish to introduce motive into general law accounts.
But in addition they want to internalize the motive, which in ordinary
use is only the case *per accidens*, as when a man's headache is taken as his
motive for upbraiding his secretary. In a hypochondriacal society, pains
and other internal disturbances may seem to provide excellent motives,
but there is clearly no reason why motives must be internal. That the
psychologist finds it necessary to suppose so is connected with the urge
toward generalization of motive accounts.

A good case is found in a recent book by David McClelland who,
beginning his study in the usual methodological fashion, says:

We need some more unique index of the presence of an aroused desire for achievement. Ideally, of course, we might favor something like a 'psychic X-ray' that
would permit us to observe what was going on in a person's head in the same way
that we can observe stomach contractions or nerve discharges in a hungry organism.[2]

Lacking this device we must do the next best thing, by cunningly con-
trived tests and measures trap the traces of the achievement motive even
where we cannot quite hang on to the thing itself. It turns out in Mc-
Clelland's study that what he has trapped are the reasons for a person
choosing one line of action or persistent habit over another. But these
reasons entitle the agent to act as he does, so that we see him acting for
these reasons. They are not theoretical constructs connecting otherwise
unintelligibly juxtaposed observables. In McClelland one sees a half-
hearted physiologizing which remains theoretical in an older and pejorative sense, that is, it remains fanciful. Moreover, the explanatory value
of his relation of the achievement motive to the behaviour he wishes to
study is dangerously close to redundancy, a problem to which he seems
on occasion to be sensitive. The upshot of his study of societies, which
he hopes will replace the old-fashioned and hopelessly unscientific ways
of historians and economists playing the role of amateur psychologists, is
that societies that have achieved (according to his measures) did so because

[2] David McClelland, *The Achieving Society* (D. van Nostrand, 1961), p. 39.

they wanted to succeed. He partially escapes obvious pleonasm by identifying wanting to succeed with the recorded 'fantasies', as he calls them, of
the subjects under examination. When they are not available for his own
tests, he examines their poems and essays, art works and other means they
had of expressing themselves. Certain scores on these tests correlate with
the success score in the politico-economic realm.

A narrow interpretation of the relation, however, is then open to a
variety of interpretations, for example, that the high success scorers in
fantasy or in literature are rationalizing their economic concerns, or
reflecting their basic interests. If the achievement motive is identified with
an independent measure, it shows only that individuals who succeed, or
spend a good deal of time in such effort, think or dream about success.
This is not too surprising, and, if McClelland were to observe closely, it
is an observation made over and over again by psychologically naïve
historians. If it means only that people who succeed want to succeed,
then it is risking tautology to stick the 'because' into the proposition.
That he does so indicates that he is burdening the concept 'motive' with
two incompatible meanings; first, the explanatory sense, according to
which a situation has been disclosed which entitles a person to act as he
does, and second, the psychological sense, which is descriptive, and
identifies motive with tendencies in behaviour.

To avoid these alternatives, McClelland, along with many psychologists, introduces a third use of motive. He rightly eschews the purely
descriptive role of motive, but, wedded to mechanistic explanations, is
led to think of motive as a force which is indirectly measured by his
fantasy and behaviour gauges. Since Freud, he says (p. 38), 'the notion
that motives are rational or can be rationally inferred from action' has
been for ever destroyed. This is owed to Freud because of his discovery
that motives 'are not what they seem', that a man can have concealed
motives, or be motivated by considerations exactly opposite of what is
revealed in his actions. This, of course, is part of the general polemic of
Freudian theory, with its efforts to set behaviour in a rather broader context. Freudian theory does not substitute causes for reasons so much as it
stretches the notion of rational to include features of the situation which
would not normally be thought of as providing grounds or reasons for
acting. This is the point argued in the previous chapter.

But Freud himself, and most psychologists following him including
McClelland, have tended to adopt a way of talking which suggests that
the newly discovered motives are irrational, for they clearly are embar-
rassingly unlike standard reasons for acting. To speak of them as irrational,
however, is to speak of them still as reasons, wrong or inadequate reasons,

it may be, but still appealing to warrants for acting. Freud and all psychologists, however, have tended to treat 'irrational' as synonymous with 'non-rational', a move which they share with most moral theorists, as we have seen. Then it becomes possible for McClelland to suggest as the best means of apprehending motives in their hidden lairs the ideal of 'psychic X-ray', and the next-best thing, inferences to such entities from carefully measured fantasy performances.

The term motive, I suggest, will simply not stand this kind of abuse. If there really were such events as McClelland would like to X-ray, we are back where we started, that is, we should have to discover a method of noting their occurrence and whatever properties they might have, and then see through repeated experiment whether they have any connexion with other events manifested by an organism. But it is not necessary to postulate such events to allow the explanatory force of motive. McClelland's general case, why should x succeed where y fails, is an extraordinarily complicated one not always requiring a motive-type answer. To the question, why did x pursue a line of conduct with such perseverance, the answer might be: the example of his father, the morality of the time, or failure in love. Any of these might provide motives, if suitable evidence is forthcoming as to the relation of son to father, the exhortations of priests and politicians, teachers and parents, of the details of private life. For each of these would explain why someone devotes himself wholly, and thus with some likelihood of success, to a particular activity. But McClelland wants nothing of piecemeal or rational accounts. Hence the internalization of motive; it is the only way he can purchase his specious generality, and justify his research as a means of explaining human conduct.

So much for motives and causes. Philosophical delicacy in this matter seems to result from accepting the view that a cause is an event invariably connected to its effect, so that causal ascriptions must always be backed by generalizations. This view, in turn, demands a hypothetical status for motives, unless we admit that in most cases motives are not assigned on general grounds. So motives become internal and dubious events, where they had been clear, but piecemeal, circumstances surrounding particular actions. If a philosopher comes to see that the use of motive depends neither on generalization nor on internal occurrences, he is apt to deny motives causal status. If neither of these conditions is necessary to speak of motives as causes, however, causal talk about the motives for action becomes innocent of Humean implications. Moreover, it is often pertinent to speak this way since the situation singled out as the motive is taken to be necessary to the occurrence of the action. The use of cause in motive-contexts should not tempt us, then, to think of invariant relations. Assigning a motive is showing that circumstances warrant actions. The investigation of circumstances is often a complicated business, calling for the routine work and the sharp eye of detective and scholar, and turning up various results from case to case. The matter of warrant is general, in a sense, for it involves reference to rules, principles, maxims, like those governing our use of emotion words. But there is nothing absolute or hierarchical about such warrants, or any among them, that would allow us to single out the circumstances that always motivate action. This is a typical gambit of moral theories.

The doctrine of egoism is perhaps the most obvious attempt to offer a general theory of human motivation, finding self-advantage at the root of every action. Its possible triviality is skirted by claiming self-advantage to be a universal maxim. This is moral universality, but it is disguised, as in Hobbes's physical universality, as if something forces us to act on our own advantage.[3] No evidence is offered for the physical doctrine, for self-advantage is never identified in any coherent way with a class or range of events which can be shown to determine behaviour in every case. Its persuasiveness is borrowed from the inclination people have to regard self-advantage as the best possible reason for doing something. Thus a moral doctrine, which of itself might seem dubious, is dressed up in a mechanical suit. Stripped of this deterministic clothing, it stands among many competitors as possible grounds for acting.

Moreover, like pleasure, self-advantage is a vacuous aim. It is the form of an aim rather than a specific objective. Normally, when we say a person is pursuing his own advantage, we mean that he is pursuing objects incompatible with the advantage of others, like the case in which an employer seeks quick returns at the expense of the company and the employees. It is not, in other words, that such motives or aims are intrinsically selfish, though some aims have a more decided tendency to conflict with the interest of others. It is surely not Hobbes's or any egoist's intention to maintain that one ought to pursue that which conflicts with the aims of others, yet it is not clear otherwise what specific actions the egoistic hypothesis entails.

---

[3] R. S. Peters, in both his *Concept of Motivation* (Routledge & Kegan Paul, 1958) and *Hobbes* (Penguin Books, 1956), argues persuasively for the view that Hobbes's joining of egoism and mechanical theory is logically misconceived. It is possible that Hobbes's view does not accommodate itself so readily to straw-man treatment, but the criticism of that view, whether it is Hobbes's or not (and it certainly is a popular view), is one which I endorse, perhaps giving Peters' arguments a slightly different twist.

Egoism attempts to combine a number of logically incompatible aims: (1) to explain what men do; (2) to do so generally, and therefore (3) to give the explanation a mechanical appearance. The result is a theory which is either vacuously true, empirically false, or morally vicious. This, of course, in no way denies the more rough-hewn generalization on which Hobbes built his political theory, that men do tend to pursue aims that all too frequently are socially disruptive. This might be called a fact about man, but equally it might be called a fact about the circumstances and environment of human life. That profit-seeking is selfish is as much a fact about the limitation of resources as it is a fact about profit-seekers.

Egoism, then, is a typical consequence of the attempt to generalize and internalize motives, wresting them in the process from the moral context in which they explain. There are undoubtedly many sources of the temptation to convert and modernize motives, the preference for mechanical models to which Wittgenstein calls attention in the *Blue Book* being one. Our general view of a subject (like explanation) is usually governed by those cases which are tidiest, surest and most successful. Motive accounts seem defective because of their rough edges, their tentativeness. Often there is no basis for deciding among competing motives, and this leads philosophers of science and psychologists to suppose that in ordinary language we simply do not have concepts or techniques precise enough to get at the real motive. But this misconstrues the case entirely. If our assigning of motives is often tentative and obscure, it is because the canons governing the use of motive terms are themselves not entirely clear. For one thing, they depend too much on the nuances of particular cases to afford the grounds for precise application dear to the hearts of scientific-minded philosophers. We can admit this vagueness or tentativeness without adopting the corollary so often taken to accompany it, that we require in place of ordinary talk more precise definitions and methods of investigation to sharpen our apprehension of what is at present obscure. There simply are cases in which the ascription of motives is tentative and vague, not because our tools are inadequate, but because human action is often fundamentally ambiguous, often aimless, frequently equivocal. To suppose that there really is a motive which we have failed to read by ordinary means is to deny what we observe and practise in acting as we do. Only the quixotic quest for certainty could have sustained the long effort to convert motives into something else, which they could not possibly be.

The pursuit of self-knowledge is another instance of the attempt to convert moral reasoning into factual discovery. Very commonly, we engage in ruminations of considerable length which appear to have self-understanding as their goal. So it seems that such a process parallels research in science; it is the introspective counterpart of discovering and experimentally manipulating data. A few examples will show, I think, how such a conception has gone off its logical rails.

Recall the thief who, until he was caught, understood why he stole. It is clear as it need be here how self-knowledge, self-explanation, is tied to patterns of justification of behaviour. Stealing was consistent, perhaps, with his conception of himself as a moral agent, but being caught was not. It led him to see the act of theft in a less romantic, less convention-protesting way, and more as something embarrassing and humiliating. It became for him less a sin than a *gaucherie*. But, in any case, his reappraisal of himself was a moral reappraisal, not a discovery of hidden mechanisms, or psychic paramechanisms.

Consider another case. A man thinks of himself as a romantic hero, a conception not shared by his wife, and so he acquires a mistress. Partly it is an excused act, for doesn't his wife fail him? But more than that, it matches a conception of himself—would it be misleading to say?—as a moral agent. Many moral philosophers would be horrified to consider this a moral conception, but that is where professional moralists have typically gone wrong. Morality, considered philosophically, needs to be thought of, not as that set of prescriptions for action or models for human agency that one affirms, but any pattern of argument, any model for behaviour that is of the persuasive or ideal-appealing form. To forget this is to misdescribe as caused or compelled by desires the behaviour of which we disapprove.

To continue the story. Pressures begin to mount. The mistress demands too much of his time, she is costing him money. He, poor fellow, is past the point where he can extricate himself without exposure and disaster. The action, originally so clear, so patent, becomes shrouded in mystery. Why does he do what he does? he mourns. Perhaps he goes to an analyst, or engages in gloomy self-accusation which he misconceives as self-research, and reads Dostoievski and Kierkegaard. But his troubles cannot be properly described as the dredging up of memories, hidden motives and other gems at the bottom of the psychic mine. Memories may, of course, feature in arguments through which he readjusts the image of himself, and new principles of action may emerge from his reflections. It is always easier for him to accept new patterns of behaviour on the supposition that what he is doing is the result of the inevitable welling up of actions from psychic depths. So it is with the mythology of the unconscious, and so with the man of letters disguising his moral point with the cloth of character, as if novelists had perceptions which we ordinary men lack. This heightened awareness is less oracular or divinatory than it is hortatory.

The poets, says Thornton Wilder in *The Ides of March*, do not give us deeper insights but express more urgent longings, an aphorism which can serve us as a text. Character portrayal in fiction and epic is not designed to report inner truths, but to project a pattern of actions and sentiments, self-consistent and capable of withstanding the buffets of objections and circumstance. We come close to understanding this when we appraise the tragic hero as 'larger than life'. But our moral hyper-seriousness leads us to forget that comic heroes, buffoons, villains are created on the same principles, Tom Jones as much as Ivan Karamazov, Panurge as well as Faust, Falstaff as well as Hamlet. If we think of the latter half of these pairings as deeper creations than the former, it is not because of deeper or more general truths about human kind contained in them, but because the noble, the distressed and the distraught seems to have greater moral appeal than the pleasure-seeking, riotous and sensual. But Tom Jones, Panurge and Falstaff are equally models of conduct, equally forceful and consistent and detailed creations which provide patterns of moral argument for specific actions and entire ways of life. The so-called psychological critics have mis-stated their case in supposing that they are assisting in the novelists' endeavours to find the hidden facts, like so many biologists uncovering the hidden secrets of life or physicists disclosing the elusive structure of the atom. All criticism is moral criticism if it is germane to the work of art, not in the sense that it praises and condemns from the standpoint of a moral code (for example, Wagner's music is 'bad' because it is sensual), but in the sense that it helps to reveal the nature of the moral point of view embedded in the work. If the work of art is bad, it is because it fails to work out its moral theme consistently, not because it disagrees with our own.

Self-knowledge, then, is not a likely candidate for the study of some fixed thing called human nature. The physiologist might with some justice claim to talk about human nature, for he can with some legitimacy claim to have discovered patterns, functions and facts that account for the observed behaviour of the organism. Psychoanalysts and psycho-logists, writers, critics and philosophers, cannot in the same sense be said to provide the lineaments of human nature, conceived as permanent and enduring features of man's life. They deal instead in the changeable patterns by which behaviour is justified. What counts as grounds for the moralist varies from time to time, person to person, and circumstance to circumstance. Criteria of this nature cannot be supposed to have the permanence or fixity of the physiologist's account.

The psychologist attempts to set the boundaries of a territory that lies between ethics and physiology. His typical concepts reflect, however, the questionable extent or existence of this territory. Drive, motive, purpose and intention represent decreasing degrees of physiologizing in the attempt to set these boundaries. The claim that these terms denote items to be discovered, directly or by inference, and that through their discovery we shall understand human nature, suggests physiological investigation. But the strategies of psychological investigations suggest that it is not physical but psychological occurrences which constitute the object of the psychologist's investigations. The question is, are there such occurrences? There are candidates for this office, the chief of which is bodily sensation, which goes half-way toward the physical in having location, and half-way toward the 'psychological' in its privacy. But we bring bodily sensations into an account of human action by seeing them as pleasant and unpleasant, desirable and undesirable, that is, from the moral point of view. So far as they enter into explanations of behaviour, they do so through justifying licenses, not through causal inferences.

INTENTION

So much for the generalizers and internalizers. Numbers of philosophers have found fault with psychological uses of motive and Cartesian internalizations of reasons for acting. But in their alternatives, they have generally ignored the role of moral categories in describing and explaining human action. The relation usually envisaged between *explicans* and *explicanda* of this type is logical. For these philosophers, rules, conventions, procedures and strategies entail, as opposed to entitle, the action to be explained. And this provides additional fuel for anti-causal fires.

This view is defended in a number of ways. A popular defence in recent years depends on the analogy of human actions to games. We shall turn to that analogy in Chapter IX. First, let us examine a concept which also serves to focus arguments against the causal interpretation of human action, namely, the concept of intention.

We may begin by noting that a man may intend to do something and not carry it out. He may have intended to catch the 8.15 to the city but missed it because his watch was slow. Such a case might tempt us to claim a similarity between intentions and motives. Motives, too, are easy to detach from those events which are alleged to be consequences of them. But intentions are attributed to individuals rather more intimately than motives. We may ascribe a motive to a man, as we have seen, without special attention to his words, actions or disclaimers. The circumstances, informed by some conception of appropriate grounds, allow the assigning of motives. But we would not attribute intentions to a man simply because he had grounds for acting in that way. Each of us, no doubt, has grounds for murder, larceny or other crimes, but we should be in a sorry way if we were accused on this account of intending to commit these crimes.

The fact that connexions of intention to action are frequently broken may seem to argue also against the supposition that intentions are causes. We are not disposed to ascribe causal efficacy to events that have no regular consequences. But the irregularity of connexion between intention and act might be thought to parallel irregularities that do also occur in nature. A housewife mixes all the ingredients for bread, but it turns out that the oven is not sealed or the yeast was stale. And so, in place of bread, a stone. It looks as if 'he intended to catch the 8.15, only his watch was slow' is like this. The reasoning is, if a normal causal sequence is broken, look for the intersection of the normal chain of events with some other chain that brings about different consequences. Ascriptions of intention could then be regarded as causal, differing from some other kinds of causal ascription only in the greater frequency of irregularities.

A major obstacle stands in the way of this temptation, however. If by cause is meant an event which, save for interfering conditions, has a given event as consequence, intentions fail to fit the pattern, quite apart from any decision as to whether intentions constitute a class of events. The man intends to catch the 8.15 *today*. It may be true as well that he intended to catch it yesterday, and so through all his drab commuter history. But the evidence we require today need have nothing to do with yesterday *or* tomorrow. We see him running from his car toward the platform, looking frantically at his watch, and cursing it and his luck, as the train pulls away yards ahead of him. We need not be utterly confounded by the failure of the Humean criterion of cause to apply, any more than we need be by its failure or lack of pertinence in cases like hitting and striking. In any case, we don't observe the interaction of intentions and action.

Perhaps intentions are logically tied to actions. We should certainly be hard put to it to give any other than the Ryleian answer to the demand, Describe your intention. It is: to mix a martini, catch the 8.15, go to the opera, and so on. Descriptions of intentions are descriptions of actions. But, it might be asked, what about intentions not carried out? There is no special difficulty here, to describe the intention is still to describe the action, only in this case, an envisaged action. Envisaged actions clearly depend on performed actions for their meaning, just as unspoken thoughts depend upon first acquiring the power of utterance. Special means for divining intentions seem out of place. An intention may be hard to read in action because of the complexities of conduct in which it is embedded. But if it is to be discovered, it is a discernable action.

If this is so, however, intention has no explanatory significance. Intentions are ways of describing actions, not explaining them. Ordinary circumstance bears this out. If I am asked, why are you going to the movies? it is no answer to say, because I intend to. This the questioner understands in being able to describe my actions as 'going to the movies'. Sometimes avowals of intention enter into an explanation. If I am raising a loan, I might explain it by saying I intend to buy a car. But this is because the sequence of actions which lead to the envisaged goal is complex, and protracted in time, so that one sometimes needs to be informed that the observed actions are designed to lead to certain further actions or occurrences. Still, by giving the intention, the whole sequence is described. To talk of intentions is thus to answer the question *what*, not *why*.

We might speak here, also, as Anscombe does in *Intention*, of mental causes, by which she means causes known without observation. I answer the doorbell, brush a fly off my nose, or recoil from a snake coiled in the grass. The actions might be described as intentional, though the latter two cases merge into involuntary reflexes. (A reflex action might fulfil an intention; but we might just as well say, fulfils a purpose, and postpone discussion until we come to that term.) But the intention in these cases would not be part of a causal chain, for example, doorbell ringing—intention—answering the door. The implication in Anscombe's account is that because the actions are intentional they are causes known without observation. Yet she admits that the patellar reflex can be known without observation (for example, to a person with his eyes shut). The contrast intended is not clear. It seems she might mean by 'known without observation', known without repeated observation, that is, known without research. This would created difficulties only if one were already committed to the Humean view of causation, while admitting to embarrassment in the face of cases like answering doorbells and awareness of patellar reflexes. The fact is, we observe many causes without research, and many of these have nothing to do with human behaviour, but solely with physical interaction.

There is, then, no special reason to encumber ourselves with a term like mental cause. Actions may be intentional, *and* may follow upon physical cues or causes. It would be pretentious to insist that a person had formed an intention in order to account for the link between doorbell ringing and rising to answer it, even more so, to speak of the intention as the link between the fly and the act of brushing it off. Notice here that the causal link answers the question *why*, the intention the question *what*. Someone might ask 'Why are you waving your hand like that?', and get the answer, 'There's a fly on my nose.' To the question, What are you doing, the answer would be 'I am swatting at a fly'. The explanation is not the intention, but a description of the action as intentional already assumes a kind of explanation. The explanation is part of the description.

If appeal to intentions explains what is being done, it does not explain causally, but by making an action intelligible. We say, 'I did *x* because of *y*' where *y* and *x* must be different events. (Otherwise, are we not involved in circularity?) The point of the causal locution is to connect one event with another. There is no particular reason why the events connected should be of the same type, as if, when our effect is an action—answering the door—the cause must somehow be mental. In the first place, both the cause and effect are physical. Both are observable; both occur somewhere at some time. In the second place, it is never quite clear what a philosopher is trying to contrast when he contrasts movements and actions. 'Doorbell's ringing' is a way of talking which clearly depends upon conventions, meanings, and the like. But it is none the less an observable occurrence. The blow on the knee with the rubber hammer also depends upon conventions, meanings. We shall see in a moment that the distinction of action and movement enters in another way. But it is clear that the general distinction between action and movement rests upon some conception of pristine observables, a notion already dismissed as incoherent.

Still, we say something different about events when we speak of them as intended, and when we speak of them as caused. It has only been shown so far that a description of intention does not exclude a causal account. But we need to explicate the sense in which an intentional description makes movements intelligible, and thus explains them. The clear sense is the one in which an action is puzzling. In a very funny scene from a recent film a bicycle-riding postman is plagued by a bee. He is watched from a neighbouring hillside by a puzzled farmer, who only sees the postman's frantic gestures. In a minute, the farmer discovers for himself why the postman indulges in his antics, for the bee comes up the hillside. It is as if we might say, where we observe the occasion of the action it is no longer puzzling. Seeing the bee entitles us to interpret the arm-flailing as 'trying to brush off the bee'. Hearing the doorbell ring entitles us to call the action 'answering the doorbell'. The relation of bee and doorbell to action is in such cases not causal; that is, our understanding the movements as intended is not merely another way of saying that the bee or doorbell caused the actions. (Though we could say this.) Rather, the bee or doorbell provide the appropriate circumstances to such actions. We say, that is the sort of thing to do in such circumstances. The bee and doorbell, looked at this way, are logical cues to the action, for we think of bees as the sort of companions to be rid of, and ringing doorbells as the sort of signals for answering doors. Notice here how much of psychology is a matter of what we *could* say, by converting the way we do talk to the form proper to causal talk, but what we do not need to say, given our ordinary techniques and information.

The doorbell case leads directly to a convention. That is what bells are put there for. It might appear, on the other hand, that the buzzing bee does not mean flailing arms, but rather that the bee's sting creates a desire to be rid of the pesky insect. But even here, though we have taken the issue back to such rudimentary human experiences as pain and fear, the force of our account is the force of justification. The relation of pain and fear is not causal, for it does not involve research into regularities, but depends upon identifying pain as that to be avoided if possible. For all practical purposes—except with untutored children, psychologists and sociologists—we might as well have stopped with the bee as the thing to be avoided. We learn by experience to segregate the stinging and non-stinging bees, poisonous and non-poisonous reptiles. We might, for philosophical reasons, wish to unpack 'That's a bee' into an argument of the form, 'Bees sting, stings hurt, therefore avoid bees.' The connexion between the hurting and the avoidance is not like that between the sting observed in the abdomen and the pain and swelling its plunging into the skin causes. 'Pain' involves 'avoidance'.

A number of philosophers have recently advanced the claim for practical, as against contemplative, knowledge. Anscombe (*Intention*, §§ 32–36) in particular notes the peculiarities of practical syllogisms, which have directives to act as their consequences. To render such arguments formally valid, a major premise is required which in fact no one who takes appropriate action (and therefore understands the point of the persuasive argument) would accept. Any other rendering of practical reasoning is so hedged round with qualifications that the arguments seem hardly necessary. This is because the terms that are used in most practical reasoning are learned in the context of acting in certain ways. So 'it's pleasant' includes the notion of worthy-of-being-pursued, 'I want it' includes actions taken toward achieving (or trying), (cf. Anscombe § 36), and 'That's a bee', the notion of getting rid of it.

All of this is a matter of appropriate contexts. And this is what has bothered so many philosophers. For they have wished to offer a criterion for the use of a term on the supposition that, if one could not be offered, our successful use of the word would be paradoxical. The difficulty has been a failure to realize that we learn terms in context, and our application of a term is by an analogy to the paradigms which inform our further applications of it.

We might then explain a person's action by saying 'the doorbell's ringing', or 'A bee is buzzing round his head', without research or the unpacking of argument. Here it is pretty clear that the relation between the 'cause' and the action is one of *entitlement*. The action is appropriate to the circumstances in accordance with either standard cases or criteria. Actions are movements seen and identified as warranted or not by circumstances. Movements, in a sense opposed to actions, are events seen as instances of interaction—push-pull, contact, collision. If I ask 'What happened?' upon hearing a loud crash in the kitchen, and my wife says 'The wind knocked over a vase on the sill', the account is of movements because it appeals to interactions with other things, processes or events that have spatial and temporal location. By extension, the same might be said of the more tenuous uses of cause described by Hume, that is, where regularity of connexion is substituted for observed interaction. If she says, 'I'm emptying ice cubes,' the account is of actions because of its ties with warrants for an occurrence.

There are many borderline cases. Someone laughs hysterically and when asked why says, 'My cat is rubbing against the soles of my bare feet'. We might wish to speak here of cause and effect; equally we might be inclined to think of laughing as 'natural,' that is, as a consequence warranted by the circumstances. We call it helpless laughter; yet we do not mean helpless in the way that a man falling from a second story window is helpless, quite unable to alter the speed of his fall. It makes sense to speak of controlling one's laughter. Might we say laughter is expressive behaviour? It is designed to convey information. The same holds for a cry of pain, which can be suppressed if circumstances warrant. Sometimes, it is true, we say that a cry of pain, a laugh, a gesture, is involuntary. But this only shows that the voluntary/involuntary distinction does not have the force of the caused/free distinction. The distinction between voluntary and involuntary is generated by the concept of free action. For consider the involuntary cry of pain. It is not like the jerk of the leg when tapped; it is certainly not like the body falling from an upper window. It might be described better as a conflict of intentions. One wants to let anyone nearby know that one is hurt; one also has special reasons for not letting the particular person nearby know. Suppose that in the course of a much desired massage, the masseur actually pinches a muscle. The cry of pain is involuntary only if it would have been suppressed in order to insure that the massage did not end. That is, it can be understood as involuntary only against a background of the action which would have accomplished the desired result or preserved the desired circumstance.

Anscombe and Melden both consider interesting cases of the involuntary which could not be accounted for this way, for example, the peristaltic motions of the gut, the involuntary recoil of the hand from a hot stove, and the familiar patellar reflex.[4] Perhaps these are all cases to which we would ordinarily apply the concept involuntary. But it must not be supposed that they are therefore alike, or contain a common ingredient, except that they are contrasted with the clear case of voluntary, that is, intended action. The cry of pain or scream of terror are different sorts of departures from this case than the patellar reflex or the action that has unforeseen consequences.[5] The clearest case is when I say, 'Stop, you're hurting me'. If I groan, howl, scream or sob, the case is perhaps not quite as clear. But standards of expressive performance still apply. If I say, 'Ouch!', we'd be inclined to say 'voluntary', if we had to say one or the other. If I moaned or screamed we might or might not. Perhaps the scream sounds put on, perhaps not. If the former, we will probably call it voluntary, if not, involuntary. But even if involuntary, what is ascribed to me can be interpreted in various ways. The cry might cause the masseur to stop his ministrations, and I might say: 'I didn't mean that you should stop.' So the cry in this case is called involuntary. This is a case of an act not having its expected consequences. If it did, if the masseur simply eased up a little with those strong hands of his, the cry would have accomplished its object and would be called voluntary. Thus voluntary and involuntary occasionally get mixed up with 'meaning to say'. A verbal slip is involuntary because the speaker meant to say something else. But this slip might receive further interpretation, as either intended or not. There are cases in which verbal slips might be accounted for phonetically, as shifts in sounds or syllables; others where the slip betrays a different intention, as amply attested to by Freud. The involuntary is not the absence of intention, but that which is contrary to some intention, and which of itself may be regarded as an intentional act, or an expression of intention. On the other hand, the patellar, or any, reflex, the sudden withdrawal of a hand from a hot surface and, on occasion, a cry, might

---

[4] Anscombe, p. 13.
[5] Cf. Anscombe's well-poisoning case, §§ 23–35.

(as Anscombe suggests) be called non-voluntary. The question of intention does not arise in such cases. The man whose leg jerks at the tap of
the hammer neither intends to do so nor intends to do something incompatible or inconsistent with this. Only if he does intend something
different is the knee-jerk involuntary.

Hume's account of caused and free acts is thus correct in application
but incorrect in formulation. He wishes to show that free (intended)
action is a sub-class of caused (determined) action, so that they can be
shown to be compatible. They are compatible, since ascribing intentions
has nothing particularly to do with causes. An action, in the clear case,
is intended if it squares with what one wants or is trying to do. And this
is a matter that is settled (when it is settled) quite independently of those
sequences of events which might be thought to provide the causes of
action. The pain is (perhaps) the cause of the cry. But the cry may or
may not achieve its intent. If it does, we call the cry intended, subject to
certain modifications, for example, how the cry is uttered. If it does not,
we are apt to say it is involuntary, that one gives way to the cry knowing
that it will lead to the cessation of what one wants continued.

The upshot is that we need not be concerned with voluntary and
involuntary, or free and constrained, in deciding how it is that we apply
the adjective 'intentional' to actions. For it is in the context of intended
action that we come to talk about voluntary and involuntary, free and
constrained.

Still, the problem of assigning intentions is not resolved by removing
these subsidiary considerations. The phrase, 'where the action matches
what one wants or is trying to do', suggests that the paradigm is connected
in a crucial way with expressions of intention. Thus, I say, 'I'm going to
the store for cigarettes,' and do so. It might appear that the decision
depends upon the performed action, a view certainly supported by the
fact that even had I not expressed my intention, my action would have
betrayed it. The same would hold for animal intentions. Anscombe
talks about a cat crouching, with a mouse or bird in view, as a case of
intentional action, and intending in acting, but not an expression of
intention.[6] This is obvious in that a cat does not tell us what he is doing.
Furthermore, denials of intention are seldom sufficient if actions reveal.
I say, 'I'm going down to the corner for cigarettes,' and my wife observes,
'Taking the car?' and when I come back three hours later, says, 'Three
hours to buy cigarettes?' My expression of intention is lightweight compared to these aspects of my actions. Compare Wittgenstein's remark:
'If you had said the words, would you necessarily have meant them quite

[6] Op. cit. p. 2, and cf. Wittgenstein, *Philosophical Investigations* (Blackwell, 1953), § 647.

seriously? (Thus the most explicit expression of intention is by itself insufficient evidence of intention).'[7] This remark brings out one feature of the difficulty about intention, that it is often neither what is done nor what is avowed that leads us to say an action is intentional. One can say, as Wittgenstein does, that it must be seriously meant to count as an intention. But where do we look for serious intentions? An obscure remark of Wittgenstein (§ 664) distinguishing surface grammar and depth grammar might suggest that something enters into 'seriously meant' speech that does not enter into casual or deceptive speech. A man, surely, may be more or less serious in declaring his intentions, and when serious, may express them in a particular tone of voice or by assuming a particular posture. This may tempt us to think of intentions as so many muscular contractions or the awareness of them. But the intention is not one with the sensation. Suppose that people generally or always had such sensations when seriously intending. It might be said then, that if I had a way of measuring muscular contractions, I could decide what was seriously intended. (Notice how the lie detector is used, for example.) But I should still not have weighed the seriousness of *my* intention by paying heed to muscular contractions.

Sometimes the puzzle is resolved by considering cases of ascription of intentions to others. So we say the death of a man shot several times with a gun equipped with a safety catch and a mechanical reloader isn't accidental. We tell the man who has driven his car over a curb, up a steep bank, and down the sidewalk, thus running down a man who is blackmailing him, that his car was not out of control. Such cases lead very readily to think of intentions as 'imbedded in human customs and institutions' (*Investigations*, § 337). The latter example suggests that a description of intentions depends on an ascription of motives, in the sense that ascribing a motive is a business of providing grounds for acting. It also shows how lack of normal physical chains of events often gives us a place to insert an intention, for example, the car would not have taken that course. But other cases easily come to mind to which these conditions are inapposite. To say an action is intentional or that a person intended to do something or other is an ascription meeting a variety of criteria and adjusting to a variety of circumstances, of which the presence of adequate grounds and the absence of normal physical circumstances are only two, and the avowal of an intention a third. Assigning intention is so complex a business that no simple discovery can solve it or sweeping rubric resolve it. The different criteria do not belong to a common hierarchy in which

[7] *Investigations*, § 641.

some have greater logical force than others. The importance of any one criterion depends upon the context. A man whose car goes out of control does not intend to run down his victim. But the line between accident and intention is not decidable in advance by a rubric defining intention in terms of degrees of ludicrousness or implausibility of the accompanying actions. Quite similar sequences of events might, in one case, be judged intentional, in another accidental, depending upon such a variety of contexts that it would be quite hopeless to attempt to state them. Any attempt to theorize about intentions is a quixotic procedure, defeated from the start.

This might very well be the answer if one thinks of ascribing intentions to others. But further troubles arise with self-ascriptions. Ascribing intentions to oneself clearly does not depend on witnessing or noting anything. Ascribing intentions to others, however, involves a great deal of observation and shrewd calculation, though it is by its nature quite distinct from the way of going about an investigation characterized by scientific research. One way of handling first person ascriptions is given by Austin, who says that 'I intend', 'I am going to . . .' and so forth are performances, and so denies that the ordinary queries with regard to truth and falsity and manner of acquaintance apply here. If it is knowledge at all to say I intend, it is a queer sort of knowledge, queer at least after one has spent all one's time examining descriptive discourse. For it is not 'knowledge about' at all. To be able to say 'I intend' correctly marks the learning of a procedure, a performance appropriate to specified circumstances.

It might be asked why should a person perform this way or that way? Will it do here to say that any number of things may occasion the performance? I open the door of the refrigerator and, finding no beer, announce my intention of going to the store for more. I am nagged by my wife day after day, and finally say, 'Tomorrow I'll wash the car'. Finding no beer, being nagged, might be thought of as the occasions for announcing intentions. A Martian observer, looking at things from the outside, might even formulate regular connexions between special circumstances and special announcements of intention. But if we ask, what do we recognize, observe, or take note of that makes for intending or expressing intentions, we should have to appeal to a desire for something plus a knowledge as to what will achieve that end. So announcements of intention assimilate to the justifying procedures characteristic of our explanatory use of desire. We assess situations in the light of the indefinite range of desirable objects and activities, and are thus led to declarations of intention and descriptions of actions.

When my wife acidly comments the following day: 'I see you didn't wash the car', can she also say I lied? Not exactly. She might say that my intentions aren't worth much. (Compare, your confederate money isn't worth the paper it's written on.) What she is saying is that my expressions of intention turn out to be very poor indices of future performance. And this is, indeed, much like Austin's standard case of promising. The accusatory 'You said you would' is not 'You lied to me' but 'You're not reliable.' We can lie only in cases in which what we say refers to an occurrence which anyone, in principle, could witness and describe. But the close similarity of the two—both are cases of unreliability, after all— leads us to think that something, the intention, is or is not present.

We can now give an answer to the question, how does a person go about intending, if not by special knowledge of ingredients of his soul, by pointing to the rules for the employment of intentional expressions. And we can forestall the question, how does a person know whether he's seriously intending or not, by taking note of sufficient examples which show when such a question naturally arises. It does not, for the speaker or hearer, arise in the simple case of announced and immediately per- formed action, but only in the case of announced (and usually repeatedly announced) but unperformed actions. 'Do you really mean to do it this time?' suggests that there is something or other to attend to or grab hold of (like the muscular contractions James talks about in his chapter on Will, for instance),[8] which he could then tell the truth (or lie) about. But to ask a person whether he's serious is really to put pressure on him to get the job done this time. Consequently, there is no particular question that a person can address to himself, 'Do I really intend?' and hope to find an answer. Seriously intending is a move in the intending game which does not arise unless the game is complicated by failures at performance or by doubts that the performance will be carried out.

Of course, a person might say of himself, 'I did intend to, after all' and thus seemingly describe himself in some peculiar way. So the wife whose husband continually brings home a lady friend for coffee manages to spill coffee all over the lady's elegant dress. 'I didn't mean to,' she cries in alarm, excusing her conduct. But later, especially after it happens for the third time, honest attention to circumstance might lead her to say, 'I suppose I meant to after all.' Here she uses intend as we generally do of others, considering actions in the light of circumstances and motives.

This is fortified by the fact that an ascription of intention to others and the denial of intention to ourselves is usually a business of praise and

---

[8] William James, *Principles of Psychology* (Dover Books, 1950), Vol. II, pp. 486 ff. and especially p. 535.

blame, a matter in which the crucial question is the justification of an action. Consider Anscombe's case of St. Peter's three denials (pp. 91–93), in which she wishes to allow that Peter did not intend to deny Jesus. Surely he did say, 'Nay, Lord, I will not,' and surely he did say, an hour later, 'I do not know the man.' If Judas, now, had professed good faith at the Last Supper, would we say he really didn't intend to go back on his word, but failed to foresee what the penalty was to be, or forgot for the moment the 30 pieces of silver jingling in his pocket? Here, though he regretted his action, we should be less inclined to say he meant well, poor man, but circumstances. . . . In both cases we see a pattern of actions militating against earlier expressions of intention. If we distinguish the two cases, it might be because in one case a man is only saving his own skin, in the other his action leads to betrayal and execution. The seriousness of the breach is one way of deciding whether the expression of intention is to be taken as an excuse or not. Incessant repetition of the act which the person promises to avoid is another. Repeated failure to perform an action intended is still another. All these criteria suggest that what is primary in ascribing intention to others is the business of justifying or excusing. The person who says, 'But I meant to' is excusing a failure to perform. If we refuse the excuse, we wish his expressions of intention to be taken seriously by attaching penalties, by holding him to them.

Still, this fails to bring out one aspect of the judgment of intention. Judas's act was premeditated, St. Peter's was not. Note how with each new formulation it looks as if we have hit upon the characterization of intention, but each in turn points to a particular feature, and sometimes only a particular oddity in the diffuse use of this term. Premeditation fails also. It is, to be sure, a way of distinguishing between actions for which we would be prepared to hold a person responsible and those we would excuse. The act for which elaborate preparation has been made counts as intentional no matter what. But we would not say the unprepared, the spontaneous act, is therefore unintentional.

Intention is thus one of those concepts calculated to rouse the psychologist to a fury of experimental investigation, and rigorous definition of variables. For one might infer from the breakdown of all criteria that ordinary speech and observation fail to get at the thing in question. Did a man intend or not looks as if it should have a straightforward answer. And when we discover that, on one occasion, we say a man intended because 'he said he would', on another because we can point to all the preparations he has made, on still another because we can note that he does the same thing every time, and still wonder, with any and all of these criteria, whether he *really* intended, it looks as if the ordinary man needs professional assistance in the quest for intentions. Often an ascription of intention on one of these grounds runs foul of an ascription on another, which makes it, from the psychologist's viewpoint, all the more hopeless. The point is, however, that that is the sort of game being played, when we intend or announce intentions and perform actions. There are built-in ambiguities in this game. Furthermore, when the various rules of application conflict, the procedure is one of *ad hoc* judgment, guided perhaps by like cases, as the law is guided by precedent, but not determinable by special kinds of discovery. The ambiguities and the indecisiveness in many cases make it appear that something ought to be discoverable which would resolve the doubts that arise from our imperfect and primitive modes of pre-scientific observation of the world. But in the case of intention, as in so many of the concepts of ordinary life, ambiguity and vagueness and indecisiveness are part of our usage. No general theory would help us out of our difficulties.

Elaborate planning, perhaps, takes precedence most frequently over other grounds in assigning intentions. The man who has a basement chock-full of cunningly-contrived explosive devices is not making toys or engaging in a hobby, whatever his avowals or the subsequent failure to perform may indicate. But occasionally what seems to be elaborate planning may turn out to be something else. It could be a hobby, especially after all opportunities to blow up the White House or the U.N. are passed up.

To sum up. We ascribe intentions to others and sometimes to ourselves (1) by seeing an action in the light of a situation (and thus seeing it in the light, also, of some vaguely defined collection of human practices, institutions and rules), (2) by noting the tendency of actions in a situation, (3) by listening to avowals of intention, and assesssing the manner of utterance as well as the character of the avower, (4) by noticing the intensity or elaborateness of planning which appears to have an action of a certain sort as consequence. In a further sense, like Austin, we can regard expressions of intention as performatives, made felicitous (in Austin's term) by the situation and the rules that bear upon it, but not in any sense to be regarded as reports.

We might be tentatively inclined to say, then, that ascribing or uttering intentions is thus very much of a piece with other kinds of human speech depending for their use upon the procedures for justifying or excusing actions. It might even be said at this point that the very concept of action, singled out by Wittgenstein, and more clearly by Melden, as what most clearly distinguishes the mental or the human act from the inanimate movement, is a consequence of our tendency to judge and appraise the motives of human and animal agents.[9] This would seem to underline Wittgenstein's comment, already quoted, that 'an intention is imbedded in its situation, in human customs and institutions' (§ 337). It is also suggested by many of Melden's .comments on the difference between action and movement. 'The movement (e.g., arm raising) just is an action', Melden says.[10] It suggests that something distinguishes rising arms from arm raisings. But when we look closely at his argument it looks rather as if the two are alternate descriptions of the same events. For, this is Melden's central puzzle, it is the same set of physical events that on some occasions will be called movements and on others actions. Melden has some interesting things to say at this point about Camus's *The Stranger*. 'The writing of this book treats actions as if they were movements' (pp. 192-3), and thus makes its point about a character to whom the very terms of human existence are alien. The point of describing human actions as movements, as in the novels of Robbe-Grillet, whose meticulous physical descriptions have much of the same alien and depressing effects, is to bring out the oddity, the abnormality of such a life. It makes its case against a background of normal descriptions of actions, as intended, meant and lived. At least this is Melden's point.

But the Camus case also shows us that it is (always?) possible to redescribe actions as movements. It does not generally suit our purposes to do so, and this is a fact of utmost importance frequently forgotten by psychologists. They have been rigorous enough in rejecting common sense methods, but quite naïve in retaining common or garden purposes in asking questions about intelligent action. In any case we see certain physical movements as movements or as actions. What leads us to make this choice of ways of describing? A man falling from a height can be described quite adequately as 'the body falling'. But a man jumping from a window ledge cannot be described as a body projected from the ledge. To say he intended or wanted to is to reflect the distinction, but since our manner of assigning intentions and desires is by way of actions, an appeal to intentions and desires as grounds for the distinction would be circular.

We might speak of a sequence of movements as an action when one or more of a variety of conditions is met. (1) It matches an expression of intention. (2) It results in what might be supposed to be a desired consequence. (3) It is a convenient substitute for a mechanical description, when difficulties stand in the way of such a description. (4) It occurs as

---

[9] Cf. also Hamlyn's article, 'Behaviour' (*Philosophy*, XXVIII (1953), pp. 32–45), which points to the importance of Aristotle's distinction between *energeia* and *kinesis* in this matter.
[10] *Free Action*, p. 187.

part of a game, as a rule-abiding procedure, entered into by numbers of players.

(1) is rather unimportant. We are quite prepared to admit intentions without expressions, or to deny them in contradiction to expressions. But we should, especially in certain vague and unusual cases, be gratified to hear an expression of intention as a way of deciding what in the world a person wanted to do.

(2) and its corollary, the repeated production of consequences, has been discussed. It amounts to this. Certain things happen in the physical world as a result of our actions, and we see them as desirable. When this occurs, especially in conjunction with extensive planning or constant recurrence, we think of the movements involved as actions. But notice especially here the borderline cases, like brushing a fly from one's nose (Melden, p. 206), which we might think of as involuntary, yet they count as actions. They seem to be instances of causal connection; certainly they can be described that way. Yet they can be looked at also as achieving a purpose, and in this way such a gesture becomes a typical purposive act. The injection of purpose into this account would make it appear as if an assemblage of movements counts as an action because it is explained this way. But of this more in the next section.

(3) is a rather different kettle of fish. It suggests that action accounts are second-best stand-ins for mechanical accounts. The latter are, after all, difficult to come by sometimes. They require a sophistication of technique which is at times all out of proportion to the importance of the material, and so we content ourselves with speaking in the rougher way. But a mechanical account of movements simply does not give us the kind of description or explanation of behaviour for which we are usually looking. The possibility of giving a mechanical account of muscular movements does not subvert the effectiveness of an action account. Melden's discussion of this point would thus seem essentially sound. He wishes to emphasize the possibility of a causal–chain description of the arm rising, while noting that in the context of typical questions about this movement, the physiological detail would be irrelevant. We want to know why he raised his arm, not why or how it rises.

But put the question another way. Suppose we ask, why do we find certain questions relevant? Two answers seem to have been given to this question. The gist of one of these answers is to be found most forcibly expressed in Austin's lectures, where he reminds us of the extent to which many of the terms we use are learned ostensively.[11] Thus, to transfer

[11] J. L. Austin, *Sense and Sensibilia* (Oxford University Press, 1962), pp. 121–2.

Austin's moral to our present case, action concepts are learned through a rich variety of paradigms. If it is asked, how can we properly speak of sequences of movements like lighting a cigarette or jumping out the window as actions, the answer is that *that* is what is meant by an action and, consequently, that *that* is what is seen or observed. Thus, the world contains actions. We are committed to explanations by reasons, intentions, motives and the like once we see what happens as a case, say, of lighting a cigarette. Dissection or analysis of such sequences, in order to find the elements which compose them, are bound to fail, for it is not in virtue of some possibly discoverable ingredients, revealed by analytic strategy, that we are able to say, 'this is an action'. One could say that the lighting of a cigarette is composed of such and such muscular and nervous elements, also such and such geometric arrangements. Other strategies of dissection could cut up the act into other kinds of elements. Such an analysis lacks point, however, unless it fortifies our assertion that this is an action of such and such a type, or clarifies the application of the concept to a case. Ultimately, in much philosophy, the grounds of analysis are connected with the demands for pristine and incorrigible elements of sense experience. Once we see our way out of that wood, it is easier to see how analysis, though possible, might be quite irrelevant. Actions are primitive in our discourse, and consequently primitive also in our recognition of features of the world.

(4) We might, however, try to show the relevance of certain questions to an account of human action by providing an analysis of a rather different type. It is suggested particularly by Wittgenstein's approach, which might be paraphrased: seek not the elements in order to understand the whole, but seek the whole (the context) in order to understand the elements. The context with respect to identifying actions, is, for Wittgenstein, that provided by games, the fourth among our conditions for applying notions like intention to human behaviour. So it will be necessary to turn (in Chapter IX) to this concept, and its putative role in providing a general methodological answer, at least, to problems in the explanation of human behaviour. In the meantime, notice that to say action concepts are learned through a variety of paradigms casts doubt on the very conception of a general answer to such a question.

PURPOSE

Much of what has already been said about motive and intention can also be said about purpose. All of these concepts belong to a common universe of discourse, which might be expressed by saying that they belong to the point of view of the actor rather than the point of view of the spectator.

This way of putting the contrast has its disadvantages. For it makes it seem as if the language of the actor is only appropriate to the actor, to the person deliberating, deciding, aiming or intending. This focuses our attention on expressions of intention and purpose as opposed to reports of them, and leaves the field of reporting to the spectator. The ideal spectator, in turn, is the scientist. Without considerable care, then, the dichotomy of actor and spectator could lead us full circle to the view against which I have been arguing all along, namely, that knowledge, discovery, truth and understanding are the exclusive properties of science.

The dichotomy is instructive in another way, however. The spectator's point of view finds its most ready expression in the language of observation, event and occurrence. The most natural way to characterize the spectator's point of view is to imagine a succession of objects wholly describable in terms of their physical properties and relations to other objects. This is the Humean picture. It is always an *occurrence* that needs explaining, and this seems to imply that the form of any explanation will consist in relating an occurrence to the occurrences that precede it. In contrast, for the actor's point of view we must imagine something operating intelligently, according to rule or plan, or in such a way as to reach a particular goal. When we superimpose one of these pictures on the other, we get the blur and distortion characteristic of the psychologist's attempt to talk in purposive terms, yet from the point of view of the spectator. The action of a man, a rat, or a pigeon is thought of implicitly as goal-seeking (that is, drive-reducing), but the form of description is that of discrete events linked by ties of resemblance and conjunction. To say that a man does something in pursuit of an aim is clearly explanatory, but the psychologist's way of representing this explanation is the event language of the spectator. Thus purposes come to be thought of as quasi-physical occurrences causing behaviour, and talk about purpose is open to all the criticisms to which positivist philosophers subject it. For there is nothing the spectator can find that will count as purpose, nor is there any idea what sort of event is being looked for.

To note that purpose talk belongs to the point of view of the actor reminds us that we need not look for an event justifying the introduction of an explanation. Purposes are not events any more than motives or intentions. Recognizing or comprehending purposes is not a matter of observing particular events or successions of them. It is rather a matter of setting what a man or animal is doing in a context that makes those movements intelligible. It is seeing that a bodily movement is consistent with or, more strongly, logically entails, a consequence, which, in its turn, can be seen as something worthy of being attained. The connexion with motive and need talk is obvious. Just as some particular circumstances can be viewed as standard occasions justifying or excusing actions, and others as standard examples of things worth resolving or achieving, so particular circumstances or the lack of them can be thought of as the most *natural* circumstances worth trying to bring about.

In one sense, then, there is no special story to be told about purpose. It is a general title encompassing motives, intentions, needs and desires, and refers to the type of understanding that consists in justifying an action by the contribution it makes to achieving or blocking some state of affairs. This is the point of view of the actor, since it is necessary, in making such judgments, to appraise a situation for what is needed, required, desired, justified or excused in it, whether we are about to act ourselves or are merely observing the actions of others.

To psychologists these are empty words. There is, for them, only one adequate or intelligible manner of describing states of affairs, the event language with its attending explanatory pattern according to which later events are to be traced to earlier. Thus if teleological explanation is possible, there must be some antecedent events that in some mysterious way embody the purpose of the organism. 'In its extreme form', Hull says, 'teleology is the name of the belief that the *terminal* stage of certain environmental-organismic interaction cycles somehow is at the same time one of the antecedents determining conditions which bring the behaviour cycle about.'[12] So interpreted, teleological explanations can easily be shown to be useless; first, because the antecedent conditions cannot be found, and second, because, even if they could be, their discovery would have to wait upon the completion of the cycle. In effect, 'this means that the task of deduction [explanation?] cannot begin until after it is completed! Naturally, this leaves the theorist completely helpless.' In short, purposive accounts won't do because they are not causal accounts. Moreover, they deny the conditions of investigation of behaviour on which Hull insists. 'An ideally adequate theory', he says, 'even of so-called purposive behavior ought therefore to begin with colorless movement and mere receptor impulses as such, and from these build up step by step both adaptive and maladaptive behavior.'[13] His criticism of

---

[12] C. L. Hull, *Principles of Behavior* (Appleton-Century Crofts, 1943), p. 26.

[13] Ibid., p. 25. Charles Taylor, *The Explanation of Behaviour* (Routledge & Kegan Paul, 1964), pp. 16 ff. and again 114 ff., quotes these passages and criticizes the views contained in them in a way similar to that undertaken here.

purposive explanation amounts to saying that purposes won't do because they are causes, and a purposive or actor's point of view won't do because it is not the point of view of events spread out in space and succeeding one another in time. It is taken as self-evident that an explanation or description in actor language is inadequate, just because it assumes that form.

The proper retort to such an argument is to point to the ease with which we offer actor's accounts of others' actions as well as our own. But this in turn requires comment. The facility is no doubt due to the fact that in ordinary life the range of likely goals, justifying circumstances, needs and desires is pretty standard. The same feature of justifying explanations, of course, is also their danger. For we too readily ascribe to others the detail of our own desires, motives and needs, only to find that people are not as similar to one another as the point of view of the actor might seem to require. Disappointments like this lead to modifications of our accounts of the behaviour of others, but these modifications are in the first place dictated within the context of justifying or purposive explanation and, in the second place, provide us, by the failure of our explanations of particular cases, with a richer store of examples of justifying occasions for action. And this enlarges the basis for our own decisions and judgment as well as the understanding of the actions of others.

Sometimes teleological explanation is regarded as extraordinarily, indeed suspiciously, easy because of failing to distinguish having a purpose and fulfilling a purpose. It is difficult to state criteria for having a purpose, for it suggests to most philosophers the mystery of internal entities or episodes which remain out of reach of scientific investigation and so can be introduced at will without fear of refutation. Obviously, if this were the case, teleological explanations would be quite generally defective. But, as I hope to show presently, the notion of having a purpose can be given meaning without recourse to such mysteries. The other half of this distinction, fulfilling a purpose, is sometimes resorted to when the difficulties of interpreting having a purpose are taken to be insuperable. The result of this is that a purposive explanation becomes a backward description, utilizing a later term in a sequence of events as the point of departure for describing earlier events. In this sense the choice of the language of purpose is little more than one of descriptive style. Anything could in that sense be purposive, for we might even give teleological form to our description of something as incorrigibly mechanical as Boyle's law. This is the sense of purpose that Nagel appears to adopt, with the result that the term can be easily removed from the range of acceptable explanatory strategies.[14] On the view that purposive accounts are no more than backward descriptions it is easy enough to show that they are inadequate devices by which to explore nature and so, by implication, human nature. When we consider almost any case of the emergence of physical or biological theory from its primitive beginnings we can see how the language of purpose is replaced by that of mechanics. Thus it was once supposed that antibody formation was 'instructive', that the body learned from the environment what to do with an invading organism and 'chose' a protein to combat it. Now it is supposed that antibody formation is 'elective'; the response to an invading organism is elicited in a purely mechanical—in this case chemical—way, determined by the genetic code.[15] Is it simply a methodologically better account? Or are we inclined to say that some events simply are not or cannot be construed as purposive without being misleading? We might say of some cases, like those described by Nagel as 'isoperimetric' or 'variational' forms of law (pp. 407–8), that the teleological formulation is simply a convenient way of calling attention to a phenomenon which is more accurately and non-committally described by the mathematical formula. An example would be Snell's law, that the angle of incidence of a beam of light equals the angle of reflection, which can be stated in teleological form by saying that light rays follow minimum paths. We might say the same of metabolism or any self-regulating mechanism, including, for instance, the pressure-temperature balance in a star. It is simpler to express what happens by talking about what is maintained than to write out complicated descriptions of causal sequences. But in other cases we might be more inclined to say that purposive vocabulary is used more seriously, as a description, and not as a mere facility of expression, which is what Nagel makes of it.

It is thus easy for Nagel to dispose of purposive explanation, since he admits only the fulfilling sense of purpose. If, on the other hand, we admit the distinction between fulfilling and having a purpose, we must ask what limits the application of purpose concepts in the latter sense. It may help to begin by considering why we are disposed to think of some goals as 'natural'.

Part of the answer to this question is surely due to the fact of human similarity. We start with paradigm aims—a baby that is wet or hungry wants to be changed or fed, a man that is alone wants company, a man working hard at unpleasant tasks wants success. There will be occasions in our experience in which paradigms no longer apply, and these we find

[14] *The Structure of Science*, pp. 421–2.
[15] The example is borrowed from Peter Medawar, *The Future of Man* (Mentor Books, 1961), pp. 88–89.

bizarre. If, none the less, the behaviour of a man exhibits a marked persis-
tence, pattern, or direction, we are apt to come to think of the terminal
point of his behaviour as an aim, and so realize that the range of human
wants is larger than we had supposed. And note that we are able to speak
of 'terminal points' because we bring a purposive point of view to bear
on the behaviour sequence.

This procedure has the appearance of circularity. For it is a purposive
way of looking at behaviour that makes it natural to describe it purposively. To talk purposively it must be possible to speak of actions as
terminating, yet our justification for talking this way seems to depend on
having already prepared ourselves to view the behaviour as fulfilling a
purpose. Chimpanzees in the wild, for example, post a sentinel who
screams angrily at the approach of something dangerous, at which the
band flees. There is an immediate and well-nigh irresistible disposition
to say that the sentinel warns the band of danger and that he is posted
for that purpose. The reason is that we have, willy-nilly, described the
chimp behaviour in purposive language. 'Posting', 'watching', 'running
away', 'screaming', 'danger' are all terms from the purposive vocabulary.

Now it is also the case that the sentinel chimp does not stop screaming
when the danger is gone, and this suggests that the action fails to qualify
as purposive on at least one ground. Hebb, for example, considers four
criteria for the appropriate application of purpose to behaviour.[16] The
fourth of these, that activity is not purposive unless it ceases when the
objective is achieved, is not met in the case of the chimpanzee. But this
might lead us to say that purposive activity is a function of intelligence,
and that the fullest possible set of conditions is perhaps never met, though
approximated by creatures like men, of higher orders of intellectual
capacity. As we have noted already, ascription of intelligent performance
is an appraisal of actions relative to specific goals, and so purpose, as a
member of the same family of concepts, that is, performance concepts,
also depends upon appraisal.

Hebb's other criteria are also instructive. The first, the capacity for
language use, he regards as too narrow, since it excludes animal behaviour.
The second, capacity for problem solving, and the third, the long-range
anticipation of future difficulties may, with the fourth, come close to
singling out the features that would allow us to correctly apply purposive
language to behaviour. But one difficulty with all these criteria is their
actual or potential application to machines. The most natural way of
talking about and making clear the workings of a machine is not, curiously
enough, by means of a 'mechanical' account, that is, a description of its

---

[16] Hebb, *Textbook*, pp. 206 ff.

interlocking parts, but purposively by showing its design. We can also, of course, think of the machine in terms of the programming of it, that is, as an axiomatic system translated into a set of physical equivalents. Leibniz, in fact, might be interpreted as one who attempted to substitute a logical for both a purposive and a mechanical account.[17] The possibility of giving different, but equivalent, accounts suggests that there are no teleologically ordered events, nor mechanical events, but only teleological or mechanical descriptions. Our preference for one or the other depends on our interests or felicity of expression. But it has no deeper significance. Anything, on this view, would count as either purposive or as mechanical, depending on what one wanted to do or say. Interest in accuracy and predictive power might lead to mechanical description, felicity of expression to purposive.[18]

None of this, however, gets at the fact that we do think it more natural to ascribe purposes to some cases, the behaviour of organisms, for example, than to others. We are also, I believe, rather inclined to suppose that, if a purposive explanation is appropriate, a mechanical explanation will not do. Part of this may be due to the fact that descriptions which make purposive talk seem natural are themselves purposive descriptions. Some of the events surrounding the signalling of the chimpanzee, for example, are described as dangerous, that is as circumstances to be avoided. When the actions bring about this result we are apt to regard the actions as purposive in a stronger sense than that characteristic of Nagel's backward descriptions. If the behaviour is perfectly attuned to the occasion by beginning at the moment of awareness of the offending or enticing circumstance and ending with avoidance or achievement, the act is purposive. If there is a response to the occasion not quite as ideally suited to achievement or avoidance we might speak instead of emotion (fear or rage, for example) rather than purpose. If this is so, note how the language of purpose is built on the basis of emotion. For in emotions, situations conceived as dangerous, enticing or satisfying are recognized and responded to, but the reaction is not always perfectly calculated to do whatever is most appropriate to achieve or avoid the situation. Purpose, then, is restricted to those cases in which a rational plan is exhibited in addition to a signal of some goal-like character.

---

[17] Cf. *Monadology*, § 17.

[18] The preference for mechanical explanation on verificationist grounds is tied in part to the fact that theories of verification have been developed by using the science of mechanics as a model. This makes it appear as if nothing could count as verified and no explanation regarded as adequate unless it has mechanical form. But this confusion of the strategy of verifying with a special blue-ribbon case of it should not lead us to overlook the fact that there are better and worse, hence both more and less verified, purposive explanations.

If we speak this way, the limitations on the use of purpose language are evident. However perfectly the movements of physical objects or processes (a river, say) fit some prefigured end (reaching sea-level) it is not as clear how we could ascribe emotion or need to the motions of inanimate objects. One could think, I suppose, of the churning of the stream as evidence of its striving to fulfil its desires. But the thing that makes all extensions of purpose-talk to inanimate things strange is the lack of any intelligible way of claiming that the water is *aware* of the object of danger, or *conceives* that an object could be the source of danger, or *feels* the pain that engenders the thought of danger. The stressed terms in the preceding sentence are intelligible only when accompanied by a method of awareness, eyes for seeing, skin for touching and feeling pain, ears for hearing, and so on. It is worth noting in passing that part of the difficulty with a sense-datum theory of perception is that it dissolves the logical bonds that join eyes to things seen. Being aware is for a special kind of thing to grasp, perceive, discover or view some feature of the world by means of some feature in its own make-up. In short, to speak of being aware it is necessary that one speak of an organism that is aware, that has the proper equipment for being aware, and to speak of purpose or emotion or need in a strict, as opposed to metaphorical, way is to speak of being aware of something in the world (including, of course, the organism) that contributes to or relieves the organism of fears and loves, needs and goals. Thus, whatever else, the language of purpose is a language that applies only to organisms.

It may be instructive to ask how it was that Aristotle and other philosophers of antiquity came to think of purpose as universally explanatory. In part it is probably due to the fact that Aristotle shares with modern philosophers a preference for a logician's approach to the issues of science and metaphysics. He wishes to lay down general criteria for explanation, applicable to all cases. In practice he does not follow his rule, putting the peculiar features of the case at hand before the general claim. But he does introduce a proviso for a complete explanation which will include reference to the reason for which, as well as the what, how, and type. Thus, if Aristotle had become convinced that natural events have no purposes or reasons, he would have been forced to conclude that explanations of nature are logically incomplete. Similarly, modern philosophers are apt to treat reasons as inadequate explanations, because they do not rest on general truths, and hence cannot predict new cases.

But there is perhaps a more fundamental reason why explanation-in-general might have been thought to require a purposive component. The idea of explanation in itself is something that only slowly emerges from the expanding experience with and grasp of a world that men acquire individually in growing up, and collectively in social lore and science. In children the question why is intimately connected with actions and desires. They first ask why, I venture to say, because someone tells them what they must not do. Consequently the answer to the question why is first exemplified in giving a rule. Rules in turn belong to the matrix of human aims, for formulating them answers to and facilitates the desires and ends of action that men in society conceive. Quoting a rule is the initial answer to puzzlement. It is natural to suppose, then, that men would seek rules governing new cases in which puzzles arise, or view the world in such a way that puzzles would take this form. Purposive answers would thus be required to questions about behaviour of inanimate objects as well as organisms. One might speculate, for the sake of clarity if not for the sake of information, that purpose is the original and univocal answer to the question why, and serves as an initial paradigm which all satisfactory explanations must meet. Dealing with nature requires other and equally primitive models, such as the model of interaction with which we began. It would at least be foolish to suppose that mechanical ideas belong to a peculiarly sophisticated and scientific point of view. But purpose is none the less a difficult concept to shake off and leads us to clothe our most mechanical ideas in the purposive language of ends.

That we do so reminds us that it is only a part, though an important part, of explaining, to devise or assert something that bears in some way on the facts, whether this is a matter of consistency with, prediction of, or verification by the facts. Equally important to our use of the concept is that explanations make something clear or plain (ex-planare) and this ingredient points to the persons to whom explanations are offered. To make plain may be to show how a perplexing action is purposive, it may be to show how discrete elements in a physical system are really connected by interlocking parts, or it may be something else still. But the intelligible form into which the perplexing facts are fitted must be part and parcel of our conceptual framework if we are to regard this case as cleared up by the given form. Our conceptual scheme, like that of the Greeks, is in many ways shot through with purposive notions. It leads us, even in the most remote by-ways of physical science, to describe movements of bodies as actions, to think, for example, of geodesics of relativity theory as minimum paths and the particle exchange of elementary particle physics as account keeping.

It is thus not surprising that we should wonder whether there is any limit to the application of the concept of purpose. Surely, we say, there is nothing unintelligible about the idea of the hand of God hurling the planets in their orbits, or the supreme intelligence contriving the universe for a purpose. Though we stumble over the attempt to give specific content to this form, a purposive account is none the less a model of intelligibility. More especially it is, as Aristotle noted, the only really decisive account of origins. For it is the only kind of answer to the question why that puts an end to further questioning. Thus it looms large in any cosmological theory, especially one that makes time finite.

But purpose also fills the gaps in much of physical explanation, for example, free-fall, thought of as a special case of action at a distance. Free-fall is as common and as uniform as anything in nature, yet it is puzzling because it lacks a characteristic typical of bodily motion, namely, the constant application of force as a cause of motion. Purpose fills the breach here, for it is the only account of movement that does not require the picture of muscular effort or bodily collision, of action without perceived and continuous contact. One might read the theory of material natures—the view that each element seeks its own place—somewhat more sympathetically if it is viewed in the light of the most intelligible model consistent with the observed facts.

In one sense at least action at a distance is still a puzzle. We introduce a theory to describe and bring out the relevant features of situations in which movements of this sort occur—mass and distance, velocity and acceleration—but no physical model exists which makes gravitational attraction more intelligible, that is, picturable. Still, we reject purpose as a stop-gap, as a picture that makes action at a distance intelligible. And it is worth inquiring why, for it shows something about the need for an account that is homogeneous in its descriptive and explanatory features. Our description of falling bodies has come to acquire mathematical form, but this is more than a matter of choice of symbols or a question of exactness. It is a matter of using a vocabulary that goes with a mechanical point of view. This point of view demands a form of language capable of describing what we mean by one body moving faster or slower than another, or the force with which one body collides with another. The resulting descriptions do not mesh with the purposive point of view. We see actions as moves that further a design, a matter to which questions of velocity and acceleration are normally indifferent, unless, of course, the design is to hurry, slow down, or speed up. Normally, the person who slowly solves the arithmetic problem is doing the same thing as the man who does it quickly, the farmer who ploughs his field in an hour and his neighbour who takes all day are still both ploughing their fields. In describing the inanimate world mechanically we have moved in a conceptual direction which the paradigm of purpose cannot follow.

Mechanical and purposive descriptions, then, exclude one another and the explanatory strategies that arise from them. This is probably not very surprising. The question of importance is why we think it proper to confine mechanical descriptions exclusively to inanimate objects, and purposive descriptions to organisms. One reason has been stated above. Having an aim, if it is to mean more than reaching a certain conclusion with relevant consistency, is tied to awareness of pains and pleasures, of objects desirable and fearful. And awareness depends on the special feature of animal organisms, their capacities for sensation and perception. Thus it is only in the context of organisms that the phrase ' . . . as if . . .' can be deleted from the ascription of aims and the notion of having an aim introduced.

Beyond this, our talk about physical movement, and Aristotle's, is always talk about classes of objects, never about individual things save by way of illustration. Normal purpose talk, on the other hand, is always in connection with individuals, or some collection of them which, because of common action, can be treated as an individual. A man may have a long-term purpose, of course, and he may share it with many others. But though many of his actions may be animated by a single and distant goal, a given item of his behaviour may serve as an element furthering quite different goals. He may lift an object to put it on a shelf, develop his muscles, or show off his strength. In contrast we look at falling objects, for example, as indifferent members of a class. The question is about the explanation of this general circumstance, that bodies in general fall, not about the way in which, on a particular occasion, a falling body fits into some special and limited design. There is no way in which a purposive account can be successfully applied to what happens in general, for the likeness of movement from case to case does not reflect necessarily (or actually) a similarity of moves as instruments in a design. We must know a good deal about the particular circumstances in which a man or animal acts in order to give a purposive account of his action *qua* action. Knowing merely the physical movements will not help at all. Thus the strategies of purposive explanation are alien to accounts of *kinds* of things. An argument from design presupposes a conception of the universe as an individual, and not as a collection of similar processes.

We might conclude then that purposive explanations are restricted to the particular behaviour of particular organisms. Generality is achieved only by the accumulation of cases of similar organisms living in similar circumstances. We do not know better why organism *A* acts as he does because we discover that organism *B* acts in the same way. We only know that organism *B* and the whole class of *B*-like organisms have the same aims and methods of achieving them as *A*. The original ascription of an aim to *A* is made possible only by seeing *A*'s behaviour as contributing to a consequence that the observer recognizes as a legitimate goal, that is, a circumstance that he can appreciate as a goal. In this sense to ascribe purpose is to see an act as *felicitous*, as right or proper, by reason of fitting logically to a certain design.

It might, last of all, be asked why we could not conceive of a discrete physical movement as a particular move in a strategy directed at achieving or avoiding something. The short way with this question is to point out that the possibility of doing so is disbarred on the grounds that we are not dealing with an organism. But it might also be noted how different the concepts are that make possible the description of movements, on the one hand, and actions (*moves*, elements in a strategy) on the other. The concepts applied to movement are generalizations, or abstractions, of physical resemblances—down-up, fast-slow, right-left and their refinements. The concepts of action are abstractions of strategies—pushing-pulling, lifting-lowering and, of course, much more rule-governed cases like buying-selling, arguing-persuading, informing-lying, and so on. A quite general frame of reference (space-time) serves to generate movement concepts. In describing an occurrence in those terms we are committed to a description that is indifferent to the individual cases. We have chosen a method that abstracts a common feature from all possible contexts in which special occurrences of the relevant type take place. In talking about acts or moves, on the other hand, we preserve in our concepts a relation to, and dependence upon, the particular contexts of which the moves form the elements. As the conceptual framework requires its own kind of description of the phenomena, so it determines also the kind of explanatory strategy that is relevant.

MEN AND MACHINES

Sometimes attention is called to the extraordinary capacities of negative feed-back machines to engage in human or quasi-human performances, in order to show that purposive accounts can be reduced to mechanical accounts without remainder. We know that robots are machines. We also find ourselves describing their behaviour in purposive ways; the machines do tasks, calculate, they take cognizance of and analyse their surroundings. The machine thus presents us with an analogy to organisms. Purposive descriptions seem equally possible in both cases. We are apt to think, then, that if we only knew about the inner workings of a man the way we know about the workings of a machine, we would see that in the organism case the distinction between mechanical and purposive explanation is only a function of our ignorance.

Philosophers have attempted in various ways to block the reduction of purposive to mechanical explanation. Technical capacity, for example, is often appealed to. Machines are rather more efficient than men at their appointed tasks; why on earth would we employ machines otherwise? But their performances are limited and inflexible. The human mind is capable of reasoning backward from conclusions, of seeing what arguments would support a given conclusion, or what tactics would reach a given end. A machine, in contrast, follows an inflexible pattern of inference that is built into it. It cannot foreshadow the course of argument or policy but only proceed step by step. This is often suggested by those who would say that a machine can't imagine or that it lacks insight.[19] Unfortunately these arguments too are arguments from ignorance. A machine has not been produced that will engage in certain kinds of human performance, but it is possible that machines might be devised that would.

The criterion that I have appealed to as basic to the use of purposive language, namely, the capacity for awareness, might also be considered applicable to machines. For we build machines with receptors that take in data and, by analysing it, act appropriately. The question is whether, awareness leads or could lead in the case of the machine to emotional reactions. It might be argued, of course, that we simply have not bothered to build a machine to feel pain or fear or love. Once again the argument depends upon our ignorance of what it would be like to install pain, fear, or love circuits. Part of the difficulty has to do with a feature of being aware that is obscured in the case of vision. We do not feel the strain on the concepts in claiming that a robot sees, in the way we would if we were to claim that the robot felt. For in the case of vision it is an outer world that is to be apprehended by eyes or eye-like mechanisms. It is the common world, and the functionally similar mechanisms, that allow us to extend a vision vocabulary to machines. But in the case of feelings we lack a coherent way of talking about the mechanism, and the common world is a world of shared attitudes, not observable things. If, then, we imagine Scriven's complete android,[20] the machine that has all the human properties—solving problems, devising theories, becoming angry, responding to electric shocks, with all too human shrieks, and is even manufactured out of protein[21]—we might still balk at including it

---

[19] Cf. 'Men and Machines', especially the contribution of J. O. Wisdom, in *Aris. Soc. Proc.* Suppl. Vol. XXVI, 1952.
[20] In Sydney Hook (ed.), *Dimensions of Mind* (Collier Books, 1961), p. 113.
[21] Ibid., p. 136,

among men, because that inclusion depends upon the machine entering into the human community as a member.

Suppose we did all this, calling the machine by name, treating him with respect and trying not to hurt him (unless we wanted to). Is there any point now to the question, is he man or machine? If he really is a machine there must be a point which at the show can be given away. But how? Perhaps someone comes along and says: '*That* a man? Why, I made him myself.' And we might shudder or feel queasy at the thought of the nature of our contact with him. Still, manner of manufacture might diminish in importance. Imagine a strikingly beautiful female or an eminently athletic male android. They do all the things that constitute normal human performance, only perhaps a bit better. A man might finally come to say, 'Origin's a mere prejudice, I love her'. Or the manager, whose team has been languishing at the bottom of the league and suddenly comes alive, with an android guiding it to victory, likewise might shrug off the manner of creation. Notice how the athletic world especially has encountered and overcome other prejudices, against negroes, for example. They were different, so the story went, yet this prejudice began to vanish when the noted differences were seen to have nothing to do with the kinds of activities in which 'we' and 'they' work and interact.

Thus, the difference between men and machines is first of all a difference of attitude. A machine, defined as that which has been devised out of simpler materials by a human artificer, could very well overcome the attitudes that govern our manner of interacting with it, if it showed itself human in performance. We might have qualms about its manner of manufacture and repair, its extraordinary capacities for endurance and survival, but the significance of these qualms will come to depend upon what is central to our human interests. The machine which cannot make a mistake, suffer pain, appreciate a joke, succumb to emotional displays is not going to raise problems as to whether we have really created a man. On the other hand, the lack of one of these characteristics is not going to eliminate a creature from some more intimate grouping with men than we might now be able to envisage. If a creature is both capable of and limited to typical human performances, we are well on the way to applying the term 'man' to him, even though his manner of origin is not quite traditional. But, of course, our conventions in calling this creature a man are not likely to be absolute, any more than calling a man an anthropoid lifts him bodily and wholly out of one Aristotelian niche and drops him into another. Matters relating to origin and repair are important, to be sure; perhaps they are important enough to retain a looseness in the application of human predicates to the android. He is, let us say, man-like, something we might also want to say of naturally born rational creatures from other worlds. Too often, the defenders of the machine want to press likenesses until they are total. Suppose a machine differs from us only in being manufactured, and then a child is born to it in the normal way. Is the new creature a machine? Compare: was Adam or Abel the first man? In short, the questions, are men machines, and could there be machines admissible to the company of men, bother us in part because we are so often committed to a genus-differentia rigidity, so that to say an x is a y is to deny altogether that x could also be a z, or in some other way enter into a rather different classificatory arrangement. We might come to say, there are machines like men; we might even come to be fooled by a machine. Such a mistake presupposes a criterion for deciding the matter, however. But if it were a genuine philosophical problem, then machines must have been devised that put a strain on our normal conceptual apparatus. Ordinarily, in such impasses, we have recourse to a new concept. So monkeys are not men, nor men monkeys, but both are anthropoids. Undoubtedly, such a procedure would be forthcoming in the machine case as well.

CHAPTER SEVEN

CONSCIOUSNESS

IT IS possible that the line I have been presenting with respect to concepts like desire and pleasure might suggest the view that there is no inner life. Since to say something is pleasant is to judge it, or to desire something is to find warrants for its pursuit, it might seem that I must be denying that there are inner states, occurrences or agitations. Man must be an appraising machine without the glow of inner life. Yet there surely are inner events of one kind or another.

To insist on an inner realm is itself innocuous. But it is also in a way an irresistible claim, and this leads to complications. A common difficulty in philosophy comes when, giving assent to something perfectly obvious, one finds that one has agreed as well to other things not nearly so unexceptionable. So it is in the philosophy of mind. It is obvious that there are mental events; difficulties arise only when one finds that with the initial admission one has also let in a whole crowd of more dubious claims. We are soon led by our incautious admission to allow that the inner life is apprehended by inward perception (introspection), paralleling outward perception (observation). One observes, on this view, one's thoughts and feelings, and sees or infers how they enter into relationships with other events. I venture to suggest that this view has served as a principal excuse for the science of psychology, just as the picture of a physics-like science of man has been its chief motive. For the idea that thoughts and feelings are observed leads readily to the view that they are events linked to other events by causal laws or statistical regularities. We shall need, then, before closing the book on the science of psychology, to come to grips with these mental concepts, and notably mental occurrences, that give life to the introspectionist view, and the way of explaining human behaviour that follows from it.[1]

When a person judges, believes, knows, opines, gropes for thought or word (especially that !) isn't something going on 'in the head' that he is attempting to convey, however fumblingly, by speech or appropriate action? What would a person be groping for, if not his thoughts, and in something like the way he gropes for the alarm button in the darkness of early morning? That is, he may find it, he may not, but it is there.

---

[1] It may strike the reader as odd that I associate behaviouristic trends in psychology with an introspectionist point of view. But psychological behaviourism is, in fact, a kind of wistful introspectionism, a resolution to avoid that which cannot be operationally defined, not a denial of its existence.

These questions suggest that something is occurring, going on, which by some special faculties of observation an individual seeks out, stumbles on, or experiences. Like the birds in Plato's aviary in the *Theaetetus*, one can by such a faculty reach in and grab such items. 'Everyone', says William James in the *Principles of Psychology* (p. 185), 'agrees that in our minds we discover states of consciousness.' He is thus led to think of the mind by analogy to a stream, whose shapes and motions can be grasped, though fleetingly, if one's eyes are sharp and attention alert enough.

Everything I have said here, on the contrary, would seem to endorse quite the opposite view. Along with the majority of contemporary English philosophers, I seem to be suggesting that notions like event, occurrence, and object are tied, necessarily, to the concept of material object or body, while the concept of mind finds its place with notions like doing or acting, performing and achieving. If we say 'not thoughts, but thinking' and suggest that this is after all much like 'not runs, but running, not plays but playing', we are perhaps not too far from a view that might be endorsed by the 'ordinary' man. But if we say, 'not feelings or sensations, but actions suitable to situations', the ordinary man is much more likely to opt for a dualistic conception of the relation of mind to body. There simply are inner occurrences which differ in obvious ways from observed behaviour; the two relate, not necessarily, but contingently.

It may be that what is common, ordinary and plain is not also consistent, intelligible or true. It may be also that to formulate an opinion at all about the nature of thoughts and feelings and our manner of acquaintance with them is to revise, correct, perhaps distort what is said in conversation and believed without reflection. (And isn't this Wittgenstein's point when he says that the ordinary man does not take a naïve realist, any more than he takes any other philosophical position?) This does not exempt a philosophical view from comparison to common sense or ordinary language, though it liberates it from a slavish devotion to it. Our bearings need to be taken in the philosophy of mind by reflecting first of all on the incoherence of ordinary talk about mind. It is possible that common speech affords a firmer anchor to philosophical reflection in considering an issue like the nature of the external world. For here object terms are firmly and clearly entrenched in ordinary usage, perhaps because we learn such terms ostensively and build our language around such references. In any case, we do know what we are talking about when we refer to tables and chairs, and how to go about illustrating the meaning of object terms without benefit of philosophical or physical theories. And so, when philosophers come to elevate objects into substances or demote them into bundles of sense-data, it is worth looking at our extraordinarily successful common use of physical object terms as a restraint to our theorizing.

In the case of mind, however, things are somewhat different. There is, I would venture to say, no ordinary use of mind, except in such phrases as 'it is all in your mind' or in the typical consolation that, whatever people say of my actions, I can nevertheless think and feel what I please. In short, the mind is a term of refuge, on the one hand from physical explanation and on the other from physical observation. To say something is all in the mind is to say that nothing can be discovered corresponding to your reports or causally accounting for your contortions. To speak of the mind as a private citadel is to suggest that you can *do* or think certain things without detection. In these functions of 'mind,' there is no conception of an entity or a special organ of apprehension which perceives one kind of occurrence just as eyes or ears or hands apprehend others. Indeed, Ryle is, to many students, quite incomprehensible, for they cannot appreciate the view he is attacking. Perhaps this is because the notion of a substance is quite outside their range of thinking, but it is clearly not because they have some alternative view as to the nature of mind. They have no view at all. Some have a conception of a soul, but this entity is, as it were, a temporarily suspended object or principle that takes over at least some of the functions that characterize human beings when the body dies. Thus thinking continues, but either pain or pleasure does not, depending upon one's afterlife fortunes. The soul is another kind of body resembling or relating to the mind no more clearly than to the material body. It is not, I gather, the essence of the soul to think or feel, however, but to receive rewards, suffer punishments, or engage in rapturous contemplation of infinity. It is the closest that ordinary people get to the notion of a non-material substance. In any event, the notion of soul has very little bearing on the concept of mind as it concerns us, whatever its importance to the philosophy of religion.

What is important in the ordinary view are the distinctions between public and private and inner and outer. All of us are confident that we can feel contempt for others while putting on a gracious manner, stand a certain amount of pain without showing it, indúlge in reveries while apparently alert to a wifely harangue or a pompous lecture. We can keep secrets, know without telling, feel without revealing. Surely (so goes a popular argument), it would be in effect to deny this if we were to deny specifically mental occurrences. And it would be peculiar and embarrassing indeed to be forced to deny that we can keep secrets and suppress feelings.

What are the implications of holding to common sense usage in this matter? Are we forced to say that there must be a special class of events which can be inviolate, which we can hide, so to speak, not behind cushions or in closets, but behind the formidable barrier of logical impossibility? Since thoughts and feelings can be suppressed in ways that occasion no fear at all of discovery, it looks as if we must say that they are distinct from the verbal, written, or pantomimed expression of them. Hence they are events, occurrences, entities of which an individual has sole ownership and to which he alone has access. In a sense, surely, this is what we have admitted. But the question is, what does this admission amount to?

And first, here, I think it would help to outline issues in the philosophy of mind which do not derive at all from these ordinary and plausible observations. So much of what the philosopher (or the psychologist) says about mind begins with problems in logic (about necessary truths) or epistemology (our manner of acquaintance with the world) or the philosophy of science (the nature of explanation). Look, for example, to problems about explanation, which, after all concern us first and foremost. If we restrict ourselves to the models of interaction or regular connexion, and wish to explain our actions by our thoughts and feelings, our thoughts and feelings must be treated as so many billard balls initiating subsequent movements. In psychology, this picture has led to two views which many people find equally unpalatable. The first is introspectionism, that kind of psychology that has fallen upon such evil days that it is called old-fashioned. The second is behaviourism. It is perhaps not always realized how closely related these views are. For introspectionism rests upon the claim that a proper explanation of human action must refer to the mental links that bridge stimuli and responses. And behaviourism takes that view seriously enough to suggest that there could not be such a realm, for if there were it would explain behaviour. Why can't there be such a realm? Because, if there were, the psychologist would have to abandon his pretensions to offer scientific accounts of human doings, accounts which depend upon the objectivity and reliability of data. Psychological behaviourism betrays a healthy respect for the explanatory powers of alleged mental occurrences, and is thus forced to deny their existence altogether. And this seems to deny that men fee¹ pains, or work problems, or are characterizable by anything other than bodily processes.

We have seen that the power of concepts like desire and reason to explain human action does not depend upon treating them as events causally linked to actions. Reasons and desires connect with actions in ways that do not require research to disclose. And this would seem to make it appear that the antagonists in the behaviourism debate defend equally implausible positions. One must see the movements of an agent as following rules, expressing desire or emotion in accordance with conventions and circumstances. It is no improvement in dealing with human action to break down actions into successions of spatio-temporal movements, even though a mathematical or a mechanical description would then become possible. Behaviourism, in short, suggests the wrong units, the wrong 'data'. But the supposed alternative to behaviourism won't do, either. We are not forced, in rejecting a radical behaviourism, to adopt an occult mentalism, in which all explanation is self-explanation. The explanatory use of concepts having a mental ring, that is, concepts which denote private occurrences or actions, does not lead us to such a mentalism. It would do so only if any explanation were assumed to be causal, as cases of the impact of one object on another. We are not forced to this extremity because, in their explanatory use, such terms as thought and feeling, mood and emotion, relate to the actions they explain by means of patterns of custom and convention, right and excuse. As explanatory concepts, they are, in a sense, not mental at all, at least, not so long as mental carries with it the sense of 'private'. Moreover, in most cases, the actions which we habitually take to be the consequences of thoughts and feelings are in fact their expression, that is, it is through characteristic actions that we define or come to understand the meaning of the alleged mental terms. It is in this sense that old philosophical saws like 'men pursue pleasure and avoid pain' or 'reason is the slave of the passions' are tautological. What men do identifies pleasures, pains and desires.

None the less, the bogy of introspection is not quite so easily laid. We could take working a problem on paper as explained by the nature of the problem, throwing things as explained by anger, or restlessness as due to nervousness, and be well within our rights in denying the importance of introspection to such explanations. For the actions are the characteristic, conventional or logical signs of thoughts, feelings and emotions. Speaking with undue solemnity, we might say that, without research, we can reconstruct the thoughts, feelings or emotions from the behaviour. It would indeed be unduly solemn, however, just as it would be to say that we inferred meanings from the written words on traffic signs or rest room doors. It might be quite correct on occasion to speak of inferring meanings from signs, for example, deciphering a code, or Linear B, but in the sense that such cases are inferential, the others cannot be.

We might, however, wish to relate thoughts or feelings to action or to other thoughts or feelings, where the connexion is not readily apparent. James's stream of consciousness is a case in point here, as are the so-called paralogical processes studied by psychiatrists. Suppose a woman becomes agitated at the sight of a steeple or a man becomes angered at some innocent remark. On these occasions we do want to say most of the things we normally say about causal connexions. *Unless* she had seen the steeple in that way, and *unless* he had given the remark that meaning, she would not have become agitated and he would not have become angry. But when we examine such extensions and attenuations of the normal links that forge together thought and action, we find, I think, that the procedure by which we related them is the same. In seeking the thought that would lead to the action, we are seeking the grounds that would justify it. Whether there is something 'within' or private that, from the agent's point of view, could be thought of as an occurrence or event, is irrelevant from the standpoint of explanation. For the thought or feeling, however disclosed, does not relate to its supposed effects after the manner in which one object impinges on another in an interacting physical system, but because it enters as a piece in a justifying, excusing or entitling manœuvre. Against this, psychologists have offered three alternatives. (1) A direct inspection of an internal occurrence is required in order to draw the connexion with subsequent internal or behavioural occurrences. (2) A procedure like (1) is impossibly at variance with scientific method, and consequently, we must deny that there are such occurrences at all (behaviourism). (3) The inner occurrence really would explain if we could get at it directly, but since, by (2), this is not compatible with scientific procedure, we must do our best to refine our method of observing what we can observe, and thus get the best index possible for constructing a model or hypothesis representing or reflecting the hidden occurrence. All three alternatives have life only so long as it is assumed that explanation is always causal in a mechanical sense. We can admit causal significance if one thing would not have happened unless something else had happened. In this sense temporal order is absolutely crucial, but our ways of providing a causally significant temporal order quite varied. One way consists in describing the interactions of bodies, another in providing statistical correlations, still another seeing an occurrence, a truth, a belief or an action as grounds for another. The thought happened and the action followed, but clearly not in the way that one billiard ball collides with another. The thought is not something that, watched closely by its owner, rolls about the head and knocks at the muscles. A person is simply engaged in thinking. That is what he is doing, and in doing it, consequences follow. Perhaps like this: I worked so hard I broke out in a sweat. Clearly a causal relationship, but not one connecting events in some discrete and readily identifiable way. Indeed, such an example serves best to illustrate the peculiar elusiveness of the concept of an event. The demand for a connexion between two discrete entities to satisfy a causal explanation is only intelligible if cause is identified with particular ways in which temporal links are forged, that is, interaction or statistical frequency. To do so, we overlook the way in which an activity, especially a thought, mood, or emotion, leads to its consequences.

Notice how easily causal talk might creep into a description of purely logical processes. Unless you take steps A and B you will be unable to reach conclusion C. The relationship of A and B to C may be *a priori*, but if our attention is drawn to a particular logician working the problem it becomes also a causal description of successive stages of his behaviour. Unless he had derived A and B he would not have derived C. The statement is temporal, but the authority for it mathematical and *a priori*. And so it is, though perhaps more vaguely, with the broader relationships of justification holding between thought and feeling and action. We are not forced to imagine, in order to explain action, that the mind is a special place in which special kinds of events must be apprehended or surmised, if we are to explain other events or actions that we suppose follow from them. On the score of explanation, then, we do not require the notion of occurrences which we can apprehend or infer by special means of intro-spection or hypothesis formation. We could, so far as the problem of explaining is concerned, rest quite content with the Ryleian reduction of mental things to species of doing, and the additional strategies of justifica-tion and excuse.

But we would still be wrong, surely, if we were on this basis to declare that there are no mental events. The reaction of the most conscientious reader of the above would still be: 'What, no pains but only recoil, no images or dreams but only bodily processes, no thoughts in the head but only those written, spoken or pantomimed?' Whatever the needs of explanation, we don't want to be driven into this corner. But we are still as far as ever from knowing what follows from our admission that there are unwritten or unspoken thoughts, felt pains and tickles, images and dreams. Perhaps some of the fog here is generated by those typical ontological pronouncements which have a way of getting out of hand and context. When someone says, there *are* so and so's, we would generally like to know 'and who denied it?' So, there are pains, not just physiological occurrences, there are tables, not just clusters of sense-data or atoms and the void. But our emphasis upon the existence of a favourite class of things has a way of recoiling from the reductionist targets at which they are aimed. 'There really are X's' suggests that there is some special virtue or property that X's share with the Y's our adversaries claim by way of ontology. Generally, when we begin to insist upon the existence of thoughts and feelings, images and dreams, it is against the materialist reduction of these to physiological occurrences and processes. Our insistence upon the reality of mental events is partly defensive. Thus it is not so surprising that we confer on them at least some of the physical properties to which the materialist claims to have reduced them. We want mental events, of course, to be radically different from physical events or objects, but at the same time to be sufficiently like them to be brought within our ontology without question, perhaps without the price of admission. This, I take it, is the familiar tension that arises for the Cartesian. He is really a confirmed materialist in his ontology, whatever he may be in his theory of explanation or his epistemology. Something like parallelism or a pre-established harmony is forced on those who follow Descartes, because they are thinking primarily of the difficulties of explaining mind-body interaction. And it is easy enough borrowing the Aristotelian distinction of efficient and final causes to construct a parallelism of explanation. A later offshoot of this view is the James-Russell theory of neutral monism. For here too the distinction between mind and body is created by different methods of explanation, a different ordering, of the same kind of stuff. Leibniz, in this sense also, retains a dualism of explanation with a monism in ontology. All such attempts are, I believe, rooted in a materialist ontology. To count as existing, one must show that something is a genuine object, characterized by interactions with its neighbours and properties like impenetrability and spatial and temporal location. Except for occurrence in time, however, none of these properties works out successfully for mental events and so the dualist is forced to an epistemological method for distinguishing minds and bodies or the mental and the physical.

It is worth noting, before turning to the epistemological question, the possible sense in which ontology could be thought of as a subject independent of epistemological or logical considerations. One might say that it depends on being able to list those properties which anything must have in order to count as real or existing, other than the property of being observed. An epistemologically based ontology, on the other hand, would make observation or experience the criterion for existence, though it might be possible to construct a Platonic ontology on the purely logical grounds that whatever serves, in virtue of its meaning, as an element of necessary or certain propositions, is real. But if we try to construct an ontology without benefit of epistemology, it becomes clear why materialism is tempting. For one thing, the natural tendency, when questioned about the existence of x, is to show that it has properties like impenetrability, that it occurs somewhere at some time, that it has shape and weight. It may be that we can only know these properties through observation, but we do not necessarily *mean* that they are only observable. In any event, if these are the properties that naturally occur to us as criteria for what exists, it is difficult to allow the existence of mental occurrences. At best we could say, mental occurrences share temporal properties with physical objects and occurrences, and at times spatial properties. But spatial properties, as exhibited by dreams and images, pains and other bodily sensations, are not three-dimensional, nor do they occur in a space relative to numbers of observers, nor are they tangible. If all these features are held to be marks of the real, so-called mental occurrences lose status, they become less real or ephemeral. And this shadowy character is reinforced by the considerations of explanation. By definition mental events do not affect the world, for the meaning of 'affect' is tied up, on this kind of view I am paraphrasing here, with the model of the inter-action of tangible bodies. So a thesis like epiphenomenalism takes shape, moulded by physicalist criteria for existence and causal criteria for explanation.

A materialist ontology can easily be extracted from common speech, for the simple reason that our most typical challenge to the question, 'Is there really one?' or 'Does it really exist?' is to produce something that can be handled and pointed to. Such questions do not normally arise with respect to events called mental, and so we are somewhat at a loss when asked, 'and now, about mental events, thoughts, feelings, emotions and the like, do they exist?' Our quandary has to do with the inability to place such a question in the context of argument. We know what is meant when someone challenges our claim to have seen Smith on the street, or a cuckoo in December, or a crocodile in the bath-tub. We could have been mistaken, we could have seen what only seemed to be Smith, a cuckoo, or a crocodile. Similarly, we can make the distinction of real and fake with respect to objects and artefacts, something that is the thing in question as against something that was made up to be the thing. These contrasts and hence these questions do not make sense with regard to thoughts and feelings. We cannot admit a claim to think or feel something while at the same time pointing out that the claim is mistaken. This, of course, has been made much of in philosophy, for it seems to make thoughts and feelings and anything else that could be brought under this general rubric incorrigible, and thus the basis for a properly founded epistemology. Wittgenstein, Austin and Ryle have in their separate ways given a rather different sense to this incorrigibility. It has in the past been construed as a kind of acquaintance with things so intimate that no slip could come, so to speak, between the observed and the observer. This view would bring thinking and feeling under the general rubric of observing. Wittgenstein, with his distinction of observing and having, Austin with his conception of performing, and Ryle with his analysis of the mental world into dispositions and attainments, have in various ways tried to show that thinking and feeling are concepts that cannot be brought within the class of observables.

I take it that the negative point made by all these philosophers is established. The concept of observation does seem to have a meaning when we talk about observing objects and people, actions and processes, which it can no longer have when extended to include thoughts and feelings. Perhaps this is because observation is linked to the business of verification. We talk about observing something as evidence for its occurrence. 'I saw Smith' is evidence that 'Smith is in town'. But we do not talk about observing our pains as evidence that we have pains, and even much less observing our thoughts as evidence that we are thinking our thoughts. The parallel construction would be rather improbable and irrelevant. I observed that I saw Smith is evidence that I saw Smith. A general contrast might be made then between observing and doing, something along the lines indicated by both Ryle and Austin. Observing is one sort of thing I can do, feeling is another, thinking another. Observation may result in reports and descriptions of what is observed, thought in speeches and arguments, feeling in expressive speech and action. There is, one might go on to say, a different sense of correctness, acceptability or, as Austin puts it, felicity, in each of these cases. The reports that issue from observation are true or false, the thoughts expressed cogent or irrelevant, logical or illogical, the feelings evinced appropriate or inappropriate, honest or sham.

Now this entire kind of analysis has a virtue which undoubtedly accounts for much of its current popularity. It is embarrassing to allow occurrences with which we have intimate and incorrigible acquaintance, because it is difficult to know exactly what we have said when we have made such a claim. There are no criteria for direct awareness or the clearness and distinctness of ideas, except that a person claims them as such. And this is as much a difficulty with Hume's forceful and vivacious impressions as it is with Descartes' clear and distinct ideas. There is no protection within this picture of the basis of knowledge against subjective excesses. We remove the temptation to think of the mental as referring to items of incorrigible acquaintance, if we speak of the mental as activities engaged in rather than events observed. We are no longer obliged to treat a person's utterances or his behaviour as reports of inner occurrences which we are in no position to challenge. It is true that his thoughts are his own, just as his movements are his own. But they are not reports of inner occurrences. And this turns out to mean that the proper way of evaluating his thoughts is not to treat them as reports of inner goings on, but in accordance with the relevant canons, that is, correctness of procedure (inference) and accuracy of representation, if the thoughts are about some objects or occurrences in the world.

Before including feelings, and perhaps other mental addenda, within this general picture, it is important to see how the question has shifted from the ontological to the epistemological status of alleged mental occurrences or acts. The new view tells us that the 'thingness' of something mental is irrelevant to the propriety of the statements or actions alleged to exhibit it. If I make my ontology dependent upon my epistemology, it looks as if I can then argue, there are no mental events, but only acts. For the concept of an event has been tied to the concept of observation; it is that in the world by which statements stand or fall. And we can say either that the language which appears to be about a mental realm does not consist of reports (in the manner of Austin) or that the truth of its claims do not depend upon inner occurrences (in the manner of Wittgenstein).

The result is a peculiar kind of epiphenomenalism. It may be that there are events which meet certain minimal ontological conditions, temporal location, perhaps spatial position and dimension, *but they do not matter*, for they cannot be enlisted as defences for statements. In a similar way, within the philosophy of science, epiphenomenalism would mean that with respect to explaining occurrences mental events do not matter. So far as explanation is causal, mental events do not cause. So far as that referred to as mental does explain, it does not do so causally, and hence does not require the status of event.

There are, then, various grounds on which the no-mental-event view might be taken. If it is a paradoxical view, it is because considerations from epistemology and the nature of explanation are taken as answering also the ontological question. Having denied that felt pains are causes of behaviour, in either the interaction or regularity senses, and having denied further that the experience of pain is necessary to decide on the propriety of certain utterances, it is then argued that they do not really exist. And then the retort comes: 'What! pains don't occur someplace at sometime?' And that, of course, cannot be what is meant. We could, in short, be explanatory or epistemological epiphenomenalists or materialists and at the same time be ontological dualists.

But the problem does not end there. An air of paradox remains even though we straighten out the sense in which the materialist, epiphenomenalist, or dualist position is maintained. This is because the terms, so often grouped together as denoting or defining a mental realm, are hard to bring under the same roof. The arguments of Ryle and Austin, for example, are very strong with respect to thought. It is highly improbable to treat thinking as a business of observing, catching, or contemplating one's thoughts, and to that degree it is very natural to suggest that there are, not thoughts but thinking, not intentions but intending, not purposes but purposing. If the question is raised as to how we come to think what we do unless thoughts occur, it is perfectly natural to answer that the promptings to our thoughts come from all sorts of things, including the objects, conversations, and other features of our environment. We do not need the concept of a mental entity different in kind from the words or actions that constitute thinking. If the question arises as to unspoken thoughts, Ryle's answer seems quite appropriate, they depend upon spoken thoughts. This perhaps does not dispel all the mystery surrounding these remarkable human capacities, but it need not be supposed that that is its purpose. It is indeed a very remarkable thing that we can think silently, or read without murmuring or moving the lips, or add without the aid of pencil and paper. These are, if you like, strange performances, but still performances. To call them shadow or imagined performances is to indicate that they share the nature of an activity with spoken or written acts. It is not to suggest that, lacking a visible performance, we must have recourse to hidden events which the mind, by some special faculty, observes. However embarrassing it may be to be forced to describe unspoken thoughts, it will not help to suppose that they are occurrences we observe, for then we will have deprived ourselves of even the rudiments of a method of description. If unspoken or unwritten thoughts are puzzling as *acts*, they are totally opaque as occurrences.

So the no-event thesis has much to recommend it in cases like thinking, intending, willing and purposing. Difficulties arise when we try to extend the analysis to other, and equally appropriate, uses of the term mental. Thoughts, it might be said, are eminently mental. But so are feelings. Therefore feelings must be susceptible to the same sort of analysis. To deny that feelings are events, however, is clearly paradoxical. It is a paradox that Ryle at times seems to embrace, in reaction to the possibly even more paradoxical view that the mind consists of entities or events or properties that are apprehended by some special means of observation. Perhaps the answer to both paradoxes lies in breaking up the concept of mind.

The division of the world into mental and physical realms has a certain plausibility so long as one thinks of the mind as a convenient repository for anything that does not count clearly as a physical occurrence. But the scope of the mental will vary, depending on the strictness and number of criteria we impose on the physical. If all we demand is spatio-temporal location, for example, pains and other bodily sensations might very well count as physical. So also might dreams and images. That we sometimes speak of physical pain is not necessarily to be thought of as an illustration of this use of physical, however. For physical pain is contrasted with mental pain in the light of their diagnoses. That is, it is the kind of explanation we give of a pain that leads us to classify it in this way. And this only shows that mental and physical are terms that enter into ordinary speech in a variety of ways and in order to make a variety of contrasts. Undoubtedly, we commonly ask that the physical meet the dual standards of the visible and the tangible, especially the latter. Pains, physical or otherwise, do not meet these standards. But when we speak of physical pain it does not reflect an inconsistent or incoherent view of the world. It is simply a different use, drawn in a different way from the visible-tangible use. Thus physical pain is associated with visible and tangible wounds, with characteristics of bodies. It is perhaps a mundane, but none the less important, observation that the starting point in talk about the 'physical' in ordinary speech is one's own body and the properties and processes that characterize it. This leads on the one hand to the visible-tangible mark of the physical, but on the other to sensations customarily experienced in the body. On either score, a cluster of concepts seems to have to do with occurrences or activities that can not be thought of as physical. Dreams, hallucinations (even though some of these are quite intimately attached to bodily sensations and processes), thoughts, images—these at least seem to be central cases of the non-physical.

But to what further extent, in being non-physical, are they alike? We need a piecemeal analysis here, for there is nothing that should lead us to suppose that they must in some further sense resemble one another. Indeed, no one, to my knowledge, has really advanced the view that they do resemble one another. That is why it becomes quite important for philosophers hankering after unity and simplicity to find a common *place* for all the putative members of this class. Like citizens of a country populated largely by immigrants, these various candidates to the mental exasperated 'I see it, there it is' reflects puzzlement as to what could be wanted. There is nothing more that could be done, and one might argue then that the absence of verifiability is not something uniquely characteristic of alleged mental phenomena. To deny mental phenomena ontological status or to downgrade them in an ontological scheme might then seem to be unwarranted on this basis, for surely I shall not downgrade current observation of the various pieces of furniture in my office just because I don't know what a person could mean in asking me to check whether they are really there.

An epistemologically derived ontology rests upon the conception of evidence, for epistemology is a business of providing warrants for statements. So a concept like the sense-datum is born, and so within a science a term like 'data' may come to be used. But it does not occur to a scientist to question what he sees, to question the data, but only the interpretation of them. Nor would it occur to him to think of his procedure of collecting or interpreting data as indicating an ontology according to which the world is composed of data. He has a special interest in occurrences which can be used as indices, measures, keys to larger patterns, general statements, laws or the behaviour and nature of invisible things. If we think of data as bits of evidence, it is because in general we are committed to looking at the data for what they may reveal. It is thus that the concept of a datum and by easy extension an occurrence or an object comes to be tied up with the notion of verifiability. The questions about the data are not with respect to whether they are there, so to speak, but whether they fit, whether the complicated measurements of them have been taken accurately, *whether they are data*. And these are questions about a whole scheme and procedure within a science. Such questions seem pertinent to the existence of an object in front of my eyes only because the procedures within a special science have been taken as the clearest instances of what in fact, though less clearly, is supposed to obtain for knowledge as a whole.

Note that a familiar way of making a distinction between observation and introspection, or between observing and having, depends upon this notion of verifiability, which in turn depends upon the notion of following a procedure. Thus it is argued that when we observe, we follow procedures which can be spelled out, but nothing like this is available if we are told to think of, imagine, feel or examine our pains. This distinction is plausible so long as we think of special and complicated manœuvres by which we adjust our vision or our touch to determine properties of objects. Measurement, for example, is a business of using the eyes, but it is also a business of laying down rulers and marking off. It is here that one can

---

state have similarity or identity conferred upon them by domesticating them to a common realm, the mind. One of the most typical moves in this direction is by means of the concept of experience. Thoughts and feelings, dreams and images are taken to occur because of or in the act of being experienced, in contrast to the way in which objects and events of the external world exist. But 'being experienced' is not the sort of positive criterion that would weld the disparate concepts included in the mind into a unity. For what counts as being experienced turns out to be another way of saying that the thing or event or occurrence in question belongs in some intimate way to the person who claims it, and this in turn seems to rest on a non-physical conception of the thing or occurrence. When an ordinary man talks about his experience, he seems to have in mind that contrast between what is his in some unchallengeable way and what is common to him and other observers, that which belongs to his point of view or his idiosyncracies as opposed to the world at large. It is easy enough to speak of thoughts and the like as experienced, because it is natural to speak of them as *mine*. It is, to be sure, a special sense of 'mine' which cannot, except by analogy, be employed when referring to my house or dog or car. But it can be illustrated by such an employment. For just as my house is legally inviolate, unless I invite others in, so my thoughts are inviolate unless I set about to share them by means of speech and action. And so we come back to the peculiarity that does seem to join thoughts to feelings and all the other items in the mental inventory, that they are private.

That they *are* private, however, must not be taken to mean that they *must* be private. To claim that they must be private is to say that even when I speak honestly, my words are not my thoughts, but signs or effects of them. This leads to the view that we infer what is going on in the minds of others from their speech and actions, an inference constructed by analogy to our own case. It has often been pointed out that the force of the inference is strangely weak in comparison to the degree to which we are convinced that other people think and feel.[2] Moreover, the supposition that we observe in ourselves the connexion of our speech and our thoughts is quite unintelligible, for we cannot give distinct descriptions of our thoughts and our speech. But we must not confuse the inadequacy of the view that we always infer what is going on in the mind of another with the plain fact that we sometimes do. For sometimes actions are opaque, speech misleading, and sometimes contexts alert us

[2] Cf. e.g. Norman Malcolm, 'Knowledge of Other Minds', *Journal of Philosophy*, Vol. 55 (1958), reprinted in V. C. Chappell, *The Philosophy of Mind* (Prentice Hall: Spectrum Books, 1962), pp. 151–9.

to the unlikelihood that a person is saying what he thinks or expressing what he feels. What we attribute to a person in such circumstances is what he would have said had he been honest, or how he would have behaved had he not heroically kept a stiff upper lip or suppressed a cry of pain.

This brings us to one last analysis of mind, beginning with logical points as to the use and the force of statements describing or asserting private phenomena. We want to know how an interpretation of the 'can't' in 'I can't know what is going on in the mind of another', or 'You can't feel my pains', affects a general conception of the way in which statements are true or false, necessary or contingent. These statements about the mind are presumably statements about the world, and ought by all odds to be contingent. But the 'can't' here is clearly not like the 'can't' in 'You can't run the mile in less than three minutes', or 'You can't see what's in the box'. It's not something you can try to do and fail. On the other hand, it's not clear either that telepathy would alter our view. If a man 'read' my thoughts, if he clutched his arm and howled when I cut my arm, or worse, if he clutched my arm and howled, would we say he's thinking my thoughts or feeling my pain? The answer to these questions would indicate the robustness with which we claim that we cannot feel the pains or think the thoughts of others. For if we persisted down to the end in saying, nevertheless it is not *his* thoughts or pains, our claim would be a somewhat anaemic one. We would be saying nothing more than we could say of a man running a race or scratching his head—no one can do his running or scratching, though he might, nefariously, get a substitute for the race or, lazily, a wife for his scratching. The alleged privacy of mental occurrences would in such a case be quite compatible with the no-event view, for the logic of the claim to privileged access would match the logic of activities. They too are privileged in the innocuous sense that only the performer can perform them.

But the inaccessibility that is ordinarily affirmed is not a logical right to having, but a logical confidence in keeping secret what is acted or owned. So it is supposed that a person knows his own mental acts or states in a way that no one else can, and this suggests the Cartesian doctrine of introspection as a special kind of inner observation. I can be haranguing a student in my office and thinking all the while of the evening martini, and he will never know. I will know, though, and this implies that I know about myself in ways that he cannot. Similarly, I know if and how my toe itches, my back aches, the content of last night's dream, the image that I am entertaining to my own subtle delight. All of this seems to restore the notion of interior observation and reflection, and with it

ontological status to thoughts, feelings, dreams and images. If we know these things about ourselves, it must be in principle possible to discove them, and if there is nothing to discover then we could hardly discove them. So there are mental events, sensations of reflections, streams o consciousness. So, at least, might go the rejoinder to Wittgenstein.

The issue here is so enormously complicated that it would require treatise to scratch its surface. It would moreover lead us somewhat awa from our concerns, so we must not enter into it, save to indicate its outline to an extent that would be germane to our purposes. It is clear in th first place that the concept of event is being treated as an epistemologic entity, that is, as the grounds for assertions. Furthermore all assertio which report or describe must be contingent. It must be possible reporting to make a mistake, for otherwise the dependence of an assertic on evidence is lost. A full-scale treatment of this issue would have come to grips with the notion of contingency, for it is the absence contingency which seems to require that we strike mental events fro the class of epistemological entities. It may be that the contrast betwe contingent and necessary has weighed too heavily on philosophers in t present kind of argument. Statements about one's pains may be co tingent in the sense that their utterance depends upon feeling pains, an not on the way in which concepts are used. But at the same time th may be certain, in that no possible evidence could be forthcoming th would overthrow them. Now this might also be held to be the case the observation that what is in front of me is a typewriter. What mak such an observation appear to be falsifiable is the gratuitous introducti of other observers. I do not know exactly what I would do if my neig bour came by and called it a piano, and the man from across the stre confused it with my cat, except that I might think them mad or go m myself. To ordinary people the demand for corroboration of such commonplace proposition about the world must seem capricious, wilf and without sense. And this in a way that contrasts very precisely w senses and cases in which corroboration would be thought relevant.

It is sometimes suggested that it makes no sense to ask a person check whether he really has his pain, and this has seemed to mark self-ascriptions of pains and other sensations from statements about oth or statements about the world. But the same senselessness may just well be taken as characterizing the request to check whether what I working at is really a typewriter. For in the pain case it is urged that o would not know how to go about checking, consequently having a pa is not having an epistemological entity. But would I know how to about checking whether this is really a typewriter in front of me? T

imagine making a mistake. One can imagine repeating the procedure and coming up with a different result. But this sort of doubt does not arise with respect to the fact that it was a ruler one was using or a table one was measuring. You cannot instruct a person in the procedure of looking, though you can outline places for him to look. You cannot instruct a person in hearing, savouring, smelling, except to the extent that some characteristic bodily movements can be imitated, like raising the hand to the ear or wrinkling the nostrils. And, of course, you cannot instruct a person to feel his pains. He does or he doesn't. But so also with a a person seeing what he sees, hearing what he hears, or feeling what he touches. If the notion of a procedure that can be carried out successfully or unsuccesfully is applied to cases of observation, it is in one of two senses. First, what we may have in mind are sophisticated observations, like measurement, or cases in which the observation figures as a last step in a chain of analysis or inference. This leaves unaccounted for a great many of the common or garden variety of observations outside the range of scientific theory, in addition to the noting of pains and other internal events. Second, the test for successful application of the procedure may be consensus. Observations of people, things and actions might thus be said to be checked by matching an individual's response against a standard answer. And this is possible with observing, but not with introspecting. But this is hardly profound, for it only reiterates that with which we began, namely, that the mental realm is a private realm. It was presumably this privacy that the Wittgensteinian analysis was designed to elucidate; instead it appears to invoke it.

We are left then with a realm of private affairs, of privileged access to possible objects of attention which can in principle be the objects of attention to only one individual. But perhaps this doctrine is not as offensive at the end of the analysis as it was at the beginning. The offence seems in the first place to be occasioned by what is thought to be the connexion between knowledge and evidence. It is assumed that anything that can be correctly asserted must be subject to check. It must make sense to look again, and hence it must make sense to be mistaken. We cannot be mistaken about the occurrence of our pains and our thoughts, therefore we could not properly be said to know about them. Epistemic considerations precipitate ontological views. When we deny that it makes sense to know that one has pains, it is all too easy to move to the view that pains do not exist but only pain behaviour. For that is something one could be said to observe and check. But when we see that the notion of checking, and thus being mistaken, is incoherent with respect to a large body of observations as well, the importance of blocking the move to a special kind of observation of one's internal states disappears.

In the second place, it must be remembered that the no privileged access (with its ontological corollary, no mental event) thesis is prompted in large measure by a view about the nature of perception. According to this view, to be found in Descartes, the British empiricists and Kant, the basis for our knowledge of the world is to be found in occurrences of the same order as our pains and bodily sensations. We perceive, according to this view, ideas, impressions, phenomena, sense-data, and these are internal occurrences. They belong to the mind. The importance, in Wittgenstein, of the distinction between observing and having is to bring out the vast differences between perceiving objects and experiencing bodily sensations. The former arise in the public context, in which, at the very minimum, consensus plays an important role; the latter occur in a private context in which consensus has no point. I am not concerned to advocate any particular view about the nature of perception here, but only to indicate what a muddle the concept of mind becomes if we allow that perceptions are just other kinds of internal sensations. So long as 'look about you' or 'reach out your hand and touch' have meaning, our notion of perceiving is radically different from our notion of introspecting, or whatever is taken to be the proper term to apply to awareness of bodily sensations. The difference could, perhaps, be formulated this way. A description of perceiving does not require mention of any particular kind of thing perceived. We look and listen, touch, taste and smell, by employing various organs of sense. We feel pains, tickles and itches, without a separately describable act of attention. The relation between perceiving and the object perceived is thus contingent, the connexion between feeling and the kind of thing felt necessary, in the sense that no separate process can be described. Or we might say, that no one can do our perceiving for us is a trivial tautology, just in the sense that no one can do our running, voting or speaking. But others can perceive what we can perceive. When, on the other hand, we say no one can feel our pains, we mean that the pains themselves are our own, and not merely that no one can do our feeling of them.

But this can be the first step toward a behaviouristic or materialist ontology, if we are not careful to distinguish the very different questions, how we know and what there is. If we make knowing dependent upon checking, then it becomes difficult to talk about knowing pains. But then we are tempted to say: and if we don't know them, how can there be any? Here we need either to divorce the epistemological and ontological questions or widen our conception of what it is to know. In either case the ontological question turns out to be primary, for the pressure is exerted on our epistemology through a prior commitment to the existence of objects with which we may be said to be acquainted in a way that does not permit checking.

But what exactly do we mean by there are pains, there are thoughts, there are feelings, moods, images, and dreams? Or better, why should such assertions appear gratuitous or peculiar? Perhaps this. When we say, there really is water on the road, it is because we see some of the properties of a possible object joined by others. We saw a rippling surface dancing in the sunlight, and now we are getting wet, the car has stalled, we feel the current around us. But contrast this with, there really are shadows or mirror images. The sense of this sort of assertion can no longer be within some initially considered class of things to which we are adding confirming properties. For shadows and mirror images have only visual properties. So in asserting the existence of shadows or mirror images a philosophical point is being made. Perhaps we have been led, by the common cases of mirages or illusions, to think of existence as meaning tactual properties, and not merely as guaranteed by them. And so we should have to deny that shadows are real. Yet they still *are* shadows, and such a statement reminds us that we must not confuse a common criterion for existence with its meaning.

Perhaps we do not feel too uncomfortable about this kind of extension of the meaning of existence. At least shadows are still spatio-temporal events. We should only be inclined to downgrade them ontologically if we were thinking of problems of explanation. We do not, within an interaction picture of explanation, think of shadows as having consequences. But now suppose we extend the case again to thoughts, feelings, dreams and images. We might say, surely we will find thoughts and feelings in the catalogue of existing things. It might be thought, for example, that thoughts survive in that they satisfy the minimum condition of duration through time. Thoughts exist in the sense that people engage in thinking. Note here that it is a little odd to say that activities exist, a man's walking, for instance. Yet there *are* activities that characterize a man or beast. We only hesitate to include them in our ontological inventory because of the addiction to the central sorts of cases where the assertion of existence has practical bearings and significance, that is, where our search for further properties seems warranted by what falls within our purview. As in the case of shadows, thoughts and feelings are remarkable in that no further properties can be cited that would satisfy us as to their existence. A pain is just a pain, a thought a thought, and so on. We do not find cases of thought and feeling which the evidence partially justifies and which further evidence will clinch. Questions about the existence of thoughts or feelings, images or pains, do not arise in any natural way, and we are forced to the oddity of asserting their existence only to make a philosophical point against those who have identified existence with some particular criterion for existing, by reducing the catalogue of things to physical objects, atoms, sense-data or spatio-temporal events.

There is still a difficulty within the philosophy of mind, however. A comparison with shadow and mirror images is instructive if it liberates us from a too oppressive materialist ontology. But if it is forced too far, it can lead us to a view which, possibly, accounts for some of Descartes' difficulties with the mind-body problem. The Cartesian mind is in many ways like a collection of shadows, visible but not tangible. It then becomes difficult indeed to understand how such ephemeral entities can play the role they do in causing action. The pineal gland is like a trans-former in this system, it beefs up the mental into physical occurrences, and steps down the physical into mental occurrences. But this surely won't do. Beefing up and toning down are processes which must begin with something that remains identical through the process. It is surely not that mental occurrences are simply less of the same sort of stuff that makes up physical objects. Indeed, Descartes would be the first to repudiate such a suggestion. Yet, as Ryle points out, Descartes seems to be committed to it in treating mind and body both as kinds of stuff, one hard and impenetrable, the other shadowy. I suspect that the preoccupa-tion with vision had a good deal to do with setting both epistemology and the philosophy of mind on their courses. Vision, certainly, accommo-dates itself to the manufacture of ghostly entities, whether ectoplasmic or mental, for one can always abstract and sometimes find purely visual entities, colour patches, after-images, illusions, shadows, mirror images and sometimes dreams. So one gets, in Descartes and much of the philo-sophy that stems from him, the cinema picture of the mind, and it is this that Ryle so rightly and devastatingly rejects.

But this rejection itself looks paradoxical. The mind, to be sure, is not a private theatre, playing films that aren't allowed to public audiences. To break the hold of this idea, Ryle has recourse to the view that we can't witness or attend to mental phenomena. By this epistemological bridge, it is but a step to the denial of goings on within altogether, a view which Ryle himself begins to find fault with, in an article coming on the heels of *The Concept of Mind*.[3] The point is, it does seem appropriate to talk

---

[3] 'Feelings', *Philosophical Quarterly*, Vol. 1 (1950).

about witnessing inner goings-on, so long as we do so without the suggestion of visual experience. We don't look at our pains, of course, but no
one, including Descartes, would really wish to suggest that we do. But
we do dwell on them, compare their quality to other pains or itches or
tingles that we have experienced, and describe them. A doctor can ask a
patient to look for certain painful signs of his illness. We could easily
enough construct experiments to inform someone as to the nature of the
pain we feel. In fact, young boys find this a particularly amusing pastime,
twisting arms, pummelling each other, and engaging in other such
pleasantries, asking all the while in eager anticipation, 'Does it hurt?'

None of this makes experiencing pain like seeing objects—or does it?
One objection to saying it does is that it seems to make the object seen
coextensive with the act of seeing, with the solipsistic consequences that
such a view entails. For the existence of a pain and the awareness of a
pain are distinct. We want to say that we come upon, look at, listen to,
touch, smell or taste objects and leave them behind. They were there
before us and remain after our departure. But we do not want to say
that pains are there, and at some moment or other we become aware of
them and then leave them behind. If this is the source of Ryle's qualms,
and Wittgenstein's too, then perhaps what they are after is a term which
will cover just those cases where we want to allow continued existence.
Very good. But the difficulty is that they are appropriate terms which
serve a rather different purpose, that of showing the *similarities* among
sights, sounds, tastes, smells, and feelings. Perhaps we could describe the
similarity among these and other cases by using terms like occurrence and
awareness. This would allow us to describe, and not merely evince or
display, feelings, and it would show also that, unlike other descriptions of
occurrences, descriptions of feelings are peculiar in not allowing for the
possibility of mistake. But nothing follows from this unless we treat the
feelings on the model of vision or touch, or vision on the model of
feeling.

It is also worth noting the radical differences within the favoured class
of observations. A world constructed out of visual experience would be
corrigible, in the sense that what one took to be an object of a certain
sort might turn out not to be an object of that sort or perhaps not even an
object at all. But this is not possible with respect to the solidity of an
object. If we touch, press, crush or in any way handle an object, we cannot
be mistaken in supposing that it is an object. If it supports the weight and
resists the fist, it satisfies what we mean by an object. Yet handling is a
mode of awareness or observation. Tastes and smells, on the other hand,
are much more apt to be thought of as temporary phenomena, coexisting

with our experience of them. Something, of course, exists before or remains behind, but we would be reluctant to say that it is the smells or tastes that survive, but rather some property which we hold to irritate the nostrils and caress the palate and so cause the sensations. Pain is like this too. We distinguish sharply between wounds and pain. It is thus, by the way, that we seem to be led to a causal theory of perception and to the concept of experience. For experience can be used to refer to that which happens to a person as a result of being affected by stimuli. In this sense it is not quite clear what can be meant by either visual or tactile experience, for we have no means of distinguishing the causes from their experienced effects.

These are random observations which, in a treatise on perception or philosophy of mind, would need to be systematized. Enough has been suggested for our purposes, I hope, to indicate the difficulties in any attempt to treat the mind or perception or experience as univocal concepts. These terms cover, in Wittgenstein's expression, a family of cases. Awareness is a term common to all members of the family. Yet this term itself has only the slightest epistemological significance, indicating that they are all, in various ways, methods of becoming acquainted with the world, inner and outer. A major division might be made, into observation and introspection, provided that nothing more was made of these notions than what could be expressed by saying that some of the items with which we are acquainted are external and others internal. But even this would not quite do. For a notion like internal may suggest something within the skin, as in the case of aches and pains, but something quite different in the case of dreams or thoughts. In the case of thoughts, again, we need to think rather of activities than observed or introspected occurrences. Mental images have contributed something to the notion that in thinking, one is witnessing internal occurrences, for images can have visual or visual-like properties and at the same time they can be the vehicles for acts of thought. The answer might be that of course images might count as occurrences, if all that was meant was that they can have the contours and qualities of visual experience, can last for stretches of time, and can even be 'seen' somewhere, for example, before the eyes. But they are, as Ryle insists, not observed, in the sense that one comes upon them, but are constructed. And looked at in this way an image is something done, not something watched. But so to a painter is a picture, or to a sculptor a statue. Only we do not or cannot watch a man constructing pictures in his head.

All of this, as I have suggested, needs a much more sober and detailed working out. I have only wished to indicate that one could admit mental events into one's ontology without incurring the dire epistemological consequences, or further ontological consequences, with which Ryle and Wittgenstein threaten us. These consequences follow only if we make too much of our distinctions and categories, and assume that, if seeing and feeling are allowed to resemble one another in one respect, they must resemble one another very undesirable and in other paradoxical respects.

But now to return home. What does the admission of mental events have to do with our topic of explanation? Can we allow such occurrences without allowing also a causal relationship between physical stimuli and mental events, and mental events and physical actions, or for that matter between one mental event and another? Once again, the answer seems to be that, allowing the status of event to the mental does not involve all the consequences that seem to come in that philosophical packet. It looks as if we are obliged to say that, in admitting events, we admit a world joined by causal connexions. But the case of images may serve as a reminder here. They qualify as events, but inasmuch as they are human doings, intended as opposed to observed, they enter into relations with other items in the network of reasons and not that of causes. Or, if you like, we could admit them as causes in the sense that, unless a person thought them he would not have acted the way he did. But this should not require us to picture these causal relations on the interaction or regularity models. The temporal order is present, but the manner of joining these links in the chain is logical; it consists in seeing the image or the thought as the grounds for acting. The same, I have urged, is the case with the relation of pain and other feelings to the kind of behaviour that ensues. Beyond that, we must construe physical cause as going on in an uninterrupted fashion from physical event to physical event. The fatal mistake lies in supposing that the mental occurrence is a link that fills a gap in a physical chain, not that it can form links with physical events.

There are further problems, of course, and very hard ones. I think that among the most difficult are the cases in which we talk about the physical causes of feelings. They are difficult because we are so prone to make them, yet have no analysis of our way of apprehending such relationships commensurate with the sureness of our observations or inferences. The interaction model of colliding bodies is clearly irrelevant to our account of the relationship between wound and pain. But the regularity model hardly conveys the force of our assurance in this connexion. And the logical or warranting model does not quite do the job. It is much easier with the effects of pain, which, as I have suggested, do well enough within the logical or warranting model. The relationship between wound and pain strikes me, in fact, as one of the most plausible bases for an epiphenomenalist position, just because it does not match any of the paradigms of explanation, yet seems to be such an obvious case of explanation. With this exception, however, enrolling mental events in our ontology is not going to force us to replace logical or moral explanations of human action with a scientific psychology in which the mental occurrences are treated as constructs to be defined and refined by precise measurements of behaviour. Status as events does not entail the kind of explanation to which the psychologist subscribes. Moreover, it is at least reasonably clear that the items which he wishes to bring into the ontological club—motives and drives, perhaps intentions and purposes—cannot be construed as events at all. They enter the language as means of isolating and describing actions in virtue of the conventions and rules that govern human life.

CHAPTER EIGHT

APPLICATIONS TO SOCIAL SCIENCE

IN CHAPTER II, I was concerned to exhibit some of the mournful consequences of the psychologist's and sociologist's addiction to methodology at the expense of genuine inquiry. In the chapters that followed I attempted to build an alternative account of the explanation of human action, testing it primarily against the methods and theories of academic psychology, though on occasion, as in the use of economics in the analysis of need, I have exploited areas in the social sciences in developing my account. By and large, however, the social sciences have been neglected in this presentation, and only the more exaggerated form of sociological theory was dealt with in Chapter II. It is now time to repair this omission, by taking up some of the major issues in anthropology, sociology, economics and political science in the light of the theory of moral explanation I have been developing.

ANTHROPOLOGY

Recall first that the anthropologist was at the beginning a traveller. By virtue of his acquaintance with parts of the world out of reach of most of us, he could tell stay-at-homes interesting stories about the diet and economy, the religious and sexual practices of alien and often exotic peoples. His talk looks to be of a piece with that of one's neighbour who has just come back (with slides) from Bermuda or a tour of the Western Parks.

Why is not every traveller an anthropologist? For one thing, it is a matter of acuity of observation. This is not something that can be formulated into anything as impressive (or oppressive) as a methodology. It is a matter of patient watching, and watching from a point of view that makes the alien behaviour intelligible by drawing likenesses and marking differences between practices abroad and at home. For another thing, the anthropologist faces barriers in communication and understanding beyond anything faced by the English traveller in France, or the American in Scandinavia. Differences are greater when it is a matter of the Englishman or the American among the Dobu or Andaman Islanders. A human practice among such groups is much more likely to be misinterpreted by the anthropologist than are the actions of one's cultural neighbours by the less venturesome tourist. Eating one's enemy's brains or dodging out of the way of an approaching sister are not easily identifiable acts, in the

way that a bargaining Italian or the ceremonial embrace among French-
men can be understood. There is a discontinuity of meaning here which
requires a way of understanding and explaining behaviour different from
anything that can be noticed in accounting for one's own or one's neighbours' behaviour.

This is the primary sense, it seems to me, in which the anthropologist
might be said to explain what he observes. He shows that a highly
puzzling act is the done thing, he exhibits the beliefs which provide the
rationale for such conventions or ceremonies. The same might be said
for sociological explanations except that they are offered with respect to
practices already understood and engaged in, and so these accounts seem
unnecessary and pretentious. Once we are able to say 'his sister is taboo',
or 'he wants to assimilate his enemy's mana', we have explained the
sudden decision to walk another and quite inappropriate way or the
peculiar fervour, not to be confused with enjoyment, with which the
brains are gulped down.

How does the anthropologist come to see behaviour in this way? For
one thing, he asks people. Of greater importance, he comes to live the
life of the people he investigates. He develops the capacity for identifying
objects and situations and ceremonies after their lights. And this might
be called research, and so be thought of as a scientific enterprise. Nothing
would be wrong with this, except that philosophers and social scientists
have interpreted terms like research and science in rather special ways.
This is our old acquaintance: scientific explanation consists either in
(a) inductive generalization or (b) the construction of hypotheses embrac-
ing a great number of cases, and from which further instances can be
shown to follow. It is difficult to assimilate the anthropological traveller
to either (a) or (b). Consequently anthropology is only a collection of
traveller's tales with no particular scientific significance, or else it is really
theoretical after all, and anthropologists of the past, in their methodological naïvety, have failed to formulate hypotheses with sufficient rigour
to allow for observations or experiments which would support them in
a decisive way.

I shall argue for the first of these options, but without prejudice, that
is, without the pejorative 'mere' or 'only' qualifying the terms. Travellers'
tales can be, as much as scientific theories, contributions to human knowledge; they can be better or worse, more or less accurate. Moreover, they
are not the first and random comments that some day will be organized
into a scientific theory. They are sufficient unto themselves. The pattern
of explanation in anthropology is not a poor approximation of the
generalizing and experimental and predictive capacities of the methods

of science, but moral explanation, within which instances may be judged more or less adequate.

Let me illustrate this, first by reference to amateur accounts, to travellers' tales, rather than to the possibly more self-conscious work and writing of the professionals. Laurens van der Post, having spent much time among the Bushmen, and being willing to enter into a strange way of life, is able to say quite different things about the practice of exposing the aged than is another man, like Robert Ruark, whose conception of the African was governed by the rituals of his own culture. The latter describes the practice of leaving the old on the savanna to die as if it were a case of complete moral indifference, animal rather than human behaviour. The Africans to him simply have no finer feelings. In van der Post, on the other hand, we see the abandonment performed in a vivid ceremony, emphasizing the continuity of the race, and ensuring its perpetuity. He does not fail to notice, as Ruark does, the solemn grief at parting, as the young leave their aged to the mercy of the lions and hyenas, if not to a worse death. He sees also the acceptance of this practice by those so condemned, and the necessity of it forced on the Africans by the rigours and want that characterize their life. Is the difference here merely a choice of prejudices or values? It is surely a matter of values. Ruark sees the practice as an isolated piece of grist for his own moral mill; he makes no attempt to place the practice in its context. And this makes the difference. Ruark makes a moral judgment, but van der Post arrives at a moral assessment. The first requires nothing beyond one's arsenal of moral convictions and a case to which to apply them. The second requires a much more detailed description of what might be called the moral ecology within which the practice is observed. The first reflects the interference of values with accurate description which social scientists rightly deplore. The second is a case of moral explanation, based upon the most detailed factual picture possible.[1]

Still, someone committed to a rather different way of talking about human affairs might argue that what is seen here is a typical pattern of apology or attack. The example betrays an inclination to count as understanding, anything that justifies conduct. This is perhaps one sort of answer that is commonly anticipated to the question 'why?' So the mother's despairing 'why?', as once more her child forgets to leave his dirty overshoes in the hallway, or the lover's bewildered 'why?' to his

[1] For the views of van der Post cf. his Lost World of the Kalahari (Penguin, 1962), and The Heart of the Hunter (Penguin, 1965). As for Ruark, this, it seems to me, was the substance of his remarks in a television interview several years ago. I am unable to recall the exact occasion. It is, in any event, a common enough attitude among colonials, and anyone looking at foreign customs simply as departures from his own.

partner's infidelities. But it can, or should, be replaced by a question having a different sense.

I do not know whether a different kind of answer *can* be given. Indeed, though it is common enough for philosophers of science or of mind to decide what questions can and can't be asked of a given subject matter, I am not quite sure what is to be accomplished by such a piece of logical legislation, or how it is to be accomplished. It often appears to be a matter of second-guessing the future course of science by constructing logical necessities out of current theories. So positivists and logical empiricists have given the green light to the construction of hypotheses in sociology, and some disciples of Wittgenstein have, on the other hand, suggested that what the sociologist must do is to provide accounts which appeal rather to conventions or rules of the game. But it can be very embarrassing to a philosopher to demarcate with papal authority the domains and procedures of the several branches of knowledge only to discover that somewhere or other someone is doing quite successfully just what the philosopher told him he couldn't possibly do.

Beyond matters of caution and self-protection, however, it does appear that such philosophical theories are usually sustained by the analysis of sample theories, explanations, or other sorts of knowledge claims taken to be standard or paradigm. Thus the question as to what *can* be merges very readily into the question what should be.

I do not believe that current practice of social scientists is vitiated because they have fixed on the wrong paradigm. They have not had success with that paradigm, but that is a different thing. Hypothetico-deductive accounts in sociology are grotesque parodies of sciences like mechanics, and the anthropologist, seeking accuracy by recording native dances on tape and film, and then analysing them into their component steps, is no doubt caricaturing rather than using 'scientific' procedures of measurement, in order to assure himself a place in science's promised land. These are misuses of the physicist's ways of devising hypotheses and gathering evidence, not because these methods cannot or should not be applied to human beings, but because this aspect of the sociologist's work is out of step with the rest of his inquiry. The concepts that shape sociological thinking include status and role, convention and function, and these concepts force us to view society in ways that defeat the application of scientific rigour and method. For these are concepts which belong to the moral realm of discourse. To identify instances of status or role, convention or function, is already to understand them. Thus, theories and statistics as means of explaining are otiose in these fields. In the remainder of this section and in the next, I shall argue this thesis, first with respect to the concepts that cluster around 'convention', and second, those that cluster around 'function'.

'Convention' embraces a number of other concepts, among them status and role. They have in common the sense of carrying out instructions, doing assigned tasks, and playing one's part. If behaviour is seen as a performance, it is automatically explained in a certain way. A priest celebrating mass, a merchant bargaining in the market-place, a Park Avenue heiress walking her poodle, are, among hosts of others, events or actions which do not need explaining. This is not because they are difficult, opaque, or too unique to afford the accommodation of general theory, but because they are transparent. A way of life provides the capacity to observe and identify such acts. Since a way of life is essentially a repository of action-guiding reasons acquired in a moral education, this observation and explanation is, properly speaking, moral observation and explanation. To know that a priest is celebrating mass is, in general, to know why he is doing it. The note of novelty and research is sustained in the anthropologist's account, because he investigates the actions of those whose moral instruction differs from his own. The discordant note of redundancy in the sociologist's account is produced by the clash of a proposed method of research with actions already explained by the moral education common to the investigator and investigated.

The picture often given of sociology is of a vast assemblage of facts or 'data' which require mathematical trimming so that the underlying structure accounting for them is revealed. This aim is most clearly seen in the work of Parsons in sociology and Nadel in anthropology. But when the structure is described, as it is by Parsons and Nadel, through the use of terms like status and role, it is no longer clear why hypotheses or more rigorous mathematical treatment are necessary or appropriate. A book like Nadel's *Theory of Social Structure* is an extraordinary remove from the anthropological data with which, allegedly, it is to cope.[2] Nadel feels that anthropology is ready for the techniques of mathematical logic, but the relationships he formalizes are conventional in nature. They are roles based on age, sex, kinship, leadership, skill, service, partnership, and a group of rather shaky (for symbolization) creative or 'belief' communicative functions, like those of the artist and the orator (compare his chart, p. 53). When the nature and prerequisites of the role are clear, formalization is neither necessary nor helpful. When they are not, symbolization only succeeds in giving a false sense of security.

[2] S. F. Nadel, *Theory of Social Structure* (Free Press, 1957).

If the relationship between two or more individuals or groups is understood as the practice of a role, the action is thereby explained conventionally. The convention that governs a role, together with the suitability of the agent to perform the role, entitles the individual or the group to act as he or it does. The relation of entitlement is a logical relation; if we understand the convention we must understand the actions which follow from it. If we are able to identify an individual as the possessor of a certain role, we also know why he acts as he does.

In a recent monograph Peter Winch argues along similar lines, suggesting that sociology ought therefore to be thought of as a business of conceptual analysis, akin to philosophy instead of empirical science.[3] His argument, it seems to me, needs a good deal of restating. It applies with some force to the logic of explanation of conventional actions. But (1) it leaves out of account the manner in which conventions are deciphered and (2) it gives the impression that the sociologist or anthropologist is concerned only with intra-cultural or intra-conventional actions.

As to (1), if we have the convention in hand, so to speak, it is perhaps only a piece of conceptual analysis that leads us to the entailed or entitled actions. But for every convention in the hand, there are two in the bush. There are obscurities in much of human action which can be clarified by deciphering the conventions governing these actions, if we can first get at the convention in question. How we discover or disclose the conventions governing action is a complicated story. But surely it is not a story of conceptual analysis, but of the arduous and detailed observation of behaviour. A book like William H. Whyte's *The Organization Man* may serve as an example. In it one sees much of the behaviour of the managerial class in the United States stemming from rules of a rather unusual game or code. But the code itself is not written up in rule books or on bronze plaques for Whyte to read and apply to the behaviour of the organization people. The code is itself extrapolated from the behaviour and the talk, which then become understandable as conventional. This is empirical research in a straightforward sense. Evidence is collected, compared and tabulated. But the explanation is not some further device, brought to bear upon the generalizations that emerge from the behaviour; it comes when the investigator sees the actions of this class as rule-abiding. It would be odd to insist that the explanation should now extend to further instances, after the manner of the application of an explanatory hypothesis in science, and in a way that implies that further evidence is required to support the explanation. Further evidence would show only that the

[3] Peter Winch; *The Idea of a Social Science* (Routledge & Kegan Paul, 1958).

rules are more widely practised; it would not support or shore up the application to the original cases.

(2) raises a different order of problems. The actions of individuals or groups may appear conventional. But what of the drift and variability in the conventions themselves? A man may act in certain ways because he is a father. But why do some cultures prescribe some kinds of conduct to fathers, and other cultures assign quite different roles? Why, even further, do kinship regulations have the kind of universal application and adoption that anthropologists can show in their surveys of cultures? These and other questions about human habits and institutions are surely legitimate, even though the answers customarily given to them are equivocal and metaphorical. Indeed, they might be regarded as among the more pressing and important questions for anthropologists to answer. One kind of answer or method of providing an answer to such questions is the thesis usually labelled functionalism. I shall now turn to an examination of this thesis, and the disputes that arise between functionalists and their methodological competitors.

FUNCTION

The functional thesis is most closely associated with the name of Malinowski, and I shall be basing my remarks largely on his sponsorship of the thesis in *A Scientific Theory of Culture*.[4] His thesis is much like that of Wittgenstein's with respect to the meaning of language. Where Wittgenstein says, ask not for the meaning, but the use, Malinowski says, ask not what the culture trait is, but what is its use (p. 118). The nature of a trait cannot be discovered by its form, which may be universal, but by the way in which it combines with other traits to carry on social activities (pp. 148–9).

Let us apply this thesis first to tools, which provide obvious cases for functional analysis. Very little has been said about a tool in classifying it according to its form or material, stone or wood, core or flake, hafted or thonged. These items of archaeological description do indeed help delineate the patterns of distribution in space and time, facts which are sometimes ignored or depreciated by Malinowski. But that we choose to call them tools in the first place implies that we look at them in addition as designed to do a certain job, as performing a certain function. When Leakey a few years ago showed that one could skin an animal with a prepared core (or was it a flake?) he was offering evidence that the chipped

---

[4] Bronislaw Malinowski, *A Scientific Theory of Culture and Other Essays* (Oxford University Press: Galaxy Books, 1960).

stones liberally deposited in Palaeolithic deposits *were* tools. They could do the job.

To say that a thing is a watch is to say that it tells time, or at least that, cleaned, repaired and set, it would tell time. To say that a thing is a knife is to say that it cuts, if properly sharpened. But it is to say also that it is *used* to tell time, or to cut. Watches and other complicated machines are obviously the central or paradigm cases here. We feel no uneasiness in speaking of the use of an artefact dug up out of the soil and out of its context, or inferring all sorts of things about its users. But there are shadings and borderlines. Cases arise in which we become less comfortable, less secure, in calling the item in question a tool. It is much the same, of course, in philosophy. Following Wittgenstein's procedure, one is tempted to find uses in the automatic way that philosophers formerly assigned meanings to any assemblage of letters. Yet clearly language contains a great deal of dead wood. There are many words in the language similar in form or context to other words to which use can confidently be assigned, but which themselves are idling expressions. This is one of the difficulties in taking paradigms of descriptive or game-playing discourse so seriously that it is assumed that any linguistic act has at least the credentials for entrance into one of the classes of language act typified by the paradigm cases. Similarly, taking tools as a paradigm of anthropological investigation can lead to possibly grotesque results when applied to typical social habits and institutions. Is it the function of marriage to insure the care of the young, or of sexual taboos to underwrite marriage arrangements by placing a brake upon the socially disruptive effect of sexual urges? (Malinowski, p. 208). At least is this the function of marriage or taboos in the sense that it is the function of Leakey's chipped core to skin an animal or of a watch to tell time?

In one sense we *describe* something as functional, like a tool; in another sense we *appraise* something as functional. It is in this latter sense that the term applies to institutions and culture traits. Most members of a community marry and beget children, and recoil from sexual contact with relatives, but they do not individually do so to preserve the species, or provide a stable environment for raising children. To individuals the institutions are conditions of the environment which shape, inhibit or promote their desires, plans and actions. Anthropologists do not regard the bounty or parsimony of nature, or the soil, rainfall, rivers, mountains and harbours, as functional. But all of these conditions of the environment may be appraised as functional, and may be made use of accordingly. A man is born into society, as he is born into a physical environment, and he may make use of both to further his or others' ends. The institution of marriage and the features of the landscape may be *assessed* as functional. Tools, on the other hand, are *designed* to perform a function; it is not that they happen to or that they are found lying around and turn out to do the job. We might call design the strong and narrow, and assessment the weak and broad sense of function.

Human institutions are easy enough to appraise as functional. Consider, for example, Lévi-Strauss's description of kinship and marriage systems in *Man, Culture, and Society*.[5] There are for him certain conditions which social arrangements are designed to fulfil. A society needs to be able to assign a status to a new-born or newly-arrived member. Marriage arrangements are required, together with sexual taboos, to insure the possibility of determining a man's lineage, which is the simplest way of assigning an individual a place in society. The family supplies the key to social order, providing continuity and rank, together with an easily ascertainable way of deciding how to act toward another person in the group.

This account derives its power from the tradition of inherited status. If we look at social organization through the imperatives of rank and place (status and role), we can assess institutions of marriage and kinship as more or less effective instruments to this end. It becomes more difficult if one wonders why there should be such imperatives in the first place. For, like tools, institutions are facts, but unlike tools, the needs against which the function of an institution is to be measured are not biological or ecological constants, but are induced in part by the very institutions that are supposedly designed to satisfy them. In the case of a tool, there are certain conditions to be met and certain clear limitations on the manner of doing the job. One may choose not to do the job; instead of skinning the animal and preparing a core to do so, one may live on nuts and berries. Still the tool is the clue to the purposes of its users, and thus exhibits its functional character. The only condition that appears to be remotely analogous to this in the case of institutions is the necessity of providing some permanent organization to provide for the young. That every society has such institutions is thus ascribable to such needs. But the great variety in form of institutions cannot be explained as accommodations to this necessity. Kinship regulations, the assigning of status, and all the usual concerns of anthropologists acquire functional importance only given a conception of rules and regulations as a background to the functioning of institutions. The social forms are assumed to begin with.

[5] Harry L. Shapiro (ed.), *Man, Culture, and Society* (Oxford University Press: Galaxy Books, 1960), pp. 282–4.

The picture of functionalism that emerges is this. We approach the investigation of habits and institutions by way of the question we can also ask of tools, namely, what are they for? But the answer to this question varies, depending on whether we are entitled to talk about a designed or an appraised artefact or activity. An institution is not a piece of machinery designed to resolve antedating needs; it is rather the form which allows anthropologists to talk about needs. The need for family life is inconceivable outside the institution of the family. Consequently it would be circular to speak of the institution as answering to that need. It is all too easy here to fall into the language of determinism. When we say marriage answers to certain needs (generated by the institution as part of the environment) it is as if we could also say circumstances caused or compelled the development of family life. But if the connexion were deterministic we would expect to find concomitant variation between the environment (physical and biological) and the institution. In a sense we don't even know quite what the scope of such variables are. How are we to pick out the relevant features in the environment, for example? And thus the putative causal relationship is apt to reduce to the trivial claim that there is family life in every physical environment. When we do succeed in disclosing relevant features of the environment, they turn out to be themselves cultural factors, that is, institutions, and thus appeal to the environment fails as an explanation of the institution.

Situations are seen as constituting needs because we have cast our observations in the language of purpose and goal. To understand that a situation embodies a need is not achieved by generalizing the connexions among observed particulars. It is to see the situation as valued. So to explain cultural phenomena functionally is to see patterns in actions and institutions in the light of goals and principles which these practices help or hinder. It follows that the institutions themselves must be in existence, as part of the situation to be appraised, for us to introduce notions like the satisfaction of need and function. Need, like function, is a term of appraisal. It notes a logical, not a factual relationship between ecology and action.

Anthropologists, like their sociologist colleagues, hanker after generality and causal laws, and the sort of fact-collecting that seems to add up to generalizations upon which theories may be built. Needs are made use of to tie together the facts by means of an explanatory theory, and so it looks as if they could be employed to state general truths about human and social development. But the generality achieved or hoped for, as Malinowski recognizes, is often so all-inclusive as to be vacuous. Social institutions are frequently explained as socially integrative. In a sense, of course, institutions are socially integrative, for that is what we mean by a society. If we break down such overblown formulae to informative size, the result is a set of piecemeal ascriptions of functions to various social practices in various groups. We don't want to talk about the function of the dance, but, for example, about the function of dancing among the Winnebagos or American teenagers. For the account of function cannot be given save in the particular circumstances which provide grounds for assessing needs, that is, within the framework of institutions and codes.

The explanatory role of function is only one of its uses in anthropology. Closer to Malinowski's heart is its use as a way of defining the unit of anthropological investigation, the elements that one describes in writing up reports of this or that culture. He argues (pp. 148–9, 176) that doctrines like diffusionism or evolutionism, or techniques like trait-comparison, rest upon the supposition that the object of anthropological interest is a physical unit, the form of an object or activity, and not the meaning of what is done, or the point of its manufacture.

I wish to endorse these arguments as they appear in the pages of *A Scientific Theory of Culture*, after having excised what I should regard as a certain intemperance in Malinowski's elimination of these alternate theories and procedures. Surely there can be nothing wrong with a description of the geographical or temporal distribution of culture traits, however defined, and it is in such descriptions that the essence of diffusionist or evolutionary hypotheses are to be found. It is or it is not the case that a core or a flake industry is found over a certain territory or that specified traits succeed each other in time. The difficulties with diffusionist and evolutionary hypotheses arise at the explanatory level, the diffusionist thesis because it rests upon the highly dubious principle of the parsimony of human invention, the evolutionist because the sorts of general evolutionary hypotheses that have been developed have confused logical and temporal orders, on the supposition, for example, that evolution is in the direction of complexity, or toward some favoured technique or manner of living. The question, *why* this or that particular pattern of diffusion or evolution, suggests a causal hypothesis, which pictures the changes in society as the result of something analogous to physical forces, like tides washing over the various human communities in the world. The evidence produced, however, suggests a very different picture. The anthropologist usually exhibits grounds for the adoption of a trait, in terms, for example, of the utility or the attractiveness of the trait adopted or modified. Frequently, of course, the story he offers is one in which traits are taken over by a community from a conquering, or more subtly dominating group, and this looks much more like a causal account. But it is not that sort of cause which would benefit from casting an account in the hypothetical or inductive forms that require predictions to nourish them. The act of conquest or manifest superiority in efficiency are the features of the context that justify or provide grounds for its adoption.

The same remarks may be offered with respect to Malinowski's criticism of the trait-comparison method. He accuses Frazer, among others, of this anthropological sin, which is, of course, the failure to see a trait embedded in its context. Thus Frazer can see, without further difficulty, the kinship of the Christian mistletoe, the castrated god of the Near East and the celebration of the mass. If the object of investigation is to assess the function of the trait, the business at hand could not be conducted out of context, and so it looks as if trait-comparison is excluded on methodological grounds. But nothing excludes trait-comparison on Malinowski's terms, providing that one shows analogous contexts as well as analogous forms. And nothing excludes the comparison of forms, for example, any ceremony where ritual eating or washing is involved, for this comparison may provide the basis for discovering the historical diffusion of traits.

The typical methodological quarrels among anthropologists thus appear to be unfounded. These arguments and anxieties have been sustained by the notion that one must first define the unit of one's investigation before engaging in substantive inquiries. Having done so, the typical anthropologist inveighs against his methodological neighbours, as if hypotheses of a different order than his own are logically misconceived. But one cannot criticize a description of the diffusion of the form of pottery on the grounds that the trait has not been defined functionally. It is simply a different, though related, enterprise. The mistake arises from the conception of anthropology as a unified science, in which a total description of culture is to follow from one set of laws harnessed together by means of a common and logically unified body of concepts. But anthropology, as Wittgenstein might say, is a medley of techniques, where the medley is a harmony of different interests and points of view, and not a dissonance of vying theories.

Having purged the Malinowskian theory of such theory-ridden excesses, it is now possible to see his arguments in a rather different light. Functional accounts do not occupy a low rung on a ladder with some envisaged or not too well envisaged theory at the top. The ladder of scientific progress is not climbed by rejecting functionalist in favour of physicalist rungs. Functional accounts are not crude approximations of physical theories, but accounts of a logically different kind. If the theoretical view is imposed on anthropologists, it is on the assumption that all successful descriptions and explanations of matters of fact begin with 'hard data'.

There is a good deal of mystique surrounding the use made of this sort of concept by philosophers, aided and abetted by the way in which mathematics is made use of in the natural sciences to define and employ descriptive concepts with exceptional accuracy and precision. So it has seemed to some social anthropologists that techniques of quantification would tie down theories firmly to genuine and reliable data. Unfortunately, the steps in the dance, or the elapsed time required for a specific shuffle, no matter how often or painstakingly recorded, do not add up to the dance. If it is the dance and its role in the life of a community that interests the anthropologist, the quantitative analysis of steps and movements is out of place. Identifying dances, ceremonies and actions are also instances of genuine descriptions and observations. Such identifications begin from a different point of view, not involving the accuracy or precision characteristic of concepts in physical theory. However, they are the sort of thing we want to talk about. They have the virtue of relevance to human conduct, if they lack, in some measure, the virtue of certainty in the formulation of hypotheses concerning it.

Anthropology, then, is a normative discipline, in the sense that its inquiries are shaped by concepts like convention and procedures like the tracing of grounds for action. The intermingling of moral and empirical matters is puzzling only if moral categories are thought of as contaminating the descriptive possibilities of discourse. And this view turns on conceptions of purely empirical data like logical atoms or sense-data, which are meant to afford a starting point for any empirical inquiry. There are many things we want to find out, and to different aims and different subjects logically different items of observation are relevant. Norms and conventions, rules and grounds are the tools of moral judgment, but they are also the tools for describing social practice. The use of such concepts and procedures cannot, then, be stigmatized as mere airings of personal preferences, or isolated from the body of empirical knowledge as *a priori* or conceptual inquiries. Talk about human institutions and practices is already a moral cutting of the empirical cake.

SOCIOLOGY

Much the same arguments can be applied to sociology and history. Once again, moral reasoning has been misconstrued as causal hypothesis or general theory.

When Max Weber advanced his thesis implicating protestant theology in the rise of capitalism, he defended it on what he called 'rational' grounds, with the suggestion that the thesis might be fortified by evidence of a statistical nature. Most of his critics have countered by pointing out that this further evidence is, or must be, lacking. Weber, so this critique goes, needs to show that whenever Calvinist-like religious beliefs turn up, so do capitalist attitudes. Or, lacking such broad instances for comparison, he needs to break down his study into a multitude of connexions drawn between individual clerics and entrepreneurs. The criticism assumes that Weber's thesis is of the type described with monotonous frequency by philosophers of sciences and sociologists of a methodological bent. First, one notes regularities and then devises hypotheses to explain them. The explanation, or successful explanation, at any rate, is to be found in the deduction of new and verifiable consequences (normally predictions) from the hypotheses. Given this pattern of explanation, Weber's thesis is treated as a special case of a general law. Since the law is empty, the case remains unproven, or worse, a bit of speculation masquerading as theory.

Now Weber opens himself to the charge by formulating his hypotheses in causal form and subscribing to a methodology which puts forward ideal types as analogous, at least, to general laws, as the sort of thing that would require evidence of regularities. Winch rightly points to the logical gulf that divides the two procedures.[6] It is as if (a not uncommon problem among sociologists) Weber's way of talking about his work got in the way of the work itself. On this interpretation the historian and sociologist appeal to reasons and motives to explain actions just in the way that scientists and ordinary men appeal to the movements of some bodies to explain the movements of others. Reasons are taken to be *events*, followed by their effects, which, generally, are actions. But since reasons are hidden by the logically impenetrable wall of the mind, it is necessary to resort to the device of the hypothetical experiment, or some means of reliving others' lives, in order to suppose that we ever do succeed in offering such accounts. Once all this is assumed, it is very natural to argue, as Nagel does in *The Structure of Science* (pp. 482 ff.), that historians and sociologists who rely on the imaginative technique of identifying themselves with the subjects of their inquiries are confusing the manner of arriving at their hypotheses with the grounds for holding them. It is always possible, Nagel argues, that our conjectured plumbing of motives is quite mistaken, a possibility amply attested to in the history of history. But it is also possible that Weber's kind of sociology is open to a rather different interpretation to which Nagel's criticisms will not apply.

Weber's ideal types in *The Protestant Ethic*, for example, might be treated as characterizations or impressions of ways of thought and styles of living which enable him to compare them. The doctrine of the calling,

[6] Winch, op. cit., pp. 111–20, especially p. 115.

with its emphasis upon worldly activity, and predestination, with its alienation of daily life from spiritual concerns, are exhibited as ways by which the emphasis upon money-making for its own sake could be justified. What Weber did *not* do was to show that, as a result of worming his way into the heads of clerics and commercial men, he could disclose in himself these religiously toned motives, and assess their influence upon economic practice and attitudes. It is not a business of discovery in that sense at all, but of the assessment of arguments. It is, as Weber himself called it, a rational inquiry, for its object is to discern logical connections among propositions expressing beliefs about the world, or one's obligations, or the supernatural. In the theological context he is calling attention to the moral consequences inherent in Calvinist religious views. In the field of business ethics, as schools of business like to call it nowadays, he is showing what sorts of economic activities are permitted and encouraged by theological precepts, how, as Sombart, writing in the same field might say, economic practice can be clothed in religious sanctity.

History and sociology, so conceived, are branches of ethics. They focus attention on prevailing or important ingredients in a way of life, and show how these relate to and follow from other presuppositions, attitudes, and practices, whether these are religious, moral, scientific, political or economic. Such connexions serve to explain practice because principles can be seen at work which would justify the practice. This is Weber's theme and method. It is also, for example, the gist of Gibbon's theme, that a classical way of life is inconsistent with Christian beliefs and the *mores* of the barbarians. It is also the nature of the connexion frequently drawn between the philosophical views of the seventeenth and eighteenth centuries and the revolutions that accompanied or followed them. And lest this be thought of as an identification of history with the history of ideas, after the manner of Collingwood, it should be noted that this is also the nature of the connexion drawn between excessive taxation and those same revolutions. It has often been thought that attention to hard economic facts helps to replace the old moralistic procedures of historians with proper scientific methods. If this means that the historian who talks about taxation instead of philosophy is seeking correlations between variables which will serve as the basis for a causal theory, his evidence is shaky indeed. We should not ordinarily advance to the general theory that tax problems always cause revolutions on the basis of the handful of instances at our disposal. Moreover, if we read the historian's record closely, it is clear that he is not interested in such a general theory at all, and has no need for such a broadening of his view in order to talk, as he does talk, about the relation of taxation to the Dutch or English revolution. For he describes the taxation as excessive, that is, as constituting grounds for revolt.

If this is the way the historian and sociologist go about their business, their explanations do not require further evidence in the way that an account of physical movement is regarded as acceptable only if it extends to or embraces further cases. The way in which the background relates to the actions within which they are performed is not causal or statistical. Nor does it have the kind of capacity which requires the invention of theoretical 'models' to render the relation between them intelligible. The explanation is instead, moral; it presents features of the background as justifying or providing grounds for the action. This relationship is logical, not empirical. This appears to support Winch's view in *The Idea of a Social Science* that social analysis is conceptual or *a priori*. The social analyst is really the social philosopher and social inquiry an examination of the tools of communication by which we initiate and describe action. It is the meaning of institutions and practices, not their outward form, that concern us.

Winch draws much of the sustenance for this view from Wittgenstein, and particularly that dark saying, 'Language is a form of life.' This is taken by Winch as meaning that human action is governed by the concepts which describe it. Consequently, to understand the actions is to understand the concepts. Understanding concepts is surely conceptual inquiry, and conceptual inquiry is just as surely philosophy. So understanding social action is a philosophical, and therefore not an empirical, enterprise.

In the preceding paragraphs I have allied my arguments to those of Winch. I hope now to show that those arguments do not have the consequences envisaged by Winch for the nature of social inquiry.

In the first place, Wittgenstein's statement is open to a rather different interpretation. To say that language is a form of life may well have been a reminder that language is embedded in life and is a response to the needs and circumstances of its users. In this sense the text could be construed as an objection to a-priorism in philosophy, not a defence of it in sociology. It appears, indeed, that Winch is the victim of the kind of philosophizing to which Wittgenstein took exception. In saying, ask not for the meaning, but the use, Wittgenstein seems to have been reminding us that philosophers' categories are not eternal verities or absolute or exhaustive categories, but reflections on uses of language that can be seen to apply only in context. The moral for the social scientist, so far as he is concerned with the deliberate communication and the expressive behaviour of those whose actions he examines, appears to be: see how these communications and actions function in social contexts. It may be that the collection of statistics or the formulation of hypotheses do not enter here as explanatory moves, and this provides Winch with arguments for his view that sociology is as much *a priori* as empirical. But it is a matter of empirical discovery that people talk certain ways, for it is only in the context of the talk that we can claim to understand what they are doing and why they are doing it. So with my own variant of Winch's thesis. In morally explaining human practices the sociologist is not merely cloaking actions in the respectability of one's own moral convictions, but enriching the factual detail so as to see what it is in the situation that could provide the agent with grounds for acting.

I suspect that Winch has fallen victim to one of the philosopher's traditional dichotomies. It is a dichotomy especially associated with the name of Hume, though Hume notes many cases which overlap or lie outside of this dichotomy. First, the distinction of relations of ideas and matters of fact appears to divide propositions into those known and those probable. But among the relations of ideas are found relations of resemblance, which do not neatly line up with Hume's further distinction between conceptual and empirical. But before long it becomes easier for Hume to think of the knowledge/probability distinction in terms of its clearest cases, mathematics and causal judgments. And these illustrate the conceptual/empirical distinction as well. In this way the two dichotomies merge, conceptual and known, as against empirical and probable.

This is a merger made by many philosophers. Winch is in good company. But it is, I think, a confusion of major importance. He argues, rightly I believe, that the explanation of an action is an inquiry which cannot benefit from the strategies which one would enlist in order to establish the probability of a causal hypothesis. It is thus easy for him to make this stand as a denial also of the relevance of empirical strategies to social inquiries altogether. It may indeed be absurd to treat propositions and theories as experimental facts (as Winch notes on p. 109), but it does not follow that our way of establishing a relation between putative theories or beliefs and the actions in which men engage is a matter only of logical implication. Weber, once again, sees capitalist attitudes as following from Calvinist theology or Lutheran social doctrine. But this inquiry cannot be conducted simply by reading the *Institutes* and Ben Franklin's autobiography and showing that the first entails the second. No logician would sanction such a deduction. It is rather that the two resemble one another in ways pertinent to the assigning of grounds for acting. The connexion is not disclosed by research into regularities, but by observation, and the collection of vast amounts of evidence designed to fill out the theological and economic pictures, so that they can be compared with authority. This was in fact a matter which Weber fudged, for his comparisons are often drawn from irrelevant stretches of time, or can be drawn between just the sort of theology and economy which he wished to claim were not so connected. Thus his critics point to the arbitrariness with which he joined sixteenth-century religious beliefs and eighteenth- or even nineteenth-century economic attitudes and to the prevalence or at least occurrence of Protestant-like moral injunctions from Italian Catholics like Alberti. If these characterizations and the objections to them are ejected from the empirical canon, it should lead us to question the appropriateness of the causal-probability conception of the empirical, and not the empirical or factual character of these claims and procedures.

That the explanation in such cases is a matter of finding grounds for the questioned action, suggests that explaining is a matter of presenting arguments or offering moral judgment. The argumentative feature seems to support Winch's *a priori* view, the moral feature the view of those who, like Collingwood, lay such stress on the historian's sympathy with his subject. But the grounds available to responsible historical or sociological scholarship consist in the events and circumstances which surround the investigated action. And this, surely, is a matter of observation, which can be done with more or less attention, thoroughness and accuracy.

Two of Winch's examples may illustrate the poverty imposed upon sociology by his interpretation. In the first, Winch points out (p. 127) that understanding the concept 'war' is both necessary and sufficient to understanding how belligerents will act. It is clear, for example, why a soldier operates a machine-gun while sitting in a foxhole. His nation is at war, and this means, among other things, that soldiers will act in this way. All well and good, but one wonders: if this is sociology, why does it need to be written at all? Assuredly, the concept war includes the notion of people trying, often under most unhappy circumstances, to kill one another. But does the concept also allow us to determine why two nations have gone to war? Winch admits (p. 130) under pressure from a colleague that certain kinds of social relation, 'particularly important for sociology and history', might not be of an intellectual, symbolic or conventional nature. He cites wars 'in which the issue between combatants [is] purely a struggle for physical survival (as in a war between hungry migrants and the possessors of the land on which they are encroaching)'. But he immediately reverts to the sense in which these wars can be stylized by the conventions issuing from the concept, that is, he reverts to an explanation of individual warlike acts. In doing so, he seems to dodge the criticism of Professor Rees, referred to in his footnote. For, if I read Winch's waiver aright, Rees's question has to do with the occasion of a war, not a description of its conduct. To appeal to the fact that, though as hungry as tigers, men do not quarrel over land as tigers do over meat, is irrelevant, for it is not the style of fighting but the occasion for it that is of major interest to the historian or sociologist.

Winch draws further comfort here from the supposition that some wars can be explained in conventional, symbolic, or intellectual terms. His case is unfortunately chosen, however. For it would lead us to think of the Crusades (his example) in terms of the propaganda which led people to go on them, that is, as Holy Wars. This would surely impoverish our historical accounts, which need to take into account sundry matters like trade routes, the position of the Papacy and its manœuvrings with increasingly powerful temporal princes, and the problems arising in a state divided between feudal and royal power. By the same token one could regard Soviet moves in Korea, Vietnam, Hungary and Czechoslovakia as wars of liberation, deducible from the premises of Communist theory, just as the Crusades are deducible from Christian theology or papal policy. Surely our understanding of these conflicts is immeasurably increased when we take into account the numerous factors in the situation suppressed or not noticed by the pamphleteers or official propagandists. The history and sociology that Winch can buy with his *a priori* currency is naïve indeed. No reputable observer would be inclined to accept it.

In the second example Winch wishes to reject a comparison of Christian baptism with other instances of ritual purification. The grounds for his rejection of these interesting comparisons are clear enough. If he is to explain baptism *a priori*, the rite must be deducible from a set of conventions or espoused theory to be found in Christian theology and ritual. If the historian were to find the roots of Christian baptism in earlier rites of purification, his thesis would entail assertions of temporal, perhaps causal sequence, requiring empirical research.

The comparison of baptism and lustral rites does not have the methodological consequence Winch fears it has, for it is not appropriate to support resemblances by the accumulation of statistics. But in the anxiety to avoid this possibility Winch is forced to exclude such comparisons altogether, and thus to insist wholly on the kind of understanding of baptism that follows from the rules that explicitly govern its practice. And so he is led by his fears to retreat from a middle ground which might well be held against his enemy. Recall that this enemy is not observation and its pertinence to social inquiry, but the kind of explanation in science that

consists of generalization and prediction. Impressions formed of a subject
or resemblances drawn among subjects are factual in the quite ordinary
sense that they are based, if they are held responsibly, on arduous observation and close attention to the surrounding circumstances. What is
irrelevant is the supposition that noting resemblances or forming impressions stands in further need of statistical evidence or hypotheses from
which predictions will follow. In explaining conduct by appeal to conventions, or to aspects of the ecology of actions which provide grounds
for them, no further factual information is required. But the descriptions
and comparisons that support such explanations are surely matters of
observation. This is the gist of Winch's objection to the remarkable
passage which he quotes from Pareto (p. 105), who seems to suggest
that we can only understand baptism by including it within a more
general theory of which lustral rites and washings would be other instances.
But his objections to Pareto should not scare him quite so quickly into
his *a priori* lair.

Social customs and practices are rather less clearly governed by code-
books than Winch can allow. Most human actions may be governed or
guided by conventions, but to discover the rules in most cases involves
close description of actions and their contexts. Winch quotes with
approval a remark of G. E. M. Anscombe that to understand certain kinds
of performance, like working a sum, is to be able to do them. This,
presumably, is to serve as a model for social inquiry generally, but taken
in that spirit it implies that the sociology of mathematics is the study of
mathematics, the sociology of religion the study of theology and prescribed rites, and sociology generally the study of rational prescriptions
of action. Sociologists and anthropologists, surely, would insist that
habits and practices differ from the uttered or written doctrine, which
has, after all, been codified by those pleading special interests. To appeal
to such documents in the case of religion is to share Samuel Johnson's
view that the proper study of Christianity is contained in the work of
theologians.[7] This is no longer a sociological or anthropological, but a
theological or philosophical study. Its method involves the logical assessment of arguments and assertions designed to support or refute their
validity or application. To suppose that such appraisal could answer the
question, 'why this religious practice?' in the way that the mathematician
could answer the question, 'why did you take that step?' or that anyone
could answer the question, 'what makes you think so-and-so is in town?'
(The answer: 'I saw him') is to assume that our grounds for engaging in

[7] The example occurs in Lienhardt's essay on 'Religion' in *Man, Culture, and Society*,
pp. 310–11.

APPLICATIONS TO SOCIAL SCIENCE

en. Winch, I think, is frightened by the charge of ambiguity into
iting himself to clear cases like games and ceremonies.
omparison of traits and practices can also serve to suggest lines of
rical and geographical diffusion. This move is blocked by Winch,
t seems to suggest a way of accounting which is at odds with his
re of social science. But there appears to be no reason why such a
e grouping of aims and subject matters as constitute the social
s should admit of anything so monolithic as a 'methodology'.
can be no social science, if this means that all the ways we talk
human doings can be deduced from a set of laws or that all our
s into human action can be characterized by a common procedure.
the theoretical models that obsess sociologists nor the game or
on models proposed by Winch can be used to legislate the scope
ion of such inquiries.

POLITICAL SCIENCE

dy of government, conceived as a scientific enterprise, may
n to warrant separate treatment; it becomes only a special case
e general study of institutions grouped together as sociology.
academic autonomy would appear to rest on the special
which political scientists look at political institutions. Tradi-
special object has been to clarify the concepts and arguments
voters and legislators and to urge upon us aims they take to
te to government. Such evaluations, it need hardly be
not mere expressions of preference. They depend, so far
ered with cogency and claim our attention, on the detail
litical circumstances are examined, facts which in turn are
e substance and support to the moral or evaluative conclu-

tists have abandoned these concerns to journalists, and
thods of inquiry which would turn them into proper
attempt to avoid the dreaded accusation that they are
political forms and actions, they have turned them-
ogical pollsters, hoping by means of correlations of
social status with voting patterns to predict elections,
ir claims to be scientists. Zealous attention to their
led political scientists unwittingly into a kind of
h is very likely to be inconsistent with their political
mocratic society it is important to keep two factors
as to do with making policy, the other passing upon
inciple, to the electorate to judge policy. This is in

religious or more generally social acts are as perfectly and as rationally
established as are the grounds for mathematical or scientific judgment or
procedure. And this surely begs a very large question.

There is a gulf between moves designed to win a game or support a
theory or carry out a prescribed ceremony and those which terminate in
acquiring a wife, walking the dog, choosing an occupation, or running
for office. It is not that these actions are unrelated to conventions. But
the manner in which they are related is a good deal more complicated
than Winch's view could allow, or than his rule-book cases indicate.
Numbers of conventions, for example, are unacknowledged by those
who engage in them. Some tribes in Africa, reported in Lévi-Strauss's
essay on the family in *Man, Culture, and Society* (pp. 273-4), encourage
marriages between two women, one of whom, through the unproclaimed
affair of the other, plays the role of father to the children of the 'wife'.
Much in this arrangement is a matter of strict convention. A marriage
ceremony is performed, rules for inheritance invoked and applied, and
roles assigned. Any reasonably intelligent member of the group could
cite chapter and verse to explain these actions. But the peripheral and
unacknowledged affair, by which children bless this union, is less easy to
account for conventionally, except in that the rules and conventions of
marriage contribute something to the background of the practice. The
anthropologist explains the affair by showing how it is necessary in order
to provide the 'husband', always a woman of noble lineage, with children
so that the noble strain will not die with her. The conventional here rubs
off on the clandestine, but one needs to assay a great number of details
of the social situation of such tribes in order to draw the connexion of
ground and action.

Such examples have an esoteric charm which might distract us from
the point, which can be made just as easily by appeal to perfectly pedestrian
cases. A businessman in Paris, after a certain amount of success, is apt to
acquire a 'five o'clock' mistress, a denizen of more privileged housing in
New York City will acquire a poodle. In America the distance between
conversing males is greater than it is in France. We should not be able to
deduce these actions from concepts or look them up in rule books, but
we do infer that they are conventional once we see evidence of their
persistent practice by a special group or class or nation. To say that an
action is conventional is to say, among other things, that it is not idiosyncratic, and this is a truth that can be discovered only by observation. It
is surely not discoverable by lexicography or grammar alone.

The conventions appealed to as explaining actions are not, in such
cases, invoked through *a priori* acquaintance with concepts, or reading

rule books or listening to the rationalizations of the actors. The last of these, taken religiously, would reflect a naïvety which would render us inadequate for the business of living, let alone anthropological observation. The second would restrict the scope of sociology to the degree that one would wonder what the point of it is. The first suggests the kind of automatic imposition of one's own ways on other patterns of life, a habit which supposedly went out with the missionary.

If Winch's a-priorism is tempting, it is perhaps because it so neatly pricks the sociologist's pretensions to provide, as newly discovered scientific truths, matters that we already know, and must know in order to live successfully in a society. The sociologist tells us in a formidable barrage of terminology and theory a good many things about our various roles which we must know about in order for the sociologist to have observed us playing them. We are able to do so as a result of instruction and example, and it is thus that we come to act as merchants or teachers or fathers or friends. For a sociologist to tell us about this with the air of novel discovery strikes us as redundant, not to say insulting.

If it is this redundancy that worries Winch, his remedy, according to which sociology is to be adopted as philosophy's foster-child, is misleading. The argument seems sound enough. Concepts make actions possible, and philosophers investigate concepts. Therefore, sociology belongs to philosophy's methodological family. But we learn concepts and we learn how to act by performing tasks, following directions, taking actions. If we understand in some transparent way why we act as we do, it is because we have learned the sort of actions which are appropriate to different contexts. It is not that sociology, in pursuing research methods, is perpetrating a logical howler like the man who would discover whether two and two make four by counting apples. It is rather that this barrage of techniques is quite unnecessary to the kinds of discoveries he proposes to make by its means. Social practice is much like playing games. The rules must be known to play, and playing is to understand what you are doing. If the game puzzles us, we need to appeal to players and umpires, and the social analogues of these in lawyers and business men, doctors and priests, patients and congregations, politicians and voters. Replies to such questions are suspect in proportion to the looseness of the conventions within which the agents act. They can only be removed by seeing very clearly *what* is done and *how* things turn out, discoveries which often serve to correct and amend the rationale of the participants. The anthropologist has the advantage over the sociologist here just because he is engaged in finding out about games which we don't all play. He learns these games by questioning the participants and learning to play himself.

But those who study man or society are engaged as kind of inquiry which involves comparison of game has usually been thought that the point of such comp comfort of added evidence to the accounts of sp practices, and so to treat these special commentaries of general laws. I have done what I can to endor of this conception of the method of social inquiry ledge must be narrowly conceived indeed to theoretical or predictive statements to its compa surprising in Winch, for it is a view much m who wish to apply the methods of theore Theoretical procedures are adopted generally thing worth saying must observe the form I would have thought, ought to be more many significant statements that depend those of a statistical or theoretical natur bulk of our non-scientific knowledge of This would have been the point, one w tions to theorizing in sociology. But h and thus forced, in rejecting the the He is thus forced as well to reject different cultures, different games, f possible point, the construction of and experimental findings.

Sometimes, it is true, social in Sometimes, however, it is a bu investigate the manner of thei place an institution like baptis the gods alongside father-chi of sacrifice alongside bribery another do not thereby be theory; rather, the familiar tions and functions that lines of geographical con tion can be taken to such and actions are in eve conventions and actio the sort of ambiguity to diagnose. If dia behaviour is often t scientific procedures is thus

part because policies directly affect the citizenry, and in part because we are not sure enough of the correctness of policy to leave it up to one man or a committee to judge for the body politic as a whole. The element of expertise and knowledgeableness, on the other hand, is preserved (again in principle) in the function of an executive whose policies are initiated not through the pressure of public opinion, but by means of the informed views of the executive as to what the best policy in a situation may be. Now it is of course in the nature of the case that the executive wants to be re-elected. If each policy can be tested for its popularity by employing teams of pollsters, the distinction between the initiators and the judges of policy vanishes. The electorate, in responding to polls, becomes potentially the maker of policy, for the executive that gives ear to this counsel merely reflects public opinion. This reduces public policy to incoherence, as Plato rightly observed with respect to a kind of democracy which we suppose to be very different from our own. But our democracy is different just to the extent that the policy-making and policy-judging powers are kept distinct. The emergence of democratic forms in nation states in modern times helped to preserve the distinction which, in Plato's city-state, could easily be broken down just because the executive ear was open to every citizen. But polling techniques, made possible by the vast sums of money provided by those who have a greater interest in holding office than living up to a political theory, threaten to restore the intimate relation of executive and electorate, with all the potential for aimless and capricious policy that Plato deplored. The pollsters pay lip-service to democratic principles, but through their preoccupation with funds for research and prediction, have forgotten the main purpose for a study of politics, which is to get at the right policy, not that which, without guidance from above, will most likely be the policy chosen or the man elected.

In any case, the political scientist as pollster is not attempting to explain political behaviour. Like so many sociological techniques, polls put in rigorous or semi-rigorous, but often also in pseudo-rigorous form, the patterns in behaviour which may serve as reliable indices to further events. There is no objection in itself to the use of such procedures, provided they are carried out with a rigour consistent with the subject under examination. Often enough, of course, questionnaires demand that subjects assign numerical values to matters of such complexity that it can only be by caprice that numbers are assigned. Scores make it easier to generalize results than do written and qualified answers, of course, but to suppose that the ratings of the importance of this issue or that on a numerical scale is a more precise way of assessing what the person would otherwise *say* about the importance of issues is clearly misleading.

But let us suppose that the polling is done accurately and modestly enough. It is still not necessarily the first-fruits of a scientific inquiry which, at later stages, will explain these regularities. It may be that the manner in which an explanation is envisaged will differ radically from a type which these or further regularities would support. For note that the point of statistical investigation is to help to guide the strategies of the moment. The questions we ask are questions to which we need to know the answers as office holders or office seekers, in order to further our plans for staying in or acquiring office. Statistics are not relevant just because they are mathematical, probabilistic findings, but because they relate to some particular political purpose. There is the danger political scientists will be putting forth claims as politically neutral facts which are intelligible only as serving quite special political aims. Thus the supposed value-neutrality has exactly the opposite effect of what is intended. We have seen often enough the problems that arise when prediction and generalization are confused with explanation. We need add in this case that a collection of data is gathered, not with a view to general theory but as a way of explicating and making rational particular political decisions. The point of the data and the way of organizing them will thus change with the aims and requirements of action.

The tendency of the political scientist to permit the entry of political values while preoccupied with the issue of scientific objectivity, could be documented over and over again in the empirical literature of political science. One case must suffice. In a recent study of presidential elections, the authors pride themselves on the fact that they confine themselves to the question what the American presidential system is, and avoid judgments as to what it ought to be.[8] They are committed to studies of competing interests and groups, for that is the sort of thing that has the empirical look about it. Their studies thus lead them, though one might just as well say their method leads them, to the conclusion that parties provide the machinery for the attainment of power and the furthering of influence. They ignore altogether the fact that parties serve also as forums for ideas, presumably because ideas and issues do not bend readily to the hard-headed empirical methods of the authors. Note, though, that what is offered is in fact a definition of the electoral system in terms of its purpose, and we are restricted by the empirical method to political views supposedly consistent with it. We are allowed to talk about 'real' politics, the manœuvrings designed to achieve concrete political aims, but we are

[8] Aaron Wildavsky and Nelson W. Bosky, *Presidential Elections* (Scribners, 1963).

barred from thinking of the party system as having point or justification as a vehicle for bringing to the electorate divergent political opinions. Here it is not statistics that seduce the authors into believing that they have addressed themselves to the real questions of politics, but something equally, if not more naïve, that ideas and issues are somehow not as real as 'power' and machinations designed to seize or secure it. But the object of the political scientist as pollster and as power analyst is the same, to substitute facts for values. Yet the end product is to secure a view as to the propriety of political decisions or the point of political institutions without any consideration of the issues relevant to such views. The use of statistics in an unexamined way merely assumes the propriety of popular government. In a similar way, the definition of a political institution, in terms of power and the strategies designed to achieve it, uses a purposive and thus an evaluative conception of government. Political scientists claim to tell us what the role of an institution is, and not what it ought to be. But to speak of a role at all, is to speak of an end to be achieved. We are led to endorse a certain and spectacularly limited view of the purpose of government in confining our attention to what is in some not too clear sense the tangible element in the political process.

The student of government has also attempted from time to time to give a scientific cast to the more philosophical aspect of his subject, political theory. The hard-headed view that questions about authority and right are only questions about power is very appealing to the political scientist, because it makes it appear that a factual question has been substituted for a moral question. Since most political scientists espouse uncritically some form of subjectivism or emotivism in ethics, claiming that moral judgments are nothing but expressions of preference, there is all the more reason for them to wish to avoid value judgments.[9]

There is, of course, much to be said for power theories of the state. Thrasymachus, bursting in on Socrates' gentle discussion of justice, has an important point to make, that discussions of justice and legitimacy have little value unless we think also of some ways for enforcing laws, and creating political power. Marsiglio, Ockham and Hobbes continue that same tradition, arguing against the dangers that ensue for the state if power is diluted through division. The first two saw conflict arising because of the inability of pope or emperor to exercise authority over the

---

[9] A popular work along these lines is to be found in T. D. Weldon, *The Vocabulary of Politics* (London: Penguin Books, 1953). The most detailed and comprehensive treatment of politics from the point of view of an emotivist theory of ethics is, of course, Hans Kelsen, *General Theory of Law and State* (Harvard University Press, 1945); and *Society and Nature* (University of Chicago Press, 1943).

other; Hobbes saw the civil conflict that ensued from a similar failure involving king and parliament. Such contexts led them to think of power as the central issue in politics. Political necessities as well as scientific urges give support to theories of legal positivism.

But to take the issue of power to be the extent of the political scientist's interests is another matter altogether. A political theorist who argues this way will congratulate himself on allowing only claims that can be backed by hard facts. He will tell you that you have to have the power to rule, he may even describe (as Lenin did, for example) how power can be achieved and what can be done with it, but he then leaves it up to you how you will employ your power. After he has told you in what power consists, he will disregard matters of policy as questions of value, and busy himself with factual studies—where power resides, how it is used, and how it is transferred.

There are two major difficulties with such a view. First, the premise that appears to give the student of politics his scientific credentials is a rather obvious truth which anyone seeking to rule must know in pursuing his object. No one, surely, has ever thought that he could assume power without an army or influential groups or the electorate behind him. If it is the substance of political theory to say authority rests on power, it is not surprising that practical politicians have come to despise it as of no conceivable use to them.[10]

But this is a relatively minor point. The major question is, what is it to recognize and identify instances of power? On this score the term power has charmed many theorists into thinking that they had found the analogue for their discipline to force in physics. They were led to stress particularly physical coercion, which could be measured by inventories of men in uniform, guns and resources. And this picture is fairly accurate with respect to revolutionary states. For here the difficulty is that authority is not settled, that there is no concept of legitimacy, or an adequate body of laws or traditions. One of the difficulties in modern Communist states is that a constitution has never been in effect, whereby power could be peacefully and legally transferred, whether by election, inheritance, or other publicly adopted machinery. This is due in part to the aura of permanent revolution that surrounds the party. Thus the classic picture

---

[10] The exception might appear to be Machiavelli. But then he is only at one with legal positivists in the object of interest, power. His discussion of it, however, comes down to the level of recipes for political action, assuming quite specific contexts. The legal positivist, in contrast, wishes his study to have a scientific bearing on political action, but eschews rather nervously the practical application to unscrupulous men seeking advice on how to get and preserve power.

of physical power holds also as an account of authority and succession in such a society.

Yet even in such a state, the story is more complex than this. To maintain a political position against competitors in a state of Hobbesian war, many other resources are available than those that might be weighed as so much physical power or brute force. Otherwise, states would always turn into police or military dictatorships or juntas. Now it can be argued, in Khrushchev's case for example, that his victory was made possible because of the power of the party. But then one is already on the way toward a redefined and elastic conception of power. A body has power because it is the repository of revolutionary theory, a man because he can charm or gain the confidence of confrères or the citizenry, or because he can solve problems. And sometimes, in states backed by strength of tradition and convention, a man has power in virtue of his office. The naked power analysis might apply to certain Latin American states, and other highly unstable regimes, as is indicated by the fact that these states turn endlessly to military rule. But the very concept of civilian rule shows that something counts as power that cannot be clearly or accurately identified as a case of the imposition of the will of one man or one group on others, or measured in terms of military, police, or economic might. There are powers to persuade, powers of tradition, and powers of authority itself, the willingness of people to follow the lead of one whom they recognize as entitled to make demands of them.

This last is not an easy thing to investigate, for it does not emerge from a close description of political phenomena so much as from an ideal from which states fall away in varying degrees. Its bearings on political life take the form of a diagnosis of political ills, though without offering, necessarily, a programme for improvement. This is perhaps a further reason why political theory has come to be discredited. We are anxious for political reform, yet a doctrine like this deprives us of the social engineering or the political strategy for achieving it. For what is being said is that a functioning government enacts its decrees through respect for the law and the authority of office. But how is such respect to be inculcated when it is absent? And how can it be restrained when it oversteps its bounds?

How indeed? Plato's political pessimism is fully justified. The ideal state is a collection of ideal citizens. Still the authority of office and respect for the law are the necessary ingredients to a functioning state. Moreover, on occasion, certain institutions, like the United States Supreme Court, have carried on their activities primarily in the milieu of such authority and respect. If political scientists reject such notions as experimentally untestable or practically unfeasible, they allow the doctrine of physical coercion to fill the vacuum of political theory, and permit philosophical justification only for the kind of state of which most of us disapprove. On the other hand, it should not be surprising if, in espousing the doctrine of authority, legitimacy and respect, or for that matter a social contract as embodying and establishing such notions,[11] it appears that we are engaging in polemic, moral suasion, or value-judgment. For political institutions are, after all, human contrivances, contributing to certain ends. The most significant things we can say about contrivances is what they are for and how well they are doing their job, and these are, of course, statements of appraisal. It may be that a mechanic or engineer, in evaluating a machine, or a physiologist or a doctor in evaluating an organism, can do so within much more rigorous and generally accepted conventions of proper performance. It follows that the business of political assessment is a much more tentative thing, more liable to contradiction and controversy, but it is still the proper business of a study of politics.

This is the gist, it seems to me, of Socrates' argument with Thrasymachus in the first book of the *Republic*. It is sometimes claimed (at least college freshmen often think so) that Socrates is unfair to Thrasymachus, by diverting him from his thesis to irrelevancies. But Socrates is asking Thrasymachus to define power, and Thrasymachus finds it impossible to do so without introducing just the sorts of considerations which his power thesis has been designed to avoid. Power, it turns out, does not mean coercion, even for Thrasymachus. He wants to be the political empiricist and realist. Political reality, however, is not to be found only in the exercise of physical constraints, but in every way in which one person or group directs or manages the actions of others. So the concept of power has to be expanded till it embraces the concept of authority, which in turn cannot be defined without recourse to notions like right and obligation, and these are just the sorts of terms that Thrasymachus had hoped to eliminate from political discussion. So he retreats from the field, and Socrates can get on with the business of analysing political institutions by appraising the jobs they do in terms of the functions they serve. There are perhaps no decisive answers to such questions, but they are none the less the questions which have to be asked if we are to back our political decisions by anything like a rational procedure.

[11] On this point, and for this theme, cf. J. Tussman, *Obligation and the Body Politic* (Oxford University Press, 1960).

These are, then, sample ways in which political institutions have been subjected to what purports to be scientific scrutiny. The issue here is one of grave importance, for the pretence of science serves as a screen to political convictions. I do not mean here that political scientists consciously disguise their convictions in scientific trappings. Some of them, indeed, may literally have no political convictions whatsoever. But the importance of explaining scientifically, together with the misconception of the study of political institutions that this need fosters, leads them often to espouse political convictions as if they were not doing anything of the sort.

One of the most grotesque forms of this confusion is to be found in B. F. Skinner's *Walden II*. His avowed purpose in that novel is to show how society might be improved by scientific planning. The method used to make the political role of the scientist plausible is to assume that there is really one aim in social life, so that everything else can be thought of as a means to that end. Means can be turned over to experts, those who through long training in particular subject matters know how to manipulate some aspect of the world to achieve desired results. But notice that, in the very act of closing the discussion of aims, one adopts as unquestionable and given a particular way of ordering a society. Popper, had he added a chapter to *The Open Society and Its Enemies* might have spoken of it as a further instance of a closed society, in which debate of policy is stifled in scientific dogmatism.

We say, of course, that science is the very essence of the undogmatic, depending as it does on the free expression and exploration of ideas. But this lack of dogmatism belongs in the beginning of a scientific investigation, when we are prepared to admit many possibilities and urge exploration of them. It is not characteristic, and indeed cannot be characteristic of the scientist's approach to his *method* of inquiry. For the method involves the search for the truth, meaning only, by this highly contested concept, that a particular way or conclusion is right: alternatives are eliminated. One might almost say, the point of science is to achieve dogmatism, except that we are inclined to use 'dogmatism' only in cases of conviction without reason.

In contrast, the method of politics is to find the workable, the felicitous. We can talk about this significantly, but only in the context of aims and desires, which, being the aims and desires of particular people, very often conflict. We cannot measure a policy in terms of some simplistic criterion by assuming that there is an overriding aim or desire to which all others must bow and by which all action must be measured. Social harmony, for example, is a laudable aim, but taken as the whole point of public policy will deny individual right, and substitute methods of coercion for freedom of action.[12]

What I am claiming, then, is that a scientific approach to politics is necessarily totalitarian, because the success of that approach must take as given what, in an open society, is taken to be necessarily debatable, that is, the aims that people have and the picture of the good society. A number of years ago, in a book designed to show how inadequate amateur politics is and how preferable the society governed by scientists, C. H. Waddington says:

The freedom to be odd and unlike one's neighbour is not, I think, a scientific value; at least I should not like to have to produce scientific reasons why a community which allowed it must be better for its neighbours than one which did not.[13]

It is clear that for him, if A is good and B can be shown with scientific reliability to contribute to A, then there is no room for discussion. But the point is, our values are not simply set in one or two or a half dozen preferences at the start, but are involved at every stage of political life. We can admit in a general way that social harmony is a good thing, but we none the less must re-examine the goal, that is, re-examine its importance for us, with every measure coming to our attention that purports to provide a way of achieving that end. The means, then, are as much a matter of evaluation and judgment as are the aims, for they bring to our attention new facts which require us to re-examine the aims. We begin, let us say, by agreeing that crime is unequivocally bad. But someone proposes a remedy, a gas that spread over a city or nation saps the energy of a people and makes them quiescent. The gas men are the scientists here; they have proposed a method discovered by means of their expertise. But now, in the light of such a means, we return to our aim and ask again, how bad is crime? Bad still, no doubt. But not so bad as to warrant the use of such techniques, however foolproof. It is in this sense that scientific government is necessarily dogmatic. There can be no re-examination of the aims, for it is only by assuming them quite dogmatically that we can claim that all the rest of the business of politics is better handled by scientific experts.

---

[12] One of the most ingenious and pernicious applications of scientism to policy is the attempt, very popular recently, to dispose of criminality by therapy, on the assumption that the only matter of importance is preventing crime, and that any method (punishment, therapy, surgery or drugs) that reduces crime is the rational course of action. This ignores the value of a legal system based on the autonomous agent and calls attention to the fact that in society we join in a common game-like enterprise, in which the conditions of fair (just) play require penalties on those who violate these conditions. See my article, 'Scientific Discovery and Legal Change', *The Monist*, Vol. 49 (1965), pp. 485 ff. Numbers of books, articles, and legal cases on this topic are cited there.

[13] C. H. Waddington, *The Scientific Attitude* (Penguin Books, 1948), p. 156.

Many philosophers would be anxious to deny political implications to their analysis of the concepts of government or of human nature. I take the opposite position. The whole point of an examination of the concepts on which our view of human nature and society rests is to come to grips with fundamental issues of ethics and politics. One of the arguments against a standard analysis of terms like reason and desire, personality and society, which might be called the scientific analysis, is the political implications that issue from a wholesale endorsement of it. By the same token one would expect the view proposed as an alternative to the scientific picture to have other political implications. In recognizing that the typical patterns of description and explanation we give of human actions are matters of appraisal and judgment, and that the application of rules and standards may, for all we know, have only local authority, we must also see that the government and law of such a society requires the flexibility of judgment and attention to unique needs of particular situations. It cannot rest on a monolithic conception of the state served by scientific experts. It would, given the fact of diversity of aim and desire, be of more use for political scientists to consider the structures of the concepts and arguments that go into moral and political reasoning than to open the door to the monolithic state while striving to be scientists.

Economics

The science of economics might appear to be an exception to my thesis. For surely economists do seek, and sometimes find, laws which describe and predict what will happen to some economic entities, quantities or processes, given variations in others. There is no talk here about purposes or appraisals or policies, but rather of the inevitable fluctuations of business cycles, depressions, inflations and booms. At different times, economists have laid stress on different factors. In so-called classical theory it is taken as the fundamental law of economic behaviour that supply varies to meet demand. Later, Marx regards it as equally inevitable that business prosperity can only be achieved by cutting labour costs, so that each boom results in the use of profit to invest in labour-saving devices, in turn creating unemployment, which inevitably results in the collapse of the consumer market, depression, a supply of cheap labour, and so the beginning of the cycle all over again. Later still, Keynes argues that economic fluctuations are attributable to the difference between aggregate income and consumption, for this simple formula will give what is available for investment, which in turn will determine productivity and employment. In a similar vein, Irvine Fisher attributed economic fluctuations to the quantity of money in circulation, Berle and Means to the drift toward control of large sections of the economy by fewer concerns, Alvin Hansen to fluctuations in population growth, and so on.

Each of these theories, and indeed most others, has a *prima facie* validity. It has been argued that all of them present an over-simple model. Other things being equal, supply would rise to meet demand; the price of labour would determine profit; savings would determine productivity; the supply of money would determine inflationary and deflationary fluctuations; and the rate of population growth would expand or contract or stagnate productivity. But against a supply-demand formula, we want to argue that a situation in which vast concerns have eliminated competition in the usual sense is not 'normal'. Against Marx we want to point out that numbers of things contribute to profit over and above the lowering of labour costs, including improved production and marketing devices. Against Keynes we want to urge that consumption is not, as he seems to regard it, a constant, which can then serve to determine what needs to be done to increase or lower the money available for investment or saving. Consumption does fluctuate with income and so destroys the sure-fire validity of predictions of what will happen with the money in excess of the alleged constant figure. Against Fisher we have the evidence of later economic activity in which, though money is plentiful, inflation does not result, because there are purchasable products to spend it on or new industries in which to invest it. And against Hansen it might be noted that a burgeoning population does not amount to a burgeoning economy; it may just as well result in unemployment unless something happens to the level of productivity or unless money is available for new industries and continued consumption.

Sometimes an economist, following the lead of his favourite formulae makes predictions which are grossly in error, such as Fisher's famous prediction of a continued prosperous plateau one week before the '29 crash. And this leads many people to disparage the results of economic theory, as so many ivory-tower descriptions of what might have been, had the situation been as simple as their theories indicated.

There are two matters which require our attention here. The first has to do with the *prima facie* validity of such principles. How are the connexions of supply and demand, labour and profit, money and inflation, population or investment and prosperity formulated and tested? The other question is, given their limited validity, are we entitled to say that any such over-simple models can be applied with any point to the actual economic situation?

Let us turn to the second of these questions first, by assuming the *prima facie* validity to any or all of the connexions described in the above catalogue. Suppose a physicist were to discover that the situation which obtained in the laboratory had no counterpart in the world. Would he be justified in pursuing his investigations as if they constituted knowledge of the world? It would, of course, be grossly misleading if the formulae which applied neatly to the experimental situations were generalized for the world at large. But the physicist might regard the experimental situation as a means to formulate concepts and laws for describing the world at large. So a body may never, except in theory, move in Euclidian straight lines, but the first law of motion may none the less afford a powerful tool for observing and recording the actual motions of bodies. In the same way, though supply does not automatically vary to meet demand, or investment record the difference between aggregate income and a constant rate of consumption, these assumptions may provide ways of describing actual changes in market conditions. So too, if it is assumed that profit is the margin of labour costs, this assumption provides a technique for describing the fluctuations in profit which would at least enable economists to assign a value to the part of profit which does not seem to be a function of labour costs. And so with all the formulae of the major economists. Whether these formulae or any formulae can be profitably used in this way is a question of fact, and there does seem some reason to suppose that all of them are potentially useful in this way. The difficulty has been that most economists have supposed that their models have a general application to the actual economy. Thus, for example, conservatives of our own generation are prepared to argue, armed with supply-demand equations, that the economy left to itself, must adjust to demand. It is this generalizing tendency that has brought discredit to much of economic theory, not the use of models as ways of getting at a more accurate description of economic processes. Beyond this, one might be inclined to note that no single model appears to have captured the field, or shown itself to be in any demonstrable fashion, a superior tool of description.

These weaknesses suggest more detailed, better controlled and more skilfully quantified studies. And this of course is the direction that economics is taking. Wesley Mitchell's study of business cycles was the beginning of this sort of movement, and governments have followed suit, so that now a kind and range of data is available to the economist beyond the conception of the theorists of the nineteenth and earlier part of the twentieth centuries. We now know a good deal about the distribution of income—who gets it, what it is spent on, and who spends it on what— that the major theorists did not have at their disposal when they tried to determine the role that variations in income might play in the economy.

We know, as a matter of empirical fact, that a bank can lend up to ten times its money reserves, for this is a figure determined by the borrowing and lending habits of the nation. There are, however, two kinds of economist's statements that we ought to distinguish before we turn back to the first of our two questions. One kind of statement tells us about economic habits of a community, nation, or the world. These are the statements whose lack or unreliability made classical economic theory so vulnerable to attack. When they are incorporated into theory they occur as 'psychological' premises, like Keynes's confidence in the constancy of consumption, Malthus' and Ricardo's assumption that a working man will not produce more for more money, or Adam Smith's belief in the rationality of market-place behaviour. But they are normally incorporated in such a way as to minimize their importance, that is, they are taken to be relatively invariant, so that the economist can busy himself with the economic factors of money and interest, goods and trade. But it is clear that propensity to invest or save, consume or fritter away income, that confidence (or lack of it) in investment, can make an enormous difference in the traffic of the market-place. So economists have increasingly poached on the sociologist's preserve, for the facts they seem to need have to do less with the relation of one economic variable to another, than with the determination of some of the economic variables by moods, attitudes, beliefs and propensities of the people involved in business transactions. By and large, economists have done a more perspicacious job of sociology than the sociologists themselves. If so, it is probably because they have gone straight at a problem, rather than constructing the methodology of some possible problem. There is much here in the way of detailed, often statistical, findings, but these findings are not themselves explanatory but descriptive. Economists have begun to investigate what does happen in the market-place, and they have discovered that many different things happen, that what a labour or capital force will do varies widely from time to time and place to place. We can go further and explain the mood or beliefs of buyers and sellers, by seeing the kind of historical and social milieu in which their actions are taken. This is explanation by warrant, of a piece with other examples we have considered.

But the heart of economic doctrine lies in other kinds of statements, where the formulae offered seem to have some kind of invariant and imperative authority which sociological or psychological descriptions and explanations do not have. These are the statements as to the relation, say, of amount and velocity of money to price level, of aggregate income to investment, of income to national product. These can be formulated with mathematical respectability. Thus the first:

$$MV = PT$$

where M is the amount of money, V the velocity with which money changes hands, P the price level and T the number of transactions. And the second:

$$Y = C+I$$

where Y is the aggregate income, C consumption and I investment. (And, since S (savings) $= Y-C$, it follows that S $=$ I.) And the third:

$$I = P$$

What gives such formulae the authority they seem to possess? I wish to suggest that the authority is based on the mechanics of book-keeping. In the last of these, this is perhaps obvious. I $=$ P is a demand that something occur on one side of the ledger for everything on the other. That books *must* balance has the authority of a rule of economic practice; it does not have the significance of law which states that product is determined by income. Sometimes it looks as if books do not balance, and the book-keeper or economist must find the source of the discrepancy. This looks like the physicist's search for a loss of energy accommodated by the postulated and later experimentally verified neutrino. But in the physical case it must be possible to reject the principle on which the supposed loss of energy is postulated, that is, the conservation of energy principle. It may turn out that the world is not accurately described by this principle. In economics, however, it is not possible to reject the book-keeping principle, for this is a way in which we have agreed to conduct our business, both individual and national. Value is an institutionalized means of recording and determining the flow of goods and the use of labour. If we operate within such a system many of our actions will be determined by the rules of the game.

Take, for example, the relation of amount of money to inflation. And suppose we conclude that prices will inevitably rise if there is more money to the proportion of goods and services for sale or hire. The inevitability is a function of our manner of conceiving the market, a manner which demands that we treat money as a commodity, and all exchange of commodities as governed by the ratio of supply to demand. Now we could institutionalize rather different relations of money to goods and services, or goods to goods. We could insist that prices remain fixed, irrespective of the supply of money or goods, and withdraw the excess money from circulation when the balance goes against goods and return it when the balance goes against money. This is not, as conservative economists maintain, tampering with the natural fluctuations of the market, for there is no such thing as the natural market. We dictate that the ratio of money to goods will determine prices, as much as we would dictate that the ratio should not affect prices, if this was our way of constructing the market.

The empirical problem in modern economics is the matter of adjusting a given kind of market to some notion of prosperity. How, in other words, can we insure that the conventional play of income, money, investment and production will insure full employment? Keynes showed that the answer to that question is not contained in the conception of the free market. Thus if full employment is the crucial issue, we have to see ways in which we can modify our conventional economic practices, including our conception of the free play of value according to supply and demand, to insure that everyone is working. Of course, we might also modify it in such a way as to insure that everyone has a certain standard of living irrespective of his doing a job; but generally we do not consider this alternative for moral reasons. That is, we think a person is better off earning his wage than receiving a dole. This again is part of the convention of social life, not some consequence of a law of human or social behaviour.

In one sense there are always jobs. We can always conceive of further goods that would be worth having or services that could be performed to our advantage. We can always conceive of better hospital care, more teachers, improved highways, and so on endlessly. So there is in society an abundance of tasks. There is, on the other hand, a paucity of resources. One can at least discern the limits beyond which a field or a territory will not support more crops, a mine or all the mines will not produce more coal, a forest or all the forests will not produce more wood and pulp. This is a function of the population consuming these products. The relation of resources to consumption is indeed an empirical issue, and an increasingly important one. But economists often add to this the paucity of money, as if it were as much a matter of the facts of economic life as is the amount of goods. Of course, within an economic convention, the paucity of money is a fact, and this makes it appear as if prosperity must be conceived of as an inevitable consequence of population, resources, and supply of funds. But the relation of the last of these to the formulae of economic life is a matter of our decision to play the economic game a certain way. We can at least imagine a situation which incorporates only the population, the resources, and the employables. When we say, 'not enough jobs', we are not referring to the number of tasks available to be performed, but the amount of funds available under certain determinations of the goods and labour market to pay for the labour. If paucity of funds is treated in the style of a law of nature, as the relation of goods to numbers of mouths, it promotes the feeling that the best we can do is operate within these inalterable laws, and by the stimulus of tax reduction, or tax raising, government spending, or government thrift, enhance the supply of funds. It may be that we shall still *want* to resolve our problems in one of these ways, but at least we ought to see the market as something of our own contrivance, made up of rules which have our blessing, and not as an inevitable consequence of the 'natural' exchange and consumption of goods.

When formulae for an economy are thought of as reflecting theories, trouble ensues. Matters of policy are elevated into unalterable law. Thus modern economic conservatives invoke the inevitability of a supply-demand equilibrium, mysteriously indicating prosperity for all, if only we don't tinker with it by taxation, government spending, or political control of business activities. But the incoherence of the position is reflected in the conservative's injunction not to tamper with the free market. It would be odd to explain the behaviour of masses by the inverse square law and then add, 'and don't tamper with it'. So a crude kind of philosophy of science penetrates even the heads of politicians and allows them, if speciously, law-like support for their policies. If, on the other hand, economic laws are seen as formulations of policy, need and value, there is no reason to suppose that they cannot or do not need to be altered. The generations of economists from Adam Smith to Keynes have not reflected progressive stages in the description and explanation of economic reality, but the formulation of different policies for conducting the business of society under various conditions of productivity, war or peace, population changes and political conditions. Thus government deficit spending, whether or not it is an appropriate or desirable move in a situation, is at least not like solving the problem of transportation by levitation. It is no more contrary to nature than is the conception that a man ought to receive a profit on his investment, which was considered unnatural by the ancestors of modern economists.

The formulae of economists, then, are, by and large, statements in precise form of policy matters. The precision is necessary in order to apply the policy intelligently, just as, behind most economies, the concept of double entry book-keeping is necessary in order that the economy will function coherently. If a man or a nation wishes to engage in an activity for profit, he must have available concepts of cost, volume of sales and precise ways of computing them. Something may go wrong—his volume of sales does not match expectations, the costs go up—and these errors require explaining. But there is no certain way of determining by reference to formulae what it is that has gone wrong. The fluctuations in demand, and in the availability of raw materials and labour, are not consequences of economic laws, but represent the confluence of many factors having to do with social, geographical, even meteorological conditions. And who can say how many more? It is usually not too difficult to determine what went awry in the particular case. But the attempt to generalize or, in what amounts to the same thing, extend the mathematical equations of economic policy to the social situation by assuming that the factors which cannot be determined by wholly economic (book-keeping) considerations are constant, cannot but turn out to be irrelevant to *most* actual situations. Consumption does vary and this makes Keynes's theory a much less adequate description of any social situation, though no doubt adequate if one can find the situation in which consumption remains constant. Gluts of money do not necessarily mean inflation, though, in a society which courts money as a commodity, and in which other alternatives are blocked, Fisher's equations will hold.

In short, the mechanics of the economy can be made clear by working out the logical consequences of the concepts that make our particular form of economic activity possible. On the simplest level, if we decide to set a value on a given commodity, and know that, in order to manufacture it, wages and rent must be paid, raw materials purchased, depreciation and a margin of profit on the investment allowed for, we will be best advised to go about this business by setting our projected needs and policies in mathematical form. We shall require formulae for determining depreciation which will involve the purchase price, length of use and costs of repairs. We shall need to see, if price and costs are determined, what volume of sales will be required to insure a profit (e.g., $P = V - C$). These mathematical formulae do not describe economic behaviour, except so far as economic agents employ them in carrying out their business strategies. They state only the formal requirements for a computation of profit, costs, depreciation or any other factor.

I should not say 'only the formal requirements', for fear of subscribing to the view that such limited and practical applications of mathematical equations are second-class citizens in the business of knowing the world. They are necessary for a man of business to survive, and that they count as practical rather than theoretical knowledge is no mark against them. Trouble ensues only when it is supposed that, because of their mathematical form, they represent the best attempts yet to describe and explain human behaviour. Why people borrow in varying amounts, why they tend to put money in stocks, diamonds, or a sock, why they gain or lose confidence, are matters which relate to the whole social sphere and can be answered, if at all, only for the specific situation. Yet these habits and practices are the stuff out of which economic activity is made, and it is these that require explaining. If the psychological assumptions introduced into classical economic theory in order to explain economic behaviour seem inadequate or somewhat tattered, it is because they were treated as variables having universal application. But situations change, and with them the grounds for action. Among the factors which relate to economic action are the social controls exercised over economic activity. A society, through its policies and its education, fosters or inhibits economic enterprise and channels it in ways that conform to some perhaps vague sense of proper conduct. So talk about the inevitable fluctuations of supply and demand, interest and savings, money and goods, have to do only with societies in which these fluctuations are institutionalized by roles assigned to the market-place, money and investment.

The aura of inevitability that surrounds the equations of economists is fostered, of course, by numbers of genuine empirical discoveries. It is as if we have been for centuries in the dark about something we are all doing or participating in doing, and now, at last, with painstaking research, economists are beginning to piece together what actually happens: the habits of borrowers, the range and extent of fluctuations between inflation and depression, the businesses most crucially involved, and the order in which they are involved. It is these factual revelations of the past fifty years or so, more than the tidy formulae of theorists, that have contributed to the attitude that while economic activities are things we *do*, in the aggregate they constitute something which *happens*. Our individual economic acts are explainable *ad hoc*, perhaps, but the total effect of the aggregate of these acts is something we can only witness and describe from the outside. So we are led to think of impersonal forces, which push the economy onward irrespective of our human decisions.

Yet this view is surely self-defeating. The emergence of controls, like anti-trust legislation or the federal reserve system, shows that the aggregate is a matter of human decision *if we wish it to be*. Our trouble with economics has been that the 'objective' or 'scientific' view of economic processes has been the chief weapon of those who want to see business unfettered by social controls, just as the dialectics of the inevitability of the historical process has been advanced from time to time to support the claims of special groups or special nations to privileged status in a state or the world.

Still, what the individual does as a rational agent, and what constitutes the sum total of individual rational actions, may be so far apart as to make rational economic action or decision a pragmatically useless means of examining the aggregate of economic activities. We might imagine a tremendously complicated game in which numbers of rules govern the moves which a player might make in the light of the pieces *in view*, but in which at the same time his moves are affected by the distribution of pieces not in view which in turn affect the total disposition of the game in ways which he cannot possibly come to realize. From any player's point of view strategy is apt to be disrupted by the capricious entry of new pieces. These come under the rules and strategies of the game, but would be considered by a given player as random or natural phenomena, whose occurrence is taken as describable, perhaps predictable, by patient research, but not explainable within the concepts and rules of the game. Yet these seemingly random appearances of new pieces on the board may well be dictated by the confluence of strategies of numbers of players, some of whom may be totally unaware of the game or the existence of other players. In such a game the moves appear to follow their *own* laws, quite independent of the desires and strategies of individual players. So, too, in the market-place, economic processes seem to follow laws having nothing to do with the strategies of individual business men. Research here has a pragmatic point, justified in so far as it predicts the outcome of the game or market-place activity. Economics in this sense becomes a highly generalized method for statistical prediction. We know why the agents of economic enterprise act as they do, but the cumulative effect is much too complex to work out, if we begin with the moves of all the economic agents. So we devise theories as to how games in general turn out. But of course we know that the results of any given game may be widely at variance with the statistical averages we obtain. If our interest is the bet on a particular game, it is going to be sorry comfort to know that the average result is, say 7-4, in favour of the team higher in the standings when in this particular instance it turns out to be 19-0 in favour of the less fortunate club. Yet, of course, without statistics of this nature it is difficult to make a rational prediction at all.

The temptation to move to the techniques of natural science in economics is the demand for rational prediction, not for explanation. At the same time, the demand for prediction on this basis, while it can be formed in general terms, does not satisfy the kind of prediction wanted for this or that game or economic enterprise. We demand laws from the economist, and at the same time berate him for providing them when they don't pinpoint the particular recession or the turn to inflation. But if economics is like the game I have described, it is not easy to see how law-like statements could provide the kind of answer we want. Moreover, however adequate the laws may be in predicting in a general way the patterns and results of any number of playings of the game or of the market, it is not clear how these laws serve to explain the actions of particular players or merchants. For these actions are still rooted in the rules of the game or market, and are explainable as warranted by the rules and the attending circumstances.

There is, I am sure, a great deal more to be said about economics. Economists have approached appreciable and readily identifiable problems in economic action without the burden of a preconceived methodology to guide them to their solutions. In consequence they have evolved a much more formidable body of doctrine than have either psychologists or sociologists. It seems to me that the conception of economic laws and formulae as policy statements, and the picture of economics as a game of the sort I have described, goes some way toward an assimilation of the activities of economists to the patterns of observation and inference I have insisted upon here for the proper study of human action.

The Charge of Relativism and Other Issues

We have now treated some of the problems connected with the conception of various disciplines within the social sciences. But there are further problems belonging to social science as such, and samples of these, too, need to be reviewed in the light of the theory of moral explanation.

One such problem arises when philosophers note, quite correctly, that explanation in history or sociology is the particular understanding of individual acts, and not a general claim supporting the particular case. These philosophers are led from this observation to the supposition that some unique method, *verstehen*, empathy or sympathy, is required to account for the historian's ability to fathom individual motives or intentions. But we can now, in the light of the theory of moral explanation, give a plausible interpretation of *verstehen* or sympathetic understanding which tempers the more extravagant and quasi-mystical overtones of the view, while leaving its criticism of theoretical explanation of human behaviour intact. Fathoming the reasons for action does not, in the absence of general law, force us to suppose that we are in some mysterious way identifying or entering into the thought processes of those whose careers we investigate. It is true, as Collingwood urges, that the historian out of sympathy with his subject is in no position to give a decent account of it. But this need not lead us to say that the good historian is the one who agrees with what his subjects do. To urge sympathetic understanding or *verstehen* as the proper method for studies of history, sociology or psychology is, on my interpretation, merely a way of drawing attention to the fact that in explaining human action we must see it as justified by circumstances and grounds. It is, in a full sense, an empirical and not a divinatory procedure, since proper explanations can be given only by close attention to the circumstances that can be seen to provide grounds for action. It sounds as if the demand for sympathy is to substitute bias for independent investigation. But sympathy needs, in such a context, to be understood, not as agreement with particular aims or actions of human agents, but a readiness (a method, if you like) to think of actions as rational, and thus backed by grounds.

My thesis may help also to answer the argument offered by J. W. N. Watkins, who among others wishes to correct the reifying tendencies in social science by his thesis which he calls methodological individualism.[14] What Watkins objects to is the habit, when taken too seriously, of talking about social entities as if they were individuals, by ascribing to them motives and purposes. To attribute this kind of explanation to social forms or processes is thus to suppose that societies or groups are organisms. If we recoil from this sort of Hegelianism, it looks as if we must insist, with Watkins, that talk about social processes must be analysable into talk about the motives and actions of many individuals. The difficulties of carrying out such a plan however are clearly insuperable. In the first place, the individuals making up society are too numerous to permit such an analysis. In the second place, it is not clear how talk about social processes can be analysed into talk about motives and interests of individuals. A conjunction of statements about individuals does not entail any particular statement about social forms.

We seem then to be faced with equally unpalatable alternatives. Either we must embrace an organismic view of society or reject the possibility of social inquiry, except in the attenuated sense in which the study of society is a compilation of studies of individuals. Watkins' dilemma, however, rests on an assumption incompatible with the thesis of moral explanation, namely, that motives are occurrences residing in individuals and functioning in scientific laws as constructs.

First, psychological concepts, we have seen, are not unobservable (and therefore hypothetical) dispositions determining behaviour, but the reasons which, in special situations, warrant action. There is no logical gulf to be crossed or logical barrier to be breached in applying moral explanations to society. And second, Watkins treats psychological explanations as hypothetical, because he endorses the view that all adequate explanation is of the hypothetico-deductive form. He views human action in the way we view physical objects, as determined by antecedent conditions. The reifying sociology to which he objects is, of course, a direct consequence of the attempt to treat social processes as physical facts. Watkins' objections seem necessary if we are to avoid the organic view of society. But it is not clear how explanation of social processes, any more than explanation of individual actions, can be deterministic in this sense. It is not clear either why methodological individualism is necessary, how it will solve our problems of social explanation or, for that matter, what problems it is supposed to solve.

If one thinks of terms like desire and need serving as names for events or processes in the organism, one seems to require a way of denying entry of such terms into social inquiry. For one surely does not want to think of the state or a jury or any band of people as an organism. But once we see such terms operating in the context of rules and values, this is no longer necessary. It is quite as possible to apply the machinery of justification and excuse, of assessment and fittingness, to the activities of groups as it is to individuals. To say that a society has needs is to see its rather complex activities as being sustained or supportable only by certain means. It is not to ascribe to it peculiar properties that somehow cause society to be as it is. The basis for the view that one must analyse all terms of social reference into terms of individual reference disappears once it is seen that psychological entities are not required to explain individual action.

Watkins ties his arguments to Karl Popper's well known attacks on holism.[15] But this is another matter entirely. For holism, as a view ascribed for example, to Hegel and Marx, is the doctrine that society follows social laws. Consequently institutions have nothing to do with the actions of individual human agents. From this a political consequence is supposed to follow, that an institution must survive without the consent of the individual membership. Popper's targets are first and foremost the political consequences of this thesis, but he sees how holistic method provides the rhetoric for the political doctrine. He is, in consequence, at pains to argue against holistic sociology as well as holistic politics. He wants to deny the use of the language of the organism to describe social forms, and sees the characteristic social action as one that might not have been done if the agents had taken care, noticed certain further facts, or had

<hr />

[15] Ernest Gellner carries this argument further, suggesting that Watkins' views are readily identifiable with another of Popper's enemies of society, psychologism. See his 'Holism versus Individualism in History and Sociology' in Gardiner, op. cit. pp. 503 ff. Popper's statements of these issues are seen in *The Open Society and its Enemies* and *The Poverty of Historicism* (Routledge & Kegan Paul, 1957).

a change of heart. In short, Popper wants to argue that social phenomena cannot be thought of as law-like, but instead must be looked upon as processes which further human agency can always change. This thesis is like my own, and it applies just as well to psychology. In fact my account of psychology points toward sociology, for it has been shown that typical psychological explanations depend upon appeal to conventions. The concept of appropriate behaviour is a social concept.

One tangle of arguments, however, leads to another. I refer to the complex and not always clearly related issues that go under the label 'cultural relativism'. This is a doctrine that has been used to restore all the mystique of insurmountable barriers to the investigation of human doings and practices of which we have only just rid ourselves. It might be argued that I have been espousing or at least flirting with just such a view, for haven't I been saying that explanation depends upon moral context, and aren't such contexts, in a way, cultural units?

It is difficult to answer this charge, if charge it is, directly, because cultural relativism is less a doctrine or position than it is a collection of them. A number of different and logically unconnected views have been put forth under this label. First is the fact of relativity. I daresay no one is surprised to discover that people in different parts of the world take very different attitudes toward wives and children, friends and enemies, or food and drink. If we try to apply missionary labels like licentiousness and cruelty to those with remarkably different standards of behaviour toward women, children, or enemies, we are clearly going to go astray. For these terms denote departures from rule or practice which cannot be applied with precisely the same reference to behaviour in various ways of life. We shall not understand or correctly describe actions if we persist in thinking of foreign ways as improper departures from our own.

One thing, then, that might be meant by cultural relativism is that people differ, another that one should be sensitive to such differences. But sometimes two further views are maintained that are at best pompous renditions of this fact or this recommendation, and at worst, completely illegitimate extensions of them. I shall call these the metaphysical and the ethical versions of cultural relativism.

The metaphysical thesis locks us up completely within the limits of our values and conception of the world. Attempts to explain the actions and beliefs of those belonging to an alien way of life can only be approximations. Even worse, we can never really tell how close we have come in our approximations, since our conceptual scheme determines what we will find and what will satisfy us that we have described and explained foreign ways correctly. This view is implied, if not positively embraced, by sociologists of knowledge, notably Karl Mannheim. It has the paradoxical flavour of many all-or-nothing views, and, like so many of them, is self-defeating. For it has the form, we can never be sure of x because we are sure of y, but y turns out to be an instance of x. So here, we can never really get out of our own cultural frame of reference, because we can see how it alters and distorts our account of other societies. But if we can mark the alteration or the distortion, we must know something about other cultures which is independent of the source of distortion. How else would we know that the frame of reference does colour the foreign reality?

Sometimes the metaphysical thesis finds its support in linguistic relativity. This is a view made very popular by professional humanists as a result of reading over-eagerly the account of language to be found in the papers of Benjamin Lee Whorf.[16] According to this view, or the metaphysical extension of it, we can never apprehend the world in the way that users of a radically different language view it, because we think through our own grammatical categories. If we are able to say this much about the role of our categories in determining our conception of the world or human society, and if we are able to describe intelligibly the differences between their conception and our own, it would seem possible to apprehend their world and describe it by employing their grammar. If, on the other hand, we are really locked within our own grammar, we would not be sensitive to grammatical differences, and this would show itself either in total failure to communicate or complete oblivion to the differences. Neither of these can be the case, for without translation and sensitivity to the differences in language structure, Whorf's hypothesis could not have been stated. The common ground of language is the world. We point to objects and pantomine actions and see what words in a foreign tongue are called forth. It is possible to see that our concepts overlap, and so to understand that they are not quite equivalent. And it is also possible to discover that concepts naming objects in the foreign tongue are subject to grammatical rules which do not obtain in ours. So, let us say, the Hopi word for table or stone is tensed, that is, its form in a sentence is determined among other things, by time. But if we allow this, we must also allow what this fact presupposes, that we live in a common world of identifiable objects and actions. If translation and language acquisition begin ostensively, a common external world that language is used to describe is presupposed, and so it becomes idle and unintelligible to suppose that language somehow creates or distorts this world. If we do not assume an ostensive procedure, it is not clear how we could become aware of such basic grammatical differences. For unless we know that a term in Hopi is used to denote a stone or a table, we could not arrive at the view that the Hopi think in terms of events or processes instead of objects and substances. What we discover is that their words used to denote objects are subject to a rather different assortment of grammatical rules than is the case in English. It is not clear what it would mean to say that these differences create different conceptions of the world, unless the Hopi behaved differently toward objects than we do. But, I take it, a Hopi will walk around rather than through a boulder in his path, exert the necessary effort to lift heavy objects, and lean with the same confidence against solid objects. The metaphysical thesis according to which someone's world hinges upon his grammar is thus incoherent.

Ethical relativism is a more subtle argument. It is nourished by a moral conviction that one ought not to condemn without a hearing, and even then to realize that no moral conviction is sufficiently established to justify blaming those who differ from us. This might be called the principle of tolerance. To quarrel with it would no doubt be regarded as morally outrageous. But this principle is often converted without notice into a rather different doctrine, that cross-culture criticism is impossible. I may, indeed, refrain from condemnation, seeing that a situation might be more complex than I know or surmise, and that a person's actions will take on different moral hues as different features of the situation come into play. Reluctance to condemn is not quite tantamount to approval, however. It is possible, short of intolerance, to see that a person's act is hardly justifiable or appropriate or beneficial to himself or others even on his own grounds. Ruth Benedict's description of different societies which in *Patterns of Culture* has popularized the relativist thesis, may help us to avoid condemnation by seeing that the actions of Dobu, Kwakiutl or Hopi stem from quite different conceptions as to what it is to be a model man or citizen. None the less, there is implicit in her account a preference for some of the practices she describes over others. Reading her account we may understand the secretive and hostile habits of the Dobu better by seeing them against the moral standards of the tribe. But seeing the whole moral fabric of the Dobu community exposed invites moral comment and criticism. That she borrows highly preferential terms from psychiatry, like paranoid to apply to the Dobu, or manic to apply to the Kwakiutl, or the Nietzschean Dionysiac-Apollonian antithesis to contrast the Kwakiutl and the Hopi, indicates that a cultural pattern as a whole is standing trial. It is true that they stand trial within some conventions, principles, or aims, but to insist that these criteria be indigenous to the society judged is to demand a favourable verdict. Nor is it made clear by defenders of ethical relativism why a whole way of life cannot be judged by principles found in another culture or in the moral musings consequent upon a survey of cultures. It often seems as if the insistence upon moral judgment from within the society judged is justified only by appeal to the doctrine of metaphysical relativism, which we have already seen to be self-defeating. Indeed, comparison of cultures is an admirable technique for coming to see one's own moral presuppositions more clearly and so getting above them in order to judge them. It is in this way that anthropology is ethics. The divorce of the two is the fault of both sides, the anthropologist thinking it is his job to be a scientist and the moral philosopher thinking it is his to show as a matter of logic the hierarchy of moral concepts and rules, or the uses of moral language. The models for the joint discipline are best found in Aristotle's *Ethics* and *Politics*, in which one sees the business of describing and assessing human practices tied firmly together. Ethics, on this view, is the study of how men live. Its business is to show what counts as the grounds or warrants of actions. It is not *a priori*, for it could not be carried on in ignorance of the ways in which people gather together to form societies. Nor is it scientific in the sense that human actions could be treated as so many events in time and space, to be explained wholly by their observed or inferred interactions with other and antecedent events.

Relativism thus means that actions can only be judged in context, and that there happens to be no universal context. Explanation of human action is context-bound. This should not be surprising. Human conduct is a response to an incalculable variety of situations. What is important is the variety, the detail, not the general features which afford grounds for the statement of laws. One can on occasion imagine or even discover a case in which the context is universal, perhaps, for example, loyalty to friends or tribe, safeguards of life, or protection of children. But we cannot look to such cases for a basic moral principle from which all others will follow, or an empirical law from which particular actions can be inferred. In the first place, the case embodying universals does not normally arise, nor is it as a rule a determining factor in human choice. Human choices are made with respect to that variety of situations in which these universals play a progressively more anaemic role. They are, perhaps, limiting cases to moral argument and to human action, but to take them as reasons for the specific actions or particular choices is to resort to generalities which on the face of it are vacuous. A universal moral principle presupposes a common life, which our differences of occupation, age, sex and income deny. If we hanker after a common moral code for the benefits it will bring, a society prosperous and at peace, it can now be seen what the attainment of such a code implies. It is not a system of moral rules from which particular maxims can be shown to follow, nor is it imposed by force. It could emerge only if men truly shared a common life in which distinctions of employment, wealth and status have disappeared. The changes in society envisaged to achieve that end are messianic, whether the messianic hope is Christian or Marxist. And perhaps this suggests that moral agreement is not worth the price of such uniformity. If so, the cardinal virtue that emerges from such musings is tolerance and the cardinal method, arbitration. The difficulty of course is that such virtues work only if they are followed by all parties to disputes. And so the only moral recommendations, as the only recommendations for the empirical study of man, come to the same thing—a move here, a move there, zig and zag, after the manner of Aristotle's recommendations with regard to the Mean, everything tentative and subject to change. It is both from overweening generalizations in ethics and the pretensions of general theory in behavioural science that we stand most to fear the sorts of impositions on our lives that make for totalitarian régimes. Things, so to say, are always bad, or at least not nearly so good as we could imagine them being; but wholesale changes, whether backed by Plato's ethics, Marx's historicism or Skinner's laws of conditioning,[17] will most likely make matters worse. For men and situations represent a variety and a changing variety, which makes the application of general laws trivial or false and universal moral principles a positive evil.

[17] Many years ago, of course, Skinner worked out the messianic implications of his supposed science in a much-abused novel, *Walden II*. It proved to be an irritant to many professional humanists, such as Joseph Wood Krutch, who launched an attack on the conditioning utopia in *The Measure of Man*. The difficulty with Krutch's attack was that it threw out the baby with the bath. Moreover, it was not a very well-identified baby. It is all very well to say that Shakespeare is a better source for knowledge of human nature than modern psychology, but if this only results in raising poets in virtue of their craft to the level of authorities on human nature, nothing of significance has been accomplished. The scientism of psychologists and sociologists makes them blunt instruments for the appreciation of the kinds of facts which contribute to our understanding of human doings. But to turn to poetry *per se* is to forget that a proper understanding does involve the meticulous attention to detail, and to a mass of detail about human doings, for which poets are not particularly noted. However, to every action there is an equal and opposite reaction, which should, perhaps, please Skinner.

CHAPTER NINE

GAMES AND METAPHORS

I HAVE argued throughout this book against the conception of a general theory of human behaviour and consequently against a general method for behavioural science. Much of the stuff of this argument is to be found in the appeal to conventions as ways of explaining human conduct. But, as we have seen, Winch in *The Idea of a Social Science* uses the same appeal to construct a general method for studying human action. Central to this attempt to reunify the sciences of behaviour is the concept of games. In this chapter I shall consider the pretensions of game theory to offer an alternative *general* account of the behavioural sciences to that given by philosophers of science and methodologically inclined psychologists and sociologists. This will take us somewhat far afield from games proper into a general discussion of the explanatory use of metaphor. For as we shall see, the burden put upon the concept of a game presses it very far in the direction of a metaphorical use.

There are two senses in which the concept of games or game theory is employed. The first is a mathematical theory by which information can be used to determine the maximum or optimum alternative in a choice situation. This kind of theory, worked out in detail by von Neumann and Morgenstern,[1] has been usefully applied in many ways, particularly as a method for calculating the appropriate move to make where a certain risk is involved, as in the stocking of inventories. The theory, when applied as a description of economic habits, could, through the precision of its concepts and methods of inference, also support or overthrow commonly accepted explanations of economic behaviour based on the notion that human behaviour in the market-place is rational. It can define rational action precisely by giving mathematical form to concepts like the most profitable or most-likely-to-be-profitable move. It can thus recommend courses of action and offer a decisive test for the conjecture that an agent's behaviour is rational. Thus, if game theory determines that a given choice will have optimum advantage to the agent, it would be quite easy to show to what extent his actual buying and selling matches the defined model of rational trading.

[1] John von Neumann and Oskar Morgenstern, *The Theory of Games and Economic Behavior* (Princeton University Press, 1947).

But there are difficulties that stand in the way of the wholesale employment of this model as a general theory of behaviour. First, the explanation, 'done for profit', is a motive-account whose explanatory significance is tied to normal or standard rules justifying conduct. Hence, the failure of behaviour to match the model does not overthrow the explanation. For we would expect many departures from the model, because men sometimes act on these motives less skilfully, or act on other motives altogether. But when the behaviour and the situation join in a way allowing for a profit-seeking account, we still think of it as the explanation of that case. The refinements provided by the mathematical theory do not serve to falsify, or verify, a general theory. It is a device that can help us to perfect rational strategies, once these are decided upon. Second, it is not clear that the economic game theory model, however successful with regard to a narrow range of market-place activities, can be extended to cover other aspects of human behaviour which lack the same degree of rationality. So it is not to be expected that the mathematical theory of games will provide the general theory desired by social theorists. Third, there is a difference between defining rational action and claiming that a given agents act rationally. For though a man's action may not match the definition because command of the facts or mathematical computation is imperfect, it will still be rational, in the sense that the actions are governed by reasons. Procedures which in the large sense may characterize an act as rational may not be at all like the act imputed by game theory equations as optimum. Similarly, it is conceivable that the mathematical description of optimum choice may not be the rational choice, since other principles or considerations may enter than those that govern a strict and narrow sense of maximizing gain. In any case, it needs to be recalled that the theory is designed to recommend a line of strategy, assuming that certain goals are wanted or intended, and not to explain why these goals are wanted, or indeed what is wanted.

The other kind of game theory is perhaps more popular among social scientists and psychiatrists. It derives from comments in Wittgenstein, and is given systematic treatment in Peters' *The Concept of Motivation*.[2] Man, so goes Peters' account, is a chess player writ large. To explain human behaviour is to show that it follows from rules, positions of the pieces, and strategies of other players. In this account, to identify behaviour as an action is to identify it as a move, hence to see it as part of a game or strategy. Thus, the ability to describe an action entails an explanation of it, for the appeal to the game, which provides identification of

[2] R. S. Peters, *The Concept of Motivation* (Routledge & Kegan Paul, 1958).

what is to be described, is also the nature of our account of the action. *What* it is and *why* it is coincide.

The verbal formula for answering the what and the why may differ: 'A player is castling' is a description, 'To protect his king' explains why he is doing it. But even here, where the answers to the what and why questions are different, it can be seen that they are enmeshed in a common logical web. The move called castling follows from the need to protect the king, which in turn cannot be understood aside from the rules of the game and the point of play. So the explanations of moves in a game is not the object of an inquiry separable from a description of the moves. If, then, the logical model of the game finds application in the larger context of human life, game analysis would provide powerful support for the anti-generality view of explanation, yet at the same time provide a universal method for investigation of the sort I have been at pains to deny.

Does game analysis find such extended application? Is man a chess player writ large? If so, it would always be possible to diagnose an action as following from a rule. Such a diagnosis does more than match rule and behaviour, it tells us that a game is being played. It is easy enough to do the matching, but *what* game is being played, and *whether* a game is being played, are questions shrouded in ambiguity. It is surely questionable whether the chess model is appropriate when applied to the variety of activities that make up human life, or whether most actions take place in the context of mutually understood rules at all. Peters rests his case on what might be called rule-dominated games, like chess and other board or card games. Moves in such games are strictly circumscribed by rule and strategy. Of course, there are many things a man does while playing which do not enter into the game at all; he may scratch his ear, or drop a pawn. These irrelevancies might represent points of intersections of games, supposing that they could be construed in the light of further rules or strategies. But the irrelevant addenda are not bound by rules as is the performance demanded by rule-book or ceremony. And this would ordinarily be construed as the difference between performances within games and those outside them.

Many genuine games, furthermore, are what might be called rule-flexible. We may understand certain actions as belonging to a game, but cannot explain them solely by reference to the rules and conventions. That a boxer throws a punch or wards off a blow is due to his role in the ring, but the choice of a punch, the hardness and accuracy of it, is not. Nor, for that matter, is the skill of a chess player rule-determined, however much his actions may be understandable through rules. Suppose we ask why the boxer dropped his guard. That he did so *is* a move in the game, but the kind of explanation we require may have nothing to do with the rules and conventions of boxing. We might explain it, for instance, by noting that he was tired, or that he often drops his guard when throwing a jab. Explanations of moves in a game often extend outside the game in directions that cannot be foreseen from the rules. To list patterns of conduct or physical conditions is the beginning of a catalogue that, if honest, would be too circumstantial to serve a useful purpose.

Finally, the appeal to rules by way of explaining an action would normally be redundant. What the questioner usually wants to know is not *that* a game is being played, but *why* it is being played in a certain manner. Sometimes the answer to this question falls comfortably within the conception of a strategy, hence a convention. So we would answer, 'Why that move?' with, 'He's playing the Spanish defence'. But just as often we are concerned with the disparity between observed action and the paradigm provided by the rules of play. The game at most determines the form of our question; it provides the background to questions about abilities, mistakes and variations. But we need to look outside the body of rules to give more than a redundant and unhelpful answer to such questions.

It is instructive, therefore, to consider questions of increasing departure from the game model:

(1) Why did he sacrifice his queen? His king was in check (quoting the rule).
(2) Why did he castle? To protect his king (rule-dependent).
(3) Why did he put his knight in jeopardy? To tempt his opponent to take the knight, thus exposing his queen (strategy nourished by rules).
(4) Why did he put his knight in jeopardy? He didn't see the danger. He was tired (a move in the game rule-allowed, but not explainable by the rules alone).

In all of these cases the explanation is tied to the rules of the game, to paradigms of performance. The question, 'Why did he put his knight in jeopardy?' is governed by the rules of the game, but the answer does not consist, always or generally, in an appeal to those conventions. And notice that what applies here to a game like chess, which involves nothing in the way of muscular skills, will apply with greater force in games like boxing or football. For physical games create wider possibilities for rule-free explanations of moves.

This strictly limits the force of Peters' claim that man is a rule-following animal. The cases of human action that require explanation are normally those that depart from the behaviour indicated by rules. Of course, if we don't understand the game or ceremony, if we don't see what the person is after, it is illuminating to have the rules quoted to us, the ceremony described, or the purpose supplied. If we do see and understand, we should be rather more inclined to say that a good deal no longer needs explaining. What remains to be explained, and what most generally requires explanation is the departure from rule and paradigm performance, directing inquiry away from the game.

Anthropologists find themselves tempted by game theory, for they try to understand strange ceremonies, games and performances. It might be argued further that game theory is the appropriate procedure for the social sciences, since these disciplines are concerned with the structure of human performance, and not the individual variations upon it. Peters' thesis has been taken in this spirit. First, it provides a possibly comforting kind of methodological unity to social science. Second, it suggests that the only ways of studying man in an organized manner are by the techniques of social analysis and physiology. Psychology of individual behaviour, thought of as a discipline, becomes an illusion, since it would amount to little more than a compilation of individual actions. Since I favour the conclusion, it seems as if I ought to accept the premises.

But social analysis is not saved from the criticism directed at psychology by the introduction of game theory. There are questions, for example, about the histories of games, or their purposes, which leave game analysis behind, unless we can construe these further inquiries as questions about larger games, of which particular collections of social games are instances.

This must seem highly unlikely. But it is the approach of a rather popular recent work of sociological analysis, Goffman's *The Presentation of Self in Everyday Life*,[3] in which a game model is proposed for the treatment of all human activities. Goffman's object is to present a novel framework for the understanding of human behaviour in social situations. He calls this framework 'dramaturgical', for it rests upon the metaphor of theatrical performance. Accordingly, a person's behaviour is to be seen as acting in such a way as to sustain an image of himself to other members of a team. The two essential concepts, the individual's acting, and the teamwork required for the staging of a social performance, are then worked out by detailed application to a great variety of human activities.

[3] Ervine Goffman, *The Presentation of Self in Everyday Life* (Doubleday: Anchor Books, 1959).

Many of Goffman's observations, as well as those he borrows from numbers of sources, are shrewd commentaries upon a variety of human doings. He notes how important it is, in baseball, for the umpire to make quick judgments. If his judgment is delayed it may be more accurate, but it will undermine the impression of accuracy with players and spectators. He describes in detail the ceremonial aspects of a variety of functions: the doctor's white coat, the etiquette followed by a Shetland Islander in one social stratum as against that followed by the same person in another, the contrast of the front-stage appearance in such an institution as a mental hospital with a back-stage operation where wards are not as tidy or treatment as tender. And we might easily add others, even that old standby, the professor, with his pipe, who as a professional academic uses this device as a stage prop to convey the impression of thoughtfulness and dignity.

But all of these descriptions, interesting though they may be as direct descriptions of the way an umpire works, a hospital operates, a community in Shetland discriminates its social behaviour, or the way the professor tries to play his role, become pretentious when elevated to their new role, as special consequences of a theory which embraces these various practices. It is perhaps interesting to the outsider to know that tours of mental hospitals are conducted so as to minimize observation of back wards and the coercive techniques practised there, though it should hardly come as a matter of surprise to anyone skilful at the business of living. But does the elevation of the features of this description to the level of a general account of social behaviour enlarge our understanding of that behaviour?

The answer to this question shows, I think, the weakness of Goffman's theory. For keep in mind that he has generalized the concept of dramatic performance in such a way that all behaviour may be so treated. And this is open to two objections. For one thing, having elevated his piecemeal descriptions to a general theory, he is led to see all sorts of behaviour as dramaturgical where it is no longer clear that such a device has explanatory value. For example (pp. 194 ff.), the sexual act becomes 'a reciprocal ritual performed to confirm symbolically an exclusive social relationship', and (p. 230), housewives who enter each others' kitchens without knocking are showing that they have nothing to hide. One can imagine that the sexual act performed by two individuals might have this significance, or two housewives might very well wish to show to a third neighbour how friendly *they* are. But the cogency of such observations is restricted to those special cases where the particular circumstances warrant such an analysis. To generalize is to assert that some fact hold regardless of context. But our grounds for making these judgments as to the meaning, the significance, the purpose of an action are restricted to individual cases. For that is where meaning, significance, and purpose reside. The point of such a comment is, then, to discriminate it from a more obvious, perhaps a more general reason for acting in these ways.

The second objection underlines the first. We mean by acting a performance at variance with a genuine role or the normal appearance of a person. The analogue in daily life to stage performances is, in other words, dissembling. But for a person to dissemble is for him to play a role which is not his or which he does not normally play. There must be a legitimate sense in which we can speak of the person as *not* acting if there is a legitimate sense in which we speak of him *as* acting. Consequently the diagnosis of a person's actions as a performance depends upon the various activities that the individual (or team) generally engages in. In the dramaturgical explanation of action, context is all. It must then be a particular and not a generalized account.

It is evident that, in appealing to the dramaturgical perspective as a way of bringing unity into the study of human behaviour, Goffman is not saying that men are always and quite literally acting. Nor is Peters saying that, in their sundry actions, men are really and always playing chess. But if their theories are designed to meet the standard of generality demanded by the hypothetico-deductive account of explanation, they are obliged to make out that games or play-acting are fruitful ways of looking at behaviour, that it is generally illuminating to say that in their conduct men generally act *as if* they were play-acting or playing games. And thus to claim that one typical way of explaining is by means of metaphor. Metaphor requires our attention, then, before we can complete our analysis of game-explanations, for it is clearly in a metaphorical sense that games are offered as an explanatory device to bring the various studies of human behaviour into some kind of systematic and unified organization.

I do not wish to deny the explanatory power of metaphor. But I do wish to argue that its effective use is context-bound, and thus, as a method of presentation, excludes theoretical generality. Goffman's dramaturgical metaphor, for example, depends on there being many cases in which men are not play-acting, if play-acting is to have explanatory force in special cases. For 'He's play-acting' has the sense of doing something now which a man does not ordinarily do, or which is to be contrasted with other ways of behaving. The account is already suspect when Goffman resorts to talk about 'perspective'. He avoids the self-defeating property of the generalization, 'Everyone's play-acting', by raising it to methodological status and immunity from falsification. And this makes it appear that the dramaturgical theory is free of context. Actually, however, it is like so many sociological accounts, no longer a theory but a 'frame of reference' for 'organizing' or 'co-ordinating' the facts. Methodological immunity is bought at the price of significance. But to ask, how does this perspective help us, is to show that in this and that case it leads to a way of describing behaviour that brings out its peculiarities, its difference from standard ways of behaving. It does not provide a methodology for social or behavioural sciences any more than it offers a general theory of human conduct. At most, the methodological prescription would have to be phrased more humbly: sometimes it is worth asking yourself, is this play-acting, implying that sometimes it may not be.

It is sometimes urged, for example by John Wisdom,[4] that the explanatory power of metaphor is to be found in its paradoxical juxtaposition of different cases. His example is a good starting point for the examination of arguments whereby theories are built out of metaphors. A lady says to her friend trying on a new hat: 'My dear, the Taj Mahal!' The juxtaposition helps the lady make a decision or form an attitude; it brings into relief the hesitation, the not-quite-right feeling she has as she contemplates the hat in the mirror. She knows now why she is unhappy with it. But the test of the appropriateness of the metaphor is that it helps pinpoint a feeling already entertained, even though vaguely. It is clearly the sort of case whose power resides wholly in the special context. It would be senseless to move to a general method: always compare hats with monuments.

Now Wisdom uses this example, among other reasons, to bring out what he regards as the power of Freudian theory to explain our actions. 'The psychoanalyst', he says (p. 275), 'tries to bring into the light models which dominate our thought, our talk, our feelings, our actions, in short, our lives.' People are victims of mistakes, much as philosophers are (Wisdom's further and no doubt major point.) Psychoanalysis, as therapy, is a special case of a more widespread activity in which we engage with friends and relatives, students and colleagues. It is persuasive argument. We say: 'But look, you're behaving just like George', or 'Just like a child'. The person addressed can see that this is so, and, of course, he doesn't want to act like George or a child. The analyst says, 'Your behaviour is infantile, a regression to an oral or an anal stage' or 'You are acting toward me as you do toward your father'. We can nod our heads and say, it is similar isn't it? And this makes us quite uncomfortable,

---

[4] John Wisdom, 'Philosophy, Metaphysics and Psychoanalysis' in *Philosophy and Psychoanalysis* (Blackwell, 1957).

and perhaps less inclined to act that way or indulge in such feelings again. For we don't like to be told, when stamping the foot, that we're acting like a child. It touches us at the level of our moral awareness, it rends the fabric of our self-conceit, and undermines the rationale for our performances. The analytic move is explanatory in the sense that diagnosing motives is explanatory. It is addressed to questions of the propriety of action, when seen in the light of moral points of view shared by analyst and patient. It is a rhetorical device of great power, enabling us to see what we are doing in the actions of another, particularly if that other is the kind of person we would not want to be. Thus Wisdom says quite rightly, psychoanalysis is ethics, for it is a species of moral persuasion. But it is by the same token bound by contexts, and is not the basis for a general theory.

Psychoanalysts, on the other hand, regard such tactics as derived from theory. Infantile sexuality is not treated by Freud as the possibly illuminating gambit, see the boy in the man, or the man in the boy. As Freud talks, it makes sense to inquire, but is infantile behaviour really sexual? This question would show complete misunderstanding of the case of the lady and the hat. We should never be inclined to retort, 'but is the hat really a building'? Freud is claiming to do more than construct metaphors, he is suggesting that the mechanisms that drive the man also drive the child. Infantile sexuality is, in intent, an application of a theory to one kind of behaviour, much as the laws of planetary motion can be construed as special cases of gravitational theory. Here the likenesses afford the basis for a general theory, and this is also Freud's claim. He is not saying that the actions of children are in a way like, but of course in ways not like, the actions of adults. Without this deterministic conception the Oedipus complex and all the more singular aspects of Freud's theory collapses. The theory states that a mechanism common to all men brings about situations like the Oedipus triangle. The evidence for it is that children do engage in erotic play, that the child's attachment to his mother is like the lover for his married mistress, that his attitude towards his father is like that of the lover for the hated husband. The force of the evidence depends on being able to say in the context of therapy that the patient's behaviour is *really like* such and such. It is the power to rearrange the patient's thoughts by forcing him to entertain new comparisons and contrasts of his actions with those of others. Among these novel rearrangements one, at least, becomes a standard gambit of analysis, and this is the focus on early life events, considered in a special way. As this way of looking at infantile behaviour is generalized, however, it also becomes more attenuated.

Freud objected, and rightly, to the definition of sexuality commonly employed in his day, that is, activity directed toward reproduction, for it is not at all clear that the word, so defined, would have a use. He wished to amend the definition to include any activity directed toward orgasm. But he wanted also to extend the use of 'sexual' so as to include, in addition to so-called normal and perverted ways of achieving orgasm, all those activities in which the child gains pleasure from the manipulation of its body. And you might say, he's right, isn't he? The infant sucking his thumb, the child playing house or doctor, the man who dresses as a woman, the man who whips and the man who is whipped— all erotic. Sometimes it appears that Freud is only saying that gratification is achieved by all these means. But the theory requires more than the observation of gratification. The boy loves his mother erotically in the sense that he hates his father with a jealous hate; the little family is like the adult triangle. But how much like? So like, Freud says, that the boy desires intercourse with his mother (implying an understanding of this mature action), he hates his father with a jealous hate (implying that he has learned the cultural standards appropriate to adults of Western society), and he fears his father because he knows the punishment will fit the crime, that is, castration. Perhaps now we want to say, 'but not *that* like'. Yet the significance of the definition of sexuality for Freud is that the Oedipus situation follows as a necessary development of the child.

Like many of Freud's statements, the theory of infantile sexuality is an eye-opener to the similarities of adult to childish behaviour. But it is an eye-closer to the differences between them, especially once one moves to the theory of personality development which the extended definition generates. Historically, perhaps, the overstatement was needed. Homosexuality, fetishes, masochistic and sadistic behaviour were bewildering, precisely because investigators were reluctant to note the strong ties of such habits to the normal or sanctified centre of sexual practice. In the same way it is illuminating to observe that the raccoon is a sort of a dog, the chimpanzee a sort of a man, for such analogies suggest a theory of genetic relationships. But the analogy must not lead us too far. Don't expect a raccoon to bark or guard your house.

So in a way it is precisely the metaphorical character of Freud's remarks that constitutes the basic objection to them. They are stated as arresting and compelling notices of likenesses that we may have overlooked, and once we have accepted them in this spirit, they are used also to drive the theory-producing mechanism. It is because they are illuminating in Wisdom's sense that they are dangerous. If we take the view that they ought to be appraised, not as theoretical statements or factual statements in a science, but as illuminating metaphors, we are asked to avoid criticizing them for the role they play, or pretend to play, and judge them instead wholly on the degree of aesthetic delight, or dramatic unity, or moral demarcation they give to the subject at hand. But this is not the spirit in which Freud or his successors wished to advance their theories. They suppose that they have solved puzzles in the behaviour of children, neurotics and psychotics by theories which, like theories generally, provide us with testable statements and workable hypotheses for answering such questions.

Two morals can now be drawn for psychoanalysis. First, our discussion provides a warning against the rigid application of theory to the individual case. This has been my general point throughout. But second, intellectual capacity is required to enter into a therapeutic session, an ability to look at one's behaviour in various lights, and draw appropriate inferences. If Wisdom's is a correct description of therapy, then therapy is a rational procedure, and the extent of its employment depends upon the extent to which we are confident that our difficulties are of an intellectual nature. I am using 'intellectual' here as an honorific label. The errors from which we suffer, if they are as Wisdom describes them, are errors which arise in consequence of our possessing certain capacities for thought. One might think here analogously of Ryle's ghost in the machine as a model from which certain philosophers have suffered. It presumes a degree of sophistication and reflection in the victims of this myth to ascribe it to them and offer a diagnosis for their mistakes. In short, Wisdom's account of the purpose of therapy and thus presumably the nature of whatever it is that the therapist treats (neurosis? problems in living?) turns therapy, and with it the theories that lie behind therapy, into the business of philosophical analysis, the business of showing, in this case and that, how a view of the world has gone wrong. Psychoanalysis is moral and in a sense epistemological in nature. By the same token it is piecemeal, for philosophical analysis, in Wisdom's sense, if it is to be carried on with any cogency, must be carried on with regard to *someone's* misconception of the world. It is not that one is providing the *correct* conception, or that one could. It is rather that the philosopher is concerned with those kinds of conceptions which have an irresistible tendency towards generalization beyond the scope of proper application. But if the business of philosophy is corrective, it must be corrective for cases where one can see that something has gone wrong. We are troubled, Ryle says, by the myth of the ghost in the machine, and perhaps very often we are. But we need to be shown this in the contexts in which the myth has troubled us. If the purpose of his book is to free us of the myth, it must be addressed to those particularly recalcitrant problems which trouble us in devising accounts of human action. It will not do simply to catalogue the variety of views which might be said to follow from the concept of the ghost in the machine. If we do not share these views the point of Ryle's analysis would appear to be lost. Many readers are puzzled by *The Concept of Mind* because they read it as a general account of the nature of mind and not piecemeal diagnoses of deceptions by myths, from which they are supposed to suffer. For its argument is general, suggesting the nothing-but-behaviour-and-tendencies-in-behaviour doctrine. And then this seems to readers like another dogma, another myth ('Surely there are feelings that are my own?').

I do not offer this as a criticism of Ryle particularly, but as a comment on the difficulties inherent in all such styles of attack on misconceptions, whether philosophical or neurotic, political or economic, physical or biological, which trouble us at certain points in certain circumstances, in science or everyday life. We are concerned with pervasive myths, but our mode of attack leads to the substitution of a new myth for an old. So with psychoanalysis. The variety of therapeutic strategies seems susceptible to a kind of generalization; the mentally ill misconceive the world, the neurotic suffers from memories. But these are not the kind of generalizations which allow us to deduce the specific complaint in the specific patient. They are, if you like, generalizations of method. But soon, various rules of thumb for beginning the attack (the role of parents, childhood experiences) are converted into laws of human development. The aim to see an overworked model in a patient's view of the world and himself is muddled by insisting that the patient's troubles are always the result of the workings of a narrow range of models.

Of course, Freudian theory could be right. Perhaps we do suffer from just those particular models which he proposes. But if that is the sense in which he is stating his theory, it needs a new kind of evidence. It needs to be stated in such a way as to allow experimental evidence for the working of these early life experiences, conceived now as conditioning the child in certain specificable ways. Freudian, neo-Freudian, Jungian, Adlerian, and all non-physical, non-medical procedures oscillate between two widely divergent aims. Psychiatric descriptions are anchored to the familiar rational accounts we give of behaviour. These are judgments that the individual makes about his world and the effect that his judgments have on his style of living. This is perhaps clearest in a psychiatrist like Harry Stack Sullivan who rewrites Freud without his physical metaphors, showing in the impressive terminology of the unconscious, the libido and the Oedipus situations the extension of devices that constitute our 'normal' modes of investigating and interpreting and reflecting on the world. Thus hallucinations and the withdrawn behaviour of the schizophrenic are tied to our ordinary notions of brown study and rumination, and unconscious processes to what Sullivan calls selective inattention. And then it becomes very natural to say: now I can see how the hallucinating adult grows out of the reflective child, now the troubles of forgotten scenes and wishes from long ago lead to hysterical paralysis or the compulsive counting of telephone poles. But if we use similarities to construct deterministic hypotheses as to the effects of childhood traumas and habits on later life, we have trespassed on territory we can lay no claim to. For these hypotheses need to be defended by showing that, when a particular kind of experience characterizes a child's life, it always leads to these kinds of consequences.

The psychiatrist stresses the similarities, draws the analogies, presents the picture in a new light with new associations, as a rhetorical device to focus attention on the patient's problems. But his tendency is then to treat his rhetoric as a theory of human development. The plausibility and success of his rhetoric leads him to think that his hypotheses of human development have been proved. The theory is surrounded by a cloud of logical operations and protected from the need for verification which, as a learning theory, it would require.

Wisdom's account is attractive, for it puts the finger on the source of the plausibility of psychoanalytic theories. But if his account is carried out in full, it indicates that the procedures of analysis of which he approves have no bearing on what analysts themselves regard as the theory of human behaviour and development with which they pretend to work. In general, we want to say that some of the more central observations of analysts *make sense*; they provide a coherent account of puzzling behaviour and talk. Sometimes, undoubtedly, we are satisfied with this. In history, for example, we often want an organized account of chronological happenings which will provide plot and significance to them. It sustains our interest and fortifies our memory. Thus we turn to historians whose work is built on some general conception, like Gibbon's grand design of the operation of barbarism and Christianity in the decay of classical culture, or the economic interpretations of history which organize the plot around changes in modes of production and centres of wealth. Of course we don't employ these unifying conceptions wholly as dramatic devices. Our choice among them is determined by some way of measuring and assessing their plausibility or their fruitfulness by illuminating old facts and bringing new ones to light. But we don't impress them upon our story with the weight of theory. The account still speaks for itself as a report of human doings, as a consideration, in the light of our ordinary ways of assessing conduct and assigning motives, of the conduct and the motives of men in responsible political, economic, cultural and religious places in society. It is only when we raise these unifying conceptions to the place of theory that something goes wrong, as in Marx, Toynbee, or for that matter St. Augustine. It is the same story with psychoanalysis.

Freudian theory is, in some puzzling sense, illuminating. It embodies statements which are not merely the artificial and redundant generalizations on explanatory accounts already given in our piecemeal day-to-day accounts of behaviour. And this is vastly different from other accounts we have considered. In those accounts, the order was observation followed by explanation, followed by generalization on the explanations given. It is only to the last stage that the would-be scientists have contributed, while claiming that through generalization they have explained human behaviour in a way not previously possible. In Freud (perhaps) the order is different: observation followed by generalization on observation, followed by explanations of the general patterns, followed by further observations. From the *look* of the theory, at least, Freudian devices are summaries of observed behaviour enabling us to incorporate new observations within their scope. It does change our views about behaviour to look at it through Freudian formulations. The theory has in this sense explanatory power, and, when one considers its rhetorical effect, it seems to be, in Wisdom's words, 'rather proved'.[5] Not proved, but *rather* proved, as if Wisdom too, in emphasizing the illumination, the shock value, the perspective-shaping of Freudian theory, recognizes that something more might be offered here.

Newtonian theory too is illuminating, a perspective-shaper; it can be described as seeing the likenesses among events where these likenesses had not been noted before. But Newtonian theory is rendered explicit in such a way that the truth of its hypotheses is independent of the rhetorical value of its fresh perspective on the world. In Freudian theory, on the other hand, this separation never occurs. Either the rhetorical effect itself (in therapy, in persuasion generally) is taken as sufficient, or else the theory, when confronted with observations which seem to show its limits, is fortified by addenda which can only be called verification insurance policies, devices which immunize the theory against possible falsifying evidence. Most typical of these devices in Freud's account is that of reaction formation, which is used in such a way that if a man, say, keeps remarrying women like his mother, he's suffering from an Oedipus

[5] *Philosophy and Psychoanalysis*, p. 267.

fixation, but if he keeps remarrying women who differ from his mother, he suffers also from an Oedipus fixation and is reacting against it. Once again there is room, quite outside Freudian psychology, for occasional explanations of actions as reactions to something or other, parental training, say. One college freshman deliberately drinks in order to spite his pious teetotaller home. Another college freshman clings rigidly to parental mandate. But if we try now to say all people suffer from parental domination (for every action can be related in some way to the prescriptions and example of parents) we lose the special explanatory significance that these accounts have for individual cases. A concept like reaction formation is another of that range of devices which finds its rationale in ordinary experience, in particular cases. At this level it is used to contrast some kinds of behaviour with others, to show the peculiarity of some actions by means of implicit or explicit conceptions of rational, normal or sensible behaviour. As used by Freud it loses this power, for he assigns to it a role of universal application and hence undermines the basis of his theory.

It is now possible to make clear the lines of argument which have been hidden in the detailed consideration of specific theories. My concern has been with the logical defects of a group of theories that rest upon *ad hoc* 'rational' accounts of behaviour of the sort we use daily in deciding to engage in action or assessing the actions of others, and the attempt to generalize such accounts. But (1) in generalizing we obliterate the explanatory force of the original piecemeal accounts. And (2) the object of both our piecemeal accounts and generalizations upon them is to explain the individual. In everyday life and putative scientific commentaries on it, we are concerned, as a rule, not with the functional dependence of one property of a class of individuals upon others, but with the actions of the individual as they follow from his history. It follows from the complexity of the individual case that our description can only be an impression. We must be able to hit upon some happy formulation of character and disposition which enables us to guess the next move, the next remark, the choice today and tomorrow and next year. But there is no technique we can learn and practise which assures us that we've got it right. In short, impression-forming cannot be the central concern of a discipline or a profession, though it does play a large part in our ordinary non-academic assessments of human behaviour. It is a matter of gifts of discernment and assessment, which some psychoanalysts, sociologists, anthropologists, historians and psychologists share with some laymen. It is not a matter of discipline and expertise. In those fields where, in the interest of creating a discipline, the attempt is made to codify rules of assessment, of impression-formation, the result is self-defeating. It imposes criteria from without where what is required is assessment within the case, familiarity with the subject and cases like his, and use of those gifts which we label as insight or flair precisely because we lack rules for their practice. Finally (3) the metaphorical interpretation of such theories shows the limitations of their use. If they are to be assessed as illuminating, it is in virtue of the role they play in this or that case. Deprived of context through elevation to the status of a general account of human doings, they lose also the kind of contact with the case which provides the basis on which we are able to call them illuminating. In short the aim at generality deprives such views of their explanatory significance.

We may now return, from this excursion into the general topic of metaphor and the account of the way in which psychoanalysis illustrates the dangers of elevating a metaphor to theoretical status, to the use of the game model in explaining human action. Along the lines indicated by this account of metaphor we might now say, 'Man is a chess player writ large' is an aphorism appropriately dealt with by saying, sometimes he is and sometimes he isn't. Or perhaps, there are ways in which social behaviour is like a game of chess—diplomacy, the eternal triangle, mother, father and child, and what have you—and ways in which it is not. And even when it is, when behaviour is strongly marked by rules, our interests cannot be restricted to game-playing, rule-abiding features of behaviour. These amount to a set of commonplaces about our conduct which do not require study by social scientists, but which do not afford, either, a particularly significant body of information about behaviour requiring university instruction. We understand, in most of the ordinary business of life, that a game is being played when it is being played, that is, actually and not metaphorically played. It simply does not occur to us to explain rule-following actions, but only the departure, in one way or another, from the rules. Perhaps Ryle had something like this in mind when he recommended in *The Concept of Mind* (p. 326) that psychologists tell us, not about the normal in human conduct, but the departures from conventions; not when we are not deceived, but when we are.

These remarks call attention to difficulties in applying the concept of a game to specific actions that, supposedly, occur as moves within some particular game. A further difficulty arises when we ask: how do we discover *that* a game is being played? How do we know that some actions that we happen to observe are ceremonial? Such questions take us back once more to the work of the anthropologist. For notice that, on the basis of what was said about anthropology in Chapter VIII, it must appear that the oddities in alien behaviour are made intelligible by seeing what is observed as ceremonial and rule-abiding.

How do we discover that a game is being played? Well, perhaps we ask the players, or purchase a rule book. In either case, we are being instructed in the rules, and our intellectual powers are employed only to the minimal degree required to see how a given rule prescribes the observed conduct. The anthropologist in a foreign culture is like the child in his own. His explanations reflect the story of his learning to live in that society. But of course very little behaviour is governed by rules that can be explicitly stated, much less by rules that are written down. To say that behaviour is conventional is to use these rule-book cases as analogies, to suggest that most behaviour obeys, as it were, unwritten rules. It would seem to require a rather different kind of mental exercise to discover in the non-paradigm conventional actions the rules that govern these actions. Is courting, for example, a game? Is modern diplomacy a game? Note how often in the modern world the puzzles as to Communist aims have to do with the breakdown of something approximating a code of international behaviour. The priest celebrating the mass is engaging in rule-book ceremonies, but is his behaviour also ceremonial when he visits the poor or gives the kind of responses he does in the confessional? In cases, one might say so, but in cases not. Is the classroom, the market-place, or the battleground the arena of a game? And are instruction, haggling, or warring games practised on these fields? The questions show the difficulties in extending the analogy.

In a limited and ordinary employment of game, a man must understand the rules in order to play. But when we come to apply this concept analogically or metaphorically this requirement is no longer met. In fact, anthropologists want to claim the right to revise the participants' account of their performances. In such a case, is the anthropologist's diagnosis of the rules a generalization upon observed actions, or a directive to act? Is he umpire or observer? The first role presumes a common set of rubrics understood alike by players and anthropologist. Anthropological criticism of actions would then consist in noting their consistency with or approximation to the rules. But his role as referee is strictly limited by his inability to say in any precise sense that such and such *is* the game being played, or that such and such *are* the rules of the game. The umpire's role depends upon rule books and mutual intentions of players. Otherwise his comments are apt to be exhortatory rather than decisive. As observer, on the other hand, it looks as if he is discovering something about the habits of a community. His account explains, in the sense that he is able to say, this is what is done. Why is this explanatory? Because the habit or practice strikes us, from within our way of life, as a departure from the done thing. The discovery that everyone in a culture acts this way shows us that other traditions and other rules obtain. Many an anthropologist would deny that he is only describing actual performances. He is getting at 'culture', not as a body of observed practice, but as the ideals or paradigms from which these practices issue. The question, how do we discover the ideals, is like the vexing question, how do we know a particular game is being played. Anthropologists talk sometimes as if they are providing a game analysis, and the temptation is strong to engage in the suspiciously easy business of inventing ceremonies and conventions to interpret or make sense of human actions on a game model. This is the sort of thing I have deprecated in Goffman's work.

When we understand that a game is being played, we see bits of behaviour as moves, explained in accordance with rules. In such cases, research is an illusion, for explanation is not provided here by some further manipulation of what is observed. We bring events within the rubrics of a game, not by inductive generalization or formulation of hypotheses from which the events are to be deduced, but by changing our focus, so that actions are seen as moves in a game. We might indeed be tempted to regard such metaphorical extensions of games as preliminaries to the construction of theories. What prevents us is a kind of indecisiveness in the move from 'Such and such is, *as it were*, a move in a game' to 'Such and such is in fact a move in a game'. The latter might count as a genuine discovery. Suppose that we are observing soldiers rushing from foxhole to foxhole under a barrage of fire, and someone says, 'It's only a game.' He might mean: 'It isn't really war, it's only manœuvres.' Or he might mean, 'War is like a game, isn't it?' Peters seems to fail to appreciate the difference between these cases and is thus able to suggest that we can talk about behaviour as moves in a game when he is entitled to say only that behaviour of this or that sort is game-like.

As a result, anything can be compared with anything and given a context, any comparison can be illuminating. But this will not do as a defence of a general theory of games, either as a theory of behaviour or as a theory about theories of behaviour. Something more would be required in order to say that a particular metaphor or model is always the appropriate one.

Many contemporary psychiatrists have seen some of the difficulties in the Freudian over-extension of metaphor into theory. Interestingly enough, they have chosen to combat this tendency by using the games and play-acting concepts in a way that is open to the same criticism. It will be worth looking at one rather radical attempt by a psychiatrist to substitute a game analysis of behaviour for the hydraulic metaphors that give illicit explanatory power to Freudian theories, for it may bring into focus a pair of points that I have tried to make in this chapter. First, the value of game analysis is in its metaphorical use, which implies quite specific *ad hoc* applications and prohibits the adding up of successful applications into a genuine theory of human behaviour. Consequently we should not expect the concept of a game to provide what the machinery of pumps and pressures could not, namely, a general theory of human action. Second, it is worth looking at a phase of psychiatric theory to which we have not paid sufficient attention. Neo-Freudian psychiatry shares at least one common ground with the point of view advanced here, that explanations of behaviour are not to be found in mechanical causes. In various ways Karen Horney and Harry Stack Sullivan exhibit these moves away from Freud's mechanical, or paramechanical, bias and toward a game-like or dramaturgical point of view.[6] But I shall base my remarks on a work that goes further in the direction of ridding psychiatry of its biological and physiological tendencies, and more consciously in the direction of a game analysis of the mentally ill. Dr. Thomas Szasz makes quite clear in *The Myth of Mental Illness*[7] that he has, for example, read Peters with approval. He joins with Peters, moreover, in claiming that a game analysis excludes a mechanical account. This is to take metaphor, if metaphor it turns out to be, very seriously indeed. For, as metaphor, it may be illuminating, but we should not ordinarily say that it excludes something else being the case. Thus Szasz's account may help determine to what extent the concept of a game is being introduced into an analysis of behaviour strictly and to what extent the success of the account (and any such account) depends upon shifting from literal to metaphorical game-playing readings without notice. Szasz wants to suggest that the mentally ill, but specifically the hysteric, can be treated as if he were playing games, putting on an act. He might more accurately speak of a strategy here; he is speaking less of performances governed by rules than

---

[6] In effect this is to say that, in mental illness, men are still acting rationally, only they have got the facts wrong, or their concept of rationality must adjust to pressures rather in excess of what ordinary men face, or they have simply not had the opportunity to test out their views about life on others (Sullivan's concept of consensual validation). Thus Horney lays stress on the use made by the hysteric of his or her symptoms to reach perfectly standard goals like attention or dominance of others. See Karen Horney, *The Neurotic Personality of Our Time* (Norton, 1937) and *New Ways in Psychoanalysis* (Norton, 1939). Harry Stack Sullivan goes even further in explaining the behaviour of the mentally ill by making it appear to be like standard behaviour, sharing with it some range of common means and goals. The most complete account of Sullivan's theories is to be found in *The Interpersonal Theory of Psychiatry* (Norton, 1953); the more detailed application to the mentally ill in *Clinical Studies in Psychiatry* (Norton, 1956).

[7] Thomas Szasz, *The Myth of Mental Illness* (Harper, 1961).

actions dictated by goals. And so it is with Wittgenstein, Peters and the rest. We might as well talk about purpose to begin with, for which game theory appears to be new-fashioned talk.

In any event, the hysteric is engaged in the business of getting attention, which he (or more usually, she) does by feigning illness, a physical abnormality of some kind or another. The hysterical performance belongs, then, to a class that includes acting and malingering, in a word, impersonating. It must be understood as playing a role designed to get people to act in certain ways toward the patient.

This allows Szasz to conclude that a physical account of the hysteric is irrelevant. We all agree that we should eschew physical explanations when explaining what someone is doing in acting on the stage or clutching at the abdomen in the face of some hated task. So, if it is proper to say that the hysteric is putting on an act, it looks as if the consequence follows here too, and psychiatry is saved from the inroads of physiologists and chemists. In the other cases of acting, cheating and malingering, however, one finds comfort in certain further characteristics. (1) Conventions clearly govern the performance, as acting on the stage; (2) conscious intent is ascribed to actors or cheats; (3) lying, acting, cheating, and so forth, have unambiguous status as actions. The first of these will be seen to resolve into the characteristics of the second and third, so let us consider these in turn.

(2) When one ascribes strategies to the mentally ill, one does so while explicitly denying that the intent is conscious. The person is not in a position to avow these intentions. The unconscious thus serves to ease the strain on the concept of strategy, when that concept is extended to include the actions of the mentally ill. It might be argued that it is no criticism to show that a concept has been extended beyond its normal use, for that surely is the stuff of which scientific revolutions are made. But the point is, exactly how is it being extended in the present case? Well, unconscious intention is just like conscious intention, except that a person is not aware. He cannot avow the intention. The action in question is not sufficiently stylized to allow that kind of avowal. But in what respects is it like conscious intention? Perhaps only that it shares a mode of action with obvious cases of intended acting or cheating, without allowing us to say that a person understands what he is doing. But there are first of all cases which we should decidedly not call cases of game playing or strategy following. A person may accidentally go through a sequence of motions which could be interpreted as following a rule. Or he might imitate the motions of others playing a game. Even if we regarded such cases as borderline or exceptional, we should not ignore

their significance in posing a question for the thesis that all behaviour is strategic, planned, or game-like. So the lack of expressed intention together with a form of behaviour which in other cases is taken to be strategic or game-playing in nature, should not be regarded as grounds for a strategy-following interpretation of that behaviour. The problem here does not arise from the claim that games are sometimes appropriate ways of viewing behaviour, but that they are always appropriate.

(3) *Unambiguous actions.* I mean by this that nothing whatever could lead us to account for an action another way, for example, as the effect of causes or as part of a chain of physiological events. The hysteric exhibits behaviour which can be classified in different ways. We all know about deliberate tears, and their more violent extensions. But we are just as often inclined to attribute such tears to helplessness in the face of calamity, sorrow or rage, or physical circumstances, like menstrual or post-partum depression. We speak of them as human actions. She cries, not, 'the eyes are secreting tears', because they are characteristic human responses, not parts of a strategy or game. Sometimes it looks as if Peters, Melden and Szasz, and behind them Wittgenstein, are arguing that if behaviour can be identified as an action, we are logically compelled to follow the explanatory road toward games and strategies. But that this is plainly not so is amply illustrated by any number of examples. An ulcer can serve as a move in a game, getting sympathy and attention for someone possibly in need of it. But it also has causal ancestry. At least, we should not be inclined to suppose that the effort of tracing such an ancestry is to commit a logical blunder. Similarly, the symptoms of hysteria—amnesia, anaesthesia, paralysis—also can be regarded as links in a chain of physical events, and sometimes we do explain them this way.

It may be instructive on occasion, even on many occasions, to think of such events as devices furthering a goal. But the thesis which Szasz wishes to draw from the case of the hysteric, and Peters for human behaviour generally, is that game analysis logically excludes physical accounting. The plausibility of a game interpretation does not support this further claim. Szasz views mental illness as a problem in living, and concludes that it cannot be the subject for mechanical treatment. But physical ailments are also problems in living. We should not conclude on these grounds that they must not be treated or explained by physical means. Most of human behaviour is ambiguous in the same sense. All sorts of actions may be moves in a game, looked at one way, and yet be shown to respond to the manipulations of the physical environment of which the action is a part, and thus be explained by reference to causes.

We can now return to the original question, whether game theory provides a theory of human behaviour, general in scope but avoiding the difficulties of mechanical or paramechanical theories. Such an attempt, we have seen, runs into two sorts of difficulties. (1) Its successful advocacy in particular cases does not oust competing explanations. It does not immunize action from causal treatment. (2) The attempt to treat all human behaviour as moves in games, ceremonies and strategies, puts a strain on these concepts, clearly reflected in the employment of notions like the unconscious. It obliterates also the enormous difference between playing a game, and engaging in game-like behaviour. The usual way in which psychiatrists and social scientists employ the concept of game, the hysteric as an instance of malingering, or status and role as determinants of action, are game-like accounts. They are illuminating likenesses which, if they are to survive competition with alternative accounts, would require further elaboration and evidence before they could attain the status of a general theory of behaviour. The mechanical account, against which Wittgensteinians rail, is also illuminating. It makes a kind of sense of human behaviour. It is a striking metaphor, for example, to think of the explosions of mental illness as like the excessive pressure in a boiler. But likenesses must lead somewhere. A mechanical metaphor requires evidence of contact and collision, the interaction of particles or objects in motion, before it can be translated into theory. The game metaphor requires evidence too that a game is being played. And this is met only in part by being able to describe what someone is doing in the language of games. If a man describes his own action in the context of rules and goals *and* obeys our instructions, we are now more clearly entitled to speak of a game being played. With this information, we can say that the concept of the game explains his action.

If we cannot find the rules, if such descriptions fail us, the behaviour remains opaque. Perhaps Szasz succeeds in describing the hysterical patient as a rule-follower. But the schizophrenic, the backward patient, remains obscure. This is not to criticize his procedure, only its too general application. It is the formula 'Man is a chess player writ large', and Szasz's formula 'Man needs games', that need to be called into question, or taken with a grain of salt, or countered with the reminder that man is also an animal. There are occasions on which possible accounts of different types intersect, and it will not do in such cases to refuse admittance to physical-istic candidates to explain, on the grounds that we are talking about actions and rule-followings and not about movements or responses. The appro-priateness of our language in these cases does not determine the kind of account we give; the kind of account leads us rather to prefer different languages.

On the other hand, the case for games is an important case to make. For it is a characteristic procedure in psychology and the social sciences to devise theories which are, in essence, game-like, but to advance and defend them in such a manner as to suggest that they are mechanical or causal theories. So Szasz's reinterpretation of Freud, and Peters' analysis of motive-talk among psychologists shows that the evidence pursued is irrelevant to the theories in question. If we are dealing with game behaviour, research into causal regularities is irrelevant. But the corollary needs to be noticed also. Game-accounting is logical and limited. It belongs to the arena of *ad hoc*, not of generalized accounting. So it is automatically disqualfied as a pretender to the throne of the general theory of human behaviour.

Still, game analogies are ambitious. It is easy, for example, to find in the activities of the con-man, material enough to explain the activities and powers of priests, politicians, doctors and, no doubt, psychiatrists as well. Perhaps even philosophers. But notice at once how much the power of such a thesis derives from its hortatory aspect. If we incline to it, it is because it gives us a rational and coherent basis for judging priest-craft, diplomacy, or medical practice. So, too, with Szasz. It is his particular interest to provide a basis for criticizing modern life as hollow, a life in which material success is the only game one can win. Children, he says, turn to delinquency and many people to psychosis as a way of filling the void by playing any *real* game. Life, on this account, is like a game. And modern life is like a game that has to be won, but whose rewards are not worth having. Such an account illuminates in that it allows us to come to grips with the facts in a moral context. Something, we want to say, is basically wrong with society, and the notion of a game which can be won only at too great a cost or where the winning is meaningless, gives a diagnosis of it. In Szasz's book, then, man's need for games is a moral need, and the psychiatrist's role a moral role. This is not to debunk Szasz's work; indeed, just the reverse. But it needs to be set forth in the proper light, not as a new road to general theory, but as a device which can bring into focus the moral problems of an age.

It becomes a rhetorical device bringing together and calling attention to various moral ills. That it strikes us as quite general has to do with the fact that men do share common moral habits and defects, and face the same problems in the business of living. This generality, however, should not be confused with theoretical generality, the mark of which is the capacity to predict new applications from the statement of the theory. If game analysis holds literally, it does not do so for an indefinite range of cases, but only for the context explicated by the rules of *that* game. If it holds analogically, its power to explain rests on the way in which, for a particular audience, or on a particular occasion, or for a particular purpose, it has its desired rhetorical or illuminating effect. It would be self-defeating to extend such rhetorical devices to all human action.

CHAPTER TEN

CONCLUSION

IT HAS been my main object in this book to attack a current but confused conception of the explanation of human conduct, and replace it with a more coherent account. In carrying out this task I have been obliged to weave together two philosophical themes, one epistemological, the other moral, which may seem to be somewhat alien to one another. I have argued first that the nature of explanation depends upon the kinds of things investigated and on the exemplary cases we bring, often unconsciously, to our inquiries. Explanation, in Wittgenstein's phrase, is a family of cases, joined together only by a common aim, to make something plain or clear. This suggests that a coherent account of explanation could not be given without attending to the audience to whom an explanation is offered or the source of puzzlement that requires an explanation to be given. There are many audiences, many puzzles, and a variety of paradigmatically clear cases that give rise, by contrast, to puzzles about other cases. The means of explaining are thus quite heterogeneous. For the behavioural scientist, however, the rationale for his activity is the univocal theory of explanation that all explanation consists in bringing a case under a law. This view has an initial plausibility when developed within the domain of the science of mechanics (though even here there are some doubts, of the sort developed in Chapter III), but as applied to human performance it is totally irrelevant, producing, to the extent that its form is religiously followed, the sterile research that characterizes much of modern psychology and social science.

This is a thesis that will be seen to have implications for epistemology and the philosophy of science. But the inappropriateness of the covering law theory of explanation to the understanding of human action can only be brought out by indicating what sort of paradigms govern our observation and description of human behaviour and thus the kinds of queries we have about it. The paradigm which I have tried to uncover in various contexts is rooted in the concept of an action itself, viewed as a performance. Performances, in turn, are actions which can only be identified as appropriate, felicitous, or successful. And so the puzzles that occur to us in contemplating conduct seen as performances are, in a broad sense, moral puzzles, requiring the techniques of justification, warrant, or excuse to make them clear. And thus an epistemological query joins with a moral inquiry.

Describing and appraising are not opposed ways of examining or commenting on the world; rather, one way of viewing and describing the world is by means of appraising, that is, moral and aesthetic categories. The hypothetico-deductive account of explanation has force only so long as one is prepared to accept an atomistic (e.g. sense-datum) account of what is observed. In rejecting this account of explanation, I have also rejected an atomistic metaphysics. That we can with complete propriety claim to observe relations, for example, is a conclusion to be drawn from the analysis of both the collision and justification paradigms of explanation. We see things happen and record these observations by means of concepts like hitting or striking, which are loaded with explanatory content. In the same way the paradigm of moral explanation commits us to the claim that we observe moral facts.

This, I suppose, is the great insight of hedonism. For the hedonist may be interpreted as claiming that pleasures and pains simply are moral facts. A pleasure-pain vocabulary would have no use unless we saw things or sensations or activities as objects to be prized or despised, sought after or avoided. The difficulty is that the hedonist thesis is usually argued in such a way as to convert pleasure and pain into morally neutral facts, perhaps, as in Bentham, to give an appearance of scientific precision and objectivity to the business of moral judgment. Thus the hedonist easily falls prey to the fact-value dichotomy, because, in his anxiety to provide a factual basis for ethics, he insists upon it. He sees, but dimly, that we simply do identify some occurrences in a moral way, but he is wedded, as a rule, to some form of the epistemological doctrine of atomism within which a claim to observe moral facts is as impossible as the claim to observe relations.[1]

The claim that we can describe the world in moral terms, and that, to speak of human actions at all, we must describe behaviour in moral terms, has obvious implications for the study of ethics as well as for the supposed scientific study of man. I have not worked out in this book the implications for ethics, that not being my purpose. But it is possible to see how the study of moral argument will be affected by the view that morality as well as social science is founded in the concept of human performance. The first step to an analysis of moral argument, like the

[1] The only view, so far as I know, that attempts to adapt the idea of moral observation and description to an atomistic metaphysics is G. E. Moore's doctrine of simple non-natural properties. But any such view dead-ends in mystery; we have no idea what such a property is like. The analogies (e.g. 'like yellow') are offered in one statement and retracted in the next, (but non-natural, i.e. 'not like yellow').

first step to an investigation of human action, is to inquire what sort of thing men are doing. The study of ethics is empty without the detail of particular human actions providing the contexts in which moral puzzles and conflicts arise. By the same token, psychologists and social scientists forsake their subject matter when they suppose that the proper object of their study is a description of human behaviour meeting the standards of an atomistic metaphysics or a methodology borrowed from the science of mechanics. Freed of the paraphernalia of pseudo-scientific methodology it becomes apparent that what gives point to these investigations is questions about the propriety, felicity, rationality or success of human actions.

Moral philosophers have come to deal with their subject in isolation from actual human performances because of their addiction to univocal conceptions of truth, argument and evidence, supposing that it is their business to exhibit these conceptions in or foist them upon moral language and argument. Psychologists and social scientists, keen on achieving status among the natural sciences, have been led to suppose that they could refine action-descriptions into quantitative descriptions, and so have failed to address themselves to what people do. What is needed, in both psychology and ethics, is not measurement, experiment, prediction and formal argument, but appraisal, detailed description, reflection and rhetoric. If science is characterized by discovery and prediction, there are no sciences like psychology and the social sciences. For the study of action does not require new and hidden events and processes, but reflection upon and reordering of what we see men doing. Its object is not to make more certain the basis for prediction, but to enlarge the grounds for rational decision and appraisal. Psychology and social science are moral sciences; ethics and the study of human action are one.

These remarks about ethics, like those about epistemology, must be taken as promissory notes. They show directions in which this more specific study leads, they do not argue claims within the larger fields. But they serve to remind us that the difficulties within psychology and social science are much deeper than the many popular attacks on these fields would suggest. Indeed, the behavioural sciences do suffer from unnecessary jargon and pointless research. But so long as they insist on a method borrowed from physics and a subject matter borrowed from moral action, these symptoms must characterize their inquiries. If we confuse the symptoms with the disease, we are apt to think that behavioural science only needs someone with greater mathematical ability or scientific insight to set it up as a genuine science. (How often does one hear the tiresome remark, psychology (or sociology) has not yet found its Galileo !)

I have tried to show that such an expectation rests on conceptual confusion and bad metaphysics. It is one thing to propose a refinement of our techniques of observing muscular movements, quite another to suppose that such refinements will improve upon or replace our observation of human action. Close physical description is the first step toward a science of physiology and thus to the study of man as an organism. But such a study neither supports nor refutes the observations we make about human beings conceived as persons or human actions viewed as performances. The view of man as an organism and as an agent are simply totally different ways of looking at his conduct. Psychology and social science, in different ways and to different degrees, occupy a no man's land in which the techniques for a biophysical description are applied to the behaviour of men as agents.

The study of human action by scientific means has seemed plausible because of the unexamined metaphysical view that all genuine description is ultimately given in terms of discrete spatio-temporal events. Among psychologists especially it has been supported by the equally unexamined Cartesian view of the mind, so far, at least, as Descartes can be held responsible for the view that thoughts, feelings, motives and intentions are episodes discovered by introspection. The psychologist's concern with proper methodology would lead him to embrace any theory of the mind congenial to that purpose. The Cartesian view lends itself to this aim, for it makes it possible to think of mental acts as quasi-physical occurrences, hidden from direct observation, and thus describable only by inferences made on the basis of the most refined and experimentally controlled methods for observing behaviour possible. But these hidden events or processes do not withstand scrutiny. They are either labels for unknown (but not unknowable) physical processes in the organism or mythical substitutes for the moral explanations we give by means of terms like motive and need. Looking at them as physical processes the psychologist is entitled to claim that muscular movements are determined by antecedent stimuli and electro-chemical processes. But, talking this way, he has said nothing about the occasions for action. His discoveries, he is prone to claim, show that free will is an illusion. But for him to suppose so only shows that he is caught in the confusion of the attempt to force the conceptual scheme of bodily movements on that of rational actions.

It is as a result of such arguments as these that I have claimed that there is no such science as non-physiological psychology, and that the social studies are not sciences characterized by their own laws, but a heterogeneous collection of inquiries strung together on the common theme of human action. There is reason, of course, for such studies—for history and anthropology, and the examination of political, social and economic institutions. But it is, in a broad sense, a moral criterion that must be met if what is said in these areas has pertinence and the unity that might seem to justify their inclusion among the subjects offered in university curricula. We know, surely, though research specialists do not always seem to be aware of it, that there is a great deal of information about what people do that is simply not worth knowing, information that does not add up to a coherent picture or account of a subject-matter worth teaching in schools. What generally brings facts about human doings into some coherent form is a thesis designed to explicate and clarify the nature of our actions. Thus Adam Smith's *Wealth of Nations* is not, like Newton's *Principia*, a statement of laws of nature, in this case of supply and demand. It is a series of reflections designed to bring into focus a new way of carrying on economic practices, and in that sense, Adam Smith was describing economic behaviour. But men of his age were engaging in these practices with something less than clarity and rationality, for they looked at their new habits in an outworn scheme of concepts brought down from feudal times. It was Adam Smith's contribution to *think through anew* what men were doing, and so to clarify the concepts that served in the economic realm as guides to action. This is moral economy, for the analysis makes clear what is being aimed at, how it is being achieved, and in what way the process is to be justified. We say, sometimes, that Adam Smith's scheme was over-simple, as if more sophisticated (perhaps mathematical) techniques could correct his mistakes and offer more adequate laws of the economic process. But we ought to say, the circumstances on which his analysis was based changed out of all recognition, and so required a wholly fresh analysis. For the same reason, economic, political and social institutions require constant re-examination, re-evaluation and renewed analysis. With changes in external circumstances and human habits the idea of a social inquiry will take on different form and complexion.

Perhaps anthropology and history are more nearly moral inquiries than the other disciplines we have examined. Our interest in different customs and the actions of men under stress or a sense of the momentousness of their decisions, aside from the natural interest in what other people do, is of importance in the daily task of clarifying our own motives and roles, our laws and customs. It is possible that there has been less taint of scientism here than in the other psychological and social sciences for this reason, though methodologists have not been lacking in these areas. Most of psychological and social inquiry, however, has been vitiated by methodological concerns that have no bearing upon the puzzles and problems that arise within a view of man as an agent.

One further point is necessary. It is not enough to note the conceptual confusion that besets these fields. The view of human nature and society fostered by this conceptual confusion is and must be pernicious. We are always ready to bow to any view advertised as scientific, and thus, in the name of scientific method, we are willing to endorse a view of human action quite inconsistent with the demands made upon us as responsible moral agents. I call this attitude scientific because it is urged upon us in the name of the success and progress of science and the ameliorating effect it has on human life. But I should much rather call it an engineering attitude, for its more natural affinities are with those practical disciplines whose object is not to understand nature so much as to bend it to our purposes. We think, especially once we are imbued with positivist metaphysics, of physics as the most obvious instance of an enterprise designed and eminently suited to control nature. Yet the major advances of physics have been reflective in nature. The major aim has been to sort out the facts, not to exercise control over them.

The scientific attitude evinced by behavioural scientists, conscious or not, is not like this; it is rather the engineers' attitude. The psychologist, it is true, advances his claims as a new way of understanding human action, and his resulting theories of motivation, habit strength and learning are vitiated, as we have seen over and over again, by ill-assorted mixtures of different strategies of description and explanation. But even without his theories the psychologist is a somewhat successful animal trainer, as, to a lesser degree, the sociologist, whatever the status of his theories of social structure and process, makes use of his surveys of voter or consumer attitudes to devise more effective propaganda techniques. The behavioural scientist, then, supports his claim to scientific expertise, and thus to our attention, by his success in making animals do things on command or men respond to subliminal cues. He succeeds in doing so because he has imprisoned his subjects in quite special experimental conditions, whether the T-maze of the psychologist's laboratory or the controlled communications of an effective propaganda or advertising machine.

Now if our only question about the human or animal subject is, what can we make it do, we shall naturally incline toward the most efficient means available. Perhaps we shall find it in Skinner's laboratory, in a military camp, or in a circus, or perhaps in the methods of thought control and forced confession that Stalin and Mao-tse-tung may or may not have borrowed from Pavlov. The scientific or engineering attitude forces us to acknowledge, even to admire, the successes of such methods.

For it leaves us no way of placing these efficient techniques in the larger context of a less laboratory-like society, in which men, conceived of as autonomous agents, pursue both harmonious and conflicting aims. The laboratory success is dangled in front of us with the promise that management of human action is possible, if only we give the psychologist and his colleagues authority over men and society. The things we don't want (he promises us), like poverty, crime and war, will disappear. His promise can be realized if only we convert society or the nation into a large-scale laboratory. But the world is not just *in fact* immeasurably more complicated than the laboratory; the complexity is a condition of any life we would think worth living. The relation between men is not just *in fact* very different from that holding between animal trainer and animal; we should, I trust, regard it as a dismal and horrifying prospect to suppose that men should be trained to respond in ways that someone (and who?) has decided is best suited to the functioning of society or the well-being of the individual.

Totalitarianism is too weak a word and too inefficient an instrument to describe the perfect scientific society. For in the totalitarian régimes known to us, one is still conscious of coercion and thus of alternatives, however disastrous to the individual such alternatives may be. In the engineers' society, perhaps unwittingly promoted by psychologists and sociologists bent on being scientists, we should have to give up the concept of an open or civil society which, however inefficiently, serves as the prop for a social order based on respect for men as persons or autonomous agents.

A programme having such ultimate consequences cries out for refutation. If I have shown that its claims to give an adequate account of human actions are unfounded, perhaps I have contributed something to its demise.

INDEX

ad hoc explanation, 3, *passim*
Adlerian psychoanalysis, 220
Allport, G., 20, 21
Anscombe, G. E. M., 96, 106, 108, 110–111, 115, 178
anxiety, neo-Freudian theory of, 91
Aristotle, 40, 86, 126, 128, 207
Augustine, St., 222
Austin, J. L., 44, 84–85, 114, 118–119, 143, 144, 145
Ayer, A. J., 62

Bacon, Francis, 6
Baptism, as purification, 177–178
Bedford, E., 85 n. 6
behaviour, molar and molecular, 34
Behaviourism, 29, 32, 134 n. 1, 137–139
Benedict, R., 206
Bentham, 234
Bergmann, G., 6
Bergson, 3
Berle, A., 191
Black, M., 47
Bosky, N. W., 184 n. 8
Boyle's Law, 122
Braithwaite, R. B., 39 n. 1
Brunswik, E., 46
Butler, Bishop J., 79

Camus, A., 117
causal interaction, 41–49
causes, and reasons, 50; and logical connections, 140
cognition, theory of, 58–59
Collier, J., 57

Collingwood, R. G., 3, 173, 176, 201
collision verbs, 41–49
conditioning, 35–36
construct, hypothetical, 28, 32
convention, in anthropology, 163–164
Croce, 3
Crusades, The, 177

Descartes, 94, 141, 143, 152, 154–155, 236
desire, as causal episodes, 65–66; relation to desirable, 67–68
diffusionist hypothesis, 169
Dilthey, W., 3
Dobu, 206
Dodd, S., 10
drive, 30–32
Durkheim, E., 17

Ebbinghaus, H., 29
economic needs, 74
economics, classical, 191
egoism, 100–101
emotion, as expressive behaviour, 83–84; feigning, 84; knowing others, 84–85; emotional and unemotional, 85–86; feelings of, 86; as conventional, 88; and anxiety, 90
emotive theory, 62
Encyclopedia of Unified Science, 6
epiphenomenalism, 142, 144, 158
epistemology, 150–154, 233–234
equilibrium, senses of, 75
ethics, 234–235